m&

July 18, 2020

CT scan Results

Philosophical Virtues and
Psychological Strengths

Philosophical Virtues and Psychological Strengths

Building the Bridge

Edited by
Romanus Cessario, O.P.,
Craig Steven Titus,
and
Paul C. Vitz

SOPHIA INSTITUTE PRESS
Manchester, New Hampshire

Sophia Institute Press
Box 5284, Manchester, NH 03108
1-800-888-9344

www.SophiaInstitute.com

Sophia Institute Press® is a registered trademark of Sophia Institute.

Library of Congress Cataloging-in-Publication Data

Philosophical virtues and psychological strengths : building the bridge : / edited by Romanus Cessario, O.P., Craig Steven Titus, and Paul C. Vitz.
      pages cm
   Includes index.
   ISBN 978-1-933184-91-3 (pbk. : alk. paper) 1. Virtues. 2. Virtue. 3. Psychology, Religious. 4. Psychology and religion. I. Cessario, Romanus, editor of compilation.
   BJ1589.P45 2013
   179'.9—dc23

                                                          2013000535

Contents

Part I: Introduction

Part II: Basic Elements

Part III: Connections

Philosophical Virtues and
Psychological Strengths

Part I

Introduction

Chapter 1

Fresh Beginnings from Classical Foundations

Romanus Cessario, O.P.

Faith and reason

Psychology and religion enjoy a relationship that converges on the point that defines the capacity of the human person to reach out for transcendence. The competing claims sometimes advanced by authors from within these two disciplines form the background for several well-known debates that have occurred, during the twentieth century especially. At times, antagonisms even erupted. The Catholic Church, to cite one example, maintained a highly standoffish position with respect to the proposals advanced by Sigmund Freud and other early clinical theorists, especially when these hypotheses touched upon the place that moral truth holds in the life of the human creature. See, for example, Pope Pius XII's reprobation of "the pansexual method of a certain school of psychoanalysis" during his address to the First International Congress on the Histopathology of the Nervous System.[1] While many religious persons now accept the general

---

[1] See Pope Pius XII, "The Moral Limits of Medical Research and Treatment" (September 14, 1952), no. 16: "In order to rid himself of repressions, inhibitions or psychic complexes man is not free to arouse in himself for therapeutic purposes each and every appetite of a sexual order which is being excited or

Philosophical Virtues and Psychological Strengths

practices of clinical psychology, this does not mean that fundamental agreement exists among them about what service psychology may render toward the pursuit of a happy human life. Still, it is the case that psychology and religion address, from perspectives proper to their first principles, basic questions about what it means to exist in the world as a human person. That those diverse starting points may eventually lead to diverse, and even contradictory, conclusions about important features of human existence should cause no surprise. Consider, for instance, the different views that religious believers and secular psychologists may hold about the value of exorcism to alleviate pathological symptoms or the power of prayer to ameliorate personal difficulties.

has been excited in his being, appetites whose impure waves flood his unconscious or subconscious mind. He cannot make them the object of his thoughts and fully conscious desires with all the shocks and repercussions such a process entails. For a man and a Christian there is a law of integrity and personal purity, of self-respect, forbidding him to plunge so deeply into the world of sexual suggestions and tendencies. Here the 'medical and psychotherapeutic interests of the patient' find a moral limit. It is not proved—it is, in fact, incorrect—that the pansexual method of a certain school of psychoanalysis is an indispensable integrating part of all psychotherapy which is serious and worthy of the name. It is not proved that past neglect of this method has caused grave psychic damage, errors in doctrine and application in education, in psychotherapy and still less in pastoral practice. It is not proved that it is urgent to fill this gap and to initiate all those interested in psychic questions in its key ideas and even, if necessary, in the practical application of this technique of sexuality." Pope Pius XII's cautions were adumbrated in earlier papal documents such as Pope Pius X's 1907 Encyclical Letter *Pascendi Dominici Gregis*, no. 35. Sigmund Freud, though expressing ambivalent views about the Catholic Church, was not directly targeted for condemnation, or at least he was not aware of any such statements. See Paul C. Vitz, *Sigmund Freud's Christian Unconscious* (New York: Guilford Press, 1988).

Fresh Beginnings from Classical Foundations

In principle, there is no reason to assume that psychology and religion must follow conflicting trajectories. Bridge-building is possible. The present volume represents an effort, not to complete the bridgeworks, but to establish the foundations for a fruitful, bridge-building dialogue between speculative thinkers and clinical psychologists. Perhaps a better metaphor would be to find a path through the waters of the Red Sea. Just as Moses led the Chosen People into the land flowing with milk and honey, psychology in its modern exposition seeks to lead people away from the slavery imposed by all kinds of personal disorders into a place where human happiness flourishes. This passage through the waters does not entail a destruction of the human person, but rather brings about liberation from those disorders that enslave. Biblical commentators recognize such disorders allegorically represented by the conditions of life imposed in Egypt on the Chosen People. Respect for the basic structure or nature of the human person, created in the image of God, dominates the biblical tradition. Christian theology thus proceeds on the assumption that nothing authentically human remains excluded a priori from incorporation into the body of knowledge that finds its origin in divine revelation.

The specific warrant for this claim flows from belief in the Incarnation of the Son of God. Orthodox Christians hold that the Second Person of the Blessed Trinity took to himself a complete human nature, unique in that it is united to his divine nature. Since the fifth century, the Church has officially termed this union of a concrete individual human and a divine nature in the person of Christ *hypostatic*. This union begins at the moment of Christ's conception in the womb of the Blessed Virgin Mary—a conception that occurs outside the ordinary way of human procreation and so leaves the Mother of the Redeemer without loss of her virginity. The Christian Church thus recognizes in the Incarnate Son the perfect realization of what it means to be human, or as the Scriptures say, "one who has similarly been tested in every way, yet without sin" (Heb. 4:15).

Theologians attuned to the great Christian tradition agree that the benefits Christ brings transcend the perfections that result from the ordinary human development of our natural capacities. Life everlasting for those who leave this world in God's friendship brings with it a promise of divine communion and Beatific Vision that exceeds the highest expectations and abilities of the human race. This bright promise casts its light onto the world here below. Even now, the grace of Christ transforms those persons who remain united with the Savior, making them active images of God.

It is difficult to ponder the mystery of the Incarnation, for example, as described in the Liturgy of the Christmas season, without contemplating the mystery of divine transformation that the Incarnation of the Son of God holds out as possible for every human being. Thus the Church prays, "God our Father, through your Son you made us a new creation. He shared our nature and became one of us; with his help, may we become more like him."[2] The Christian Church recognizes in the Exodus from Egypt a prophetic announcement of the saving waters of Baptism, which makes of the baptized a "new creation." Sacramental liberation from destructive disorders is available now to every member of the human race.[3] From a theological point of view, liberation from what enslaves always perfects the nature of the human person, making him or her become more like Christ and free to pursue a chosen vocation toward everlasting life. Again the Christmas Liturgy captures what is at stake. So marvelous is this oneness

---

[2] *Roman Missal* (1974), Opening prayer for the Mass of the Saturday after Epiphany.

[3] For further development, see my "Sonship, Sacrifice, and Satisfaction: The Divine Friendship in Aquinas and the Renewal of Christian Anthropology," *Letter & Spirit* 3 (2007): 69–91.

between God and man that "in Christ man restores to man the gift of everlasting life."[4]

To bring this distinctive announcement into the world, which properly occurs only through an officially deputed preacher, the Christian Church relies on an instruction that surpasses what is available to the ordinary ways of human knowing. Divine revelation makes known to the human race a teaching about God and the way to God that surpasses the choicest expressions of human wisdom. Because the way to God engages the actions of free agents—for divine communion and beatific friendship are open only to intelligent creatures, that is, to angels and men—divine revelation extends to providing instruction about the human person and his or her actions. Anthropology, psychology, and ethics remain legitimate philosophical disciplines and initiate authentic philosophical lines of inquiry. The same inquiries, however, complemented by the findings of empirical and statistical sciences, may be taken up by a higher discipline or science such as theology. The Catholic tradition situates theology within the *sacra doctrina*, or holy teaching. Theology thus draws from the very knowledge that God possesses of himself and of all that exists. The privileged communication of this *sacra doctrina* is called revelation, and the equally privileged reception of this divine knowledge occurs, at least systematically, in the discipline that we call theology, the science of faith and of the saints of faith.

Christian believers order their lives so as to conform to two kinds of practical knowledge. The first kind of knowledge is faith knowledge. This supernatural knowledge, as said above, concerns God himself and the things of God. It is acquired only by the assent of faith, which comes freely as a gift from God. The second knowledge is that which develops from the exercise of the ordinary and unaided powers of human intelligence. The perfection of this

---

4 *Roman Missal* (1974), Preface III for the Christmas Season.

kind of knowledge is found in philosophy and in the various disciplines that serve the development of philosophical reflection. Philosophy always seeks within its own sphere of competence the highest explanations of things. It would make no ultimate sense, for example, to master the mathematical rules of quantum mechanics without knowing what quantum mechanics is about. To discover, however, what quantum mechanics is about entails knowledge of a science other than and superior to that of quantum mechanics. This sort of ordered reflection eventually leads to the highest wisdom, which brings with it knowledge of the highest causes. In his magisterial study of philosophy, Benedict Ashley speaks about the way toward wisdom.[5]

The dual tutelage of reason and faith does not generate in those who respect the limits of each discipline, human and divine, a spiritual schizophrenia. Since God is the author of both faith and reason, the Christian thinker expects to find complementarity where other inquirers sometimes perceive separation or even opposition. Thus Pope John Paul II begins his 1998 encyclical on faith and reason:

> Faith and reason are like two wings on which the human spirit rises to the contemplation of truth; and God has placed in the human heart a desire to know the truth—in a word, to know himself—so that, by knowing and loving God, men and women may also come to the fullness of truth about themselves (cf. *Ex* 33:18; *Ps* 27:8-9; 63:2-3; *Jn* 14:8; *1 Jn* 3:2).[6]

---

[5] Benedict M. Ashley, *The Way Toward Wisdom: An Interdisciplinary and Intercultural Introduction to Metaphysics* (Notre Dame, Indiana: University of Notre Dame Press, 2005).

[6] John Paul II, Encyclical Letter *Fides et ratio* (1998), Introduction. For further reflection on this principle, see my *"Duplex Ordo Cognitionis,"* in *Reason and the Reasons of Faith*, eds. Paul J.

Fresh Beginnings from Classical Foundations

No one can escape the urgency that attaches to the requirement that all come to the fullness of truth about the human person, "the only creature on earth that God has created for himself."[7] This lapidary phrase from the Second Vatican Council (1962–1965) captures the reason that prompted the research that led to the composition of this volume. The present exercise seeks to understand the highest causes of human well-being within a context illuminated by the revelation of that supernatural beatitude that is open to the human creature. To put it otherwise, the present volume looks at the psychological well-being of the human person within the parameters set by what the same council refers to as the universal call to holiness.

Philosophical Virtues and Psychological Strengths is not a book reserved for those who profess the Catholic faith. The authors have relied on the enormous intellectual achievement that has been sustained throughout two millennia by those who have adhered to the Christian faith or who, at least, have welcomed what the Catholic faith holds out for acceptance. These formers of the Catholic tradition include theologians, philosophers, and psychologists. Many are well known and find a place even in secular curricula. Think of St. Augustine or St. Thomas Aquinas. Their voices and those of others echo throughout these pages. The present volume aims to make the best of the interdisciplinary model. Together, theologians, philosophers, and psychologists inform the authors who have contributed to the pages of this volume.

Roger Scruton reports that the phrase *philosophical anthropology* dates from the eighteenth century. This now familiar coinage reflects the fragmentation of the philosophical disciplines within university settings, which developed during the period of the

---

Griffiths and Reinhard Hütter (New York: T&T Clark, 2005), 327–338.

7 See the Pastoral Constitution on the Church in the Modern World, *Gaudium et spes*, no. 21.

Enlightenment, with its encyclopedic penchant for identifying academic specializations. It also announces the academic implementation of the anthropological turn or the turn to the subject. Traditionally, Catholic theology treats "anthropology" alongside the themes that fall under the general heading of creation, which include the human creature composed of body and soul.

Philosophical psychology opens up different perspectives. In this book at least, the phrase *philosophical psychology* is used to designate the special field of inquiry that our research opens up for students of the psychological sciences. *Philosophical psychology*, in other words, describes an ordered multidisciplinary inquiry into the basic structure of the human person. It is this same person who appears as the everyday client in search of the clinician's psychological ministrations. Philosophical psychology is designated "philosophical" inasmuch as it aims to examine the structures and capacities that define the nature of the human person.

Psychology too has a special meaning. In a certain sense, the present volume employs the term *psychology* as theologians and philosophers originally understood it, that is, before the dawn of what today is known as empirical or clinical psychology. This choice rests on the conviction that classical anthropology, which includes attention to the psychological capacities of the human person as they have been understood within classical Thomist theology, can contribute to the development of the present-day psychological sciences. Although they may not have thought of psychology as a distinctive *practical* discipline, classical theorists such as St. Thomas Aquinas, nonetheless devote considerable attention to the psychological capacities of the human person. The term *psychology* to designate a specific academic field of inquiry distinct from metaphysics dates from the late sixteenth century, although the popularization of this discipline happened in the early eighteenth century and owes much to the work of the German Enlightenment philosopher Christian Wolff (1679–1754), who subordinated both his "empirical" and "rational" psychology to the overarching scheme of his ontology.

The present study represents an innovative undertaking. The research takes a fresh beginning from recent Catholic thought about faith and reason, especially as this has been expressed in Pope John Paul II's 1998 Encyclical *Fides et ratio*. Further, there exists among the essayists who have contributed to the section of this book that treats the basic elements of human psychology a general agreement on the composition of the human. Specifically, they hold that the mind-body distinction introduced at the start of the modern period and usually associated with the writings of René Descartes (1596–1650) represents a distracting and generally unfortunate evolution for the history of psychology of all stripes. The authors share instead a general anthropological assumption that the human person should be regarded as a body and soul composite, where the soul represents the seat of those psychic powers, including the felt emotions that are considered proper to the human person.

Speculative truths ordered to practical lessons

The Christian Church is committed to regarding the human creature as a composite of body and soul.[8] This tenet of Christian faith does not close off philosophical exploration of what it means to be a body informed by a living soul. It does, however, exclude monistic anthropologies. The human creature is not exclusively spiritual. (Even after death, the separated soul retains an ordination to its body.) The human creature is not exclusively material. Throughout history, each viewpoint has enjoyed its exponent. Contemporary outlooks favor a genetic-based materialism. No Catholic scholar has done more to remind philosophers

---

8 See *Catechism of the Catholic Church*, nos. 363–368, especially the reference to the text of *Gaudium et spes*, no. 14.

and theologians alike that the human person is not reducible to one or the other of its component parts than Dominican Father Benedict M. Ashley. His seminal work, *Theologies of the Body*, remains the definitive exposition of Catholic teaching on the human person as well as an authoritative account of the history of the departure from this teaching that has gradually taken hold of Western thought from the fifteenth century to the present.[9] In many respects, the findings of Ashley's scholarly work undergird whatever is said in the essays contained in part 2 of this volume. *Theologies of the Body* further supplies theoretical and historical background to what Father Ashley says in his essay on the nature of mental health and human well-being.

Although there are a number of philosophical masters who try to persuade their readers that the natural starting point of all philosophical investigation is the human psyche, the authentic Christian tradition chooses another starting point. The proper study of mankind is not man. Alexander Pope's eighteenth-century "Essay on Man" may bring poetic pleasure to the classical ear, but its anthropocentrism reflects the empiricism of his age: "Know then thyself, presume not God to scan,/The proper study of mankind is Man."[10] Without adopting the apriorisms of continental rationalism, Catholic thought shoots for the stars.

---

[9] Benedict Ashley, *Theologies of the Body: Humanist and Christian* (Braintree: Pope John XIII Medical-Moral Research and Education Center, 1995).

[10] Alexander Pope, "Essay on Man," Epistle Two: "Of the Nature and State of Man, With Respect to Himself as an Individual" (1732), I. Pope, a Catholic, wrote his essay within the context of an absolute and reverential respect for the determinations of divine providence: "All Nature is but Art unknown to thee;/All chance direction, which thou canst not see;/All discord, harmony not understood;/All partial evil, universal good:/And spite of Pride, in erring Reason's spite,/One truth is clear, Whatever is, is right."

Fresh Beginnings from Classical Foundations

The Catholic tradition embraces realist metaphysics. Philosophers inquire about being *qua* being and created being. We see this philosophical stance expertly set forth in the essay by Professor Kenneth Schmitz, which was written as an introduction to the eight essays that discuss the basic elements of a philosophical psychology. The task of the philosopher has been described as distinguishing in order to unite. Professor Schmitz remains a master of uniting, of bringing together. By locating the various elements of human psychology within the classical transcendentals of being, Professor Schmitz provides a number of overarching considerations that brings together the various distinctions articulated in the several essays that form part 2 of this volume. The philosopher's task entails searching, and so there is no final resting place other than the eventual contemplation of the Highest Truth. Where others introduce fragmentation, philosophers of excellence aim to resolve in favor of first principles. Professor Schmitz sets before us a vision of psychological pathology and psychological health situated within an understanding of the human person as a whole. He also introduces the person of Gladys Maria Sweeney, whose faith convictions have inspired her to seek out and to implement a contemplative vision of the psychological sciences.

Dr. Sweeney enjoys the credentials of a distinguished clinical psychologist. Her participation in the three-year research project that provides the matrix for this book ensured that discussion among the participants remained focused on the specific interests of the psychological sciences. Case studies referenced in the basic essays serve to illuminate from a clinical psychological point of view the major theoretical points considered under the heading of "basic elements." Obviously no claim is made to offer specific instruction for therapeutic discussions or other such mediations. The cases rather represent the métier of the psychologist inserted into a global presentation of what a Christian philosophy can say about the human creature and the destiny of each human person. The present volume may be considered a useful resource for students of psychology who would like to know more about the nature of the human person whose distresses they set out to relieve. It is assumed that the development of one's psychological skills will proceed with more alacrity and success to the extent that the practitioner understands the interactions that transpire among the various operative capacities that enable the human person to act consciously.

Synthesis

It would be impossible to foresee the various uses that students of the psychological sciences may discover in the speculative resources contained in parts 1 and 2 of this volume. To illustrate how those who study the psychological sciences may put these theoretical materials to work, the final section of the book contains two essays that suggest ways to talk about mental health issues within a context that is congenial to the vision of the human person expressed especially in section two. One author imagines a conversation between a contemporary psychotherapist and a representative of the views expressed in this book, whereas the other author, a senior researcher in the field, recapitulates the salient points made in the essays of part 2 and reminds us of the formal distinctions that separate the several disciplines that inform this volume's content. The task that remains to accomplish entails training a corps of psychological personnel who are prepared to compose their own practical essays on the basis of their appropriation of the philosophical psychology described in part 2 and also, as a result of their own research in the classroom and in their clinical practice, to put this knowledge at the service of others.

There is something arguably revolutionary about the project that the essays in this volume represent. The classical vision of the human person that animates the contents of this book may appear as something altogether novel to the thinker of the twenty-first century. No better indication of this possibility exists than the essay by Roger Scruton included in this volume. Roger Scruton illustrates by an appeal to the history of modern Western thought that many present-day common conceptions of the human person owe a great deal more to Western European philosophies of the eighteenth century than they do to the collective wisdom from both East and West developed during the course of more than fifteen hundred years, roughly from the patristic to the contemporary periods. It is nonetheless within this ancient, centuries-old history that the Catholic tradition finds its center and moorings.

This volume aims to retrieve selectively, with an eye toward psychological mediations, the best of what is contained in the Christian philosophical and theological traditions and to put this wisdom at the service of the psychological sciences. At the same time students of philosophy and theology will benefit from the lessons contained in the various essays. The realization of the practical eclipse of the Catholic tradition from contemporary discussions that transpire under the heading of psychology, a fact that Roger Scruton draws to our attention in a lapidary and still eloquent fashion, is not the occasion for lament. The participants in the research project that generated the essays in this volume do not encourage a romantic nostalgia for ancient and medieval thought, nor do they imagine some earlier time when things were better than they have been since the flowering of the Enlightenment. On the contrary, the participants, each of them, the old and the young, stand with two feet set squarely on ground hallowed by two millennia of Christian reflection and research and learning. The authors contained in this volume do not take fright at what Roger Scruton reports to be the stasis of philosophical psychology. Rather, they regard what Roger Scruton reports as a challenge issued to a new generation of theologians, philosophers, and especially psychologists, to put out into the deep. The challenge is a perennial one for Christian thinkers. Christ himself announced the goal when he reminded us that every steward instructed in the kingdom of heaven brings forth from his storehouse both "the new and the old" (see Matt. 13:52).

Chapter 2

Overarching Considerations

Kenneth Schmitz

The essays that follow are the product of a larger project initiated by Dr. Gladys Sweeney, the Academic Dean of the Institute for Psychological Sciences. It was and is her conviction that the study and therapy of psychological conditions will be enhanced by placing it within wider circles of interpretation and concern. An inner circle within psychology situates the study of specific pathologies, not only for the amelioration of disease, but also for the development and maintenance of mental and emotional health.[11] A wider circle, drawing upon another field, situates the study of psychological disorders and psychological health within an understanding of the human person as a whole. With this end in view, the present volume is dedicated to philosophical anthropology and philosophical psychology. It has been shaped and honed by a series of conversations among philosophers of the classical tradition, inspired by St. Thomas Aquinas.[12] And it has been

---

[11] The work of Martin Seligman is of especial value here: Martin Seligman and Mihaly Csikszentmihalyi, "Positive Psychology: An Introduction," *American Psychologist* 55 (2000): 5–14.

[12] Fr. Romanus Cessario, O.P. has provided invaluable guidance and counsel in this process; consult his book *The Virtues, or the Examined Life* (New York: Continuum, 2002).

tempered by conversations with practicing psychotherapists and by the study of the psychosocial conditions that they face daily.

The attempt to situate psychotherapy, at least in some of its versions, within a wider context and deeper foundations, calls for reflection upon the human person as a being within the community of beings. And so the classical philosophical understanding of psychological disease and health places the person within the comprehensive and fundamental texture of being. The background against which the present essays move is provided by a shared understanding of that texture, and draws upon metaphysics and philosophical anthropology in its classical sources. This is a daring and adventurous project in an era in which classical metaphysics is often considered a detritus of past thought, worn away by the advance of the positive sciences.

Moreover, in an era that owes so much that is beneficial to specialized disciplines of inquiry, intercommunication among the disciplines, especially so diverse as psychotherapy and philosophy, must converge at the borders drawn up and required by that same specialization, boundaries, not only in terminology, but in thought and purpose as well. It would be premature to anticipate an integration of classical philosophy and psychotherapy, but the intention of these essays is to respect their difference and yet to build a buttress in philosophy that looks toward bridging the gulf that separates the two disciplines and that invites a response from psychotherapists.

The distance between the disciplines is considerable, and the separations are several. Already mentioned is the distinction within psychology itself between human pathology and human well-being. There is also the difference between theory and practice, within psychology itself, but even greater between the effort to understand that inspires the theoretical aspect of philosophy and the hope to heal that above all animates the therapist. More important is the distinction between the psyche and the whole person. Then, too, there is the distinction between the person and his situatedness within society. And finally, the person is situated within the very texture of being itself; for no matter how distinctive the human person is, nevertheless he or she is a citizen in the community of beings. At this point one may well ask whether reflections upon the human person within the community of beings has any appreciable contribution to make to psychotherapy, and conversely, whether psychotherapy has anything to say to the philosophy of being. These essays set out to provide a beginning from the side of philosophy for a conversation that hopes to prove beneficial to both inquiries.

We may ask: What has a classical philosophy of being to offer to the study of psychological condition? And, what has psychotherapy to contribute to philosophy? As to the latter, we might propose that it offers what any special science does, but in an even more significant way, for in addition to a sense of the concrete and the specific, it offers a distinctive entry into the interiority of the human person, special insights into the concrete problems of order and disorder and of ease and dis-ease in relation to the human being.

Conversely, what might philosophy contribute to psychotherapy? We shall see in the following essays, but we might initially propose that philosophy directs attention to a sense of the pervasive presence of unity, truth, goodness, and beauty, what I have called the texture of being and what classical philosophy has termed the transcendental — that is, all-pervasive — properties of being. For philosophy distinguishes between the species-specific qualities of things (categories) and certain properties (transcendentals) that accompany being wherever it is found, even residually, in its distortions and even in its dis-ease.

What comprises the texture of being? Every being exhibits a certain core identity that remains relatively stable throughout its existence: this is the transcendental property of unity (*unum*).

This unity also embraces a more or less stable or variable set of characteristics that constitute a being in its complex totality. Traditional philosophy distinguishes the core (the substantial unity of the thing) from its secondary traits (termed *accidents*).[13] Together these comprise the concrete totality of an individual being (*ens*).

The term *essence* (*essentia*) gives expression in the strict sense to the specific nature of the being, to the substantial unity that constitutes it as a thing (*res*) of a certain kind: a lion or a sheep or a human. In an expanded sense, the term *essence* may refer to all that makes up whatever the being is, including its secondary or accidental traits. Finally, all of this—the essence in the broad sense—is distinct from the fact that it is, which refers to its existence (*esse*).

Individual beings do not stand alone, but are members of the community of beings related to and interrelated with one another in more or less intimate or distant ways. Traditional philosophy speaks of this property as *relationality* (*aliquid*).[14]

Now, it is this unfolding texture that gives to each being and the whole of being its intelligibility, its meaningfulness or truth (*verum*), some at least of which we can discover through inquiry, experience, and study. Upon our encounter with other beings we

[13] The terms *accident* and *accidental* are particularly unsuitable in present-day English to communicate the meaning intended by the terms. For they do not mean an unfortunate incident—an accident in ordinary English—but *simply that* which "comes to" (*accidere*) and adheres to or inheres in the core identity of the individual being. Or one might say that the term stands for those characteristics that are additional to the core identity. It is as though, coming upon an animal's track, we were to identify its species (a lion or a sheep), but in addition to its specific character (its substance) we were to add: "and a large one, too" (its size, one of its accidentals).

[14] I use the term *relationality* to express "reference to another" or "something other."

22

instinctively derive at least some intelligible meaning from them, a meaning that we may elaborate through further investigation and reflection.

At the same time, however, in our encounter we may be drawn toward others or away from them, responding to a certain value or disvalue in them. Usually we measure the value or disvalue in terms of our own needs and interests (*bonum utile*), but we are also capable of appreciating the excellence of another being, even if it does not serve our needs, as when we admire the strength and fluid beauty of a caged beast. Such a value-charged appraisal testifies to the good (*bonum simpliciter*) that is ingredient in each being, even if that good may not be good for us. With this review, we have just traversed the transcendental, all-pervasive properties that make up the texture of being.

With the introduction of the characteristic of the good that is attendant upon being, we enter upon the domain of therapy, both as the remedy of disease and as the restoration to health. And with this we touch upon the boundary that both separates and joins philosophy and psychotherapy.

Let me now indicate how the essays engage that border. In the first essay, Christopher Thompson acknowledges the differences that must be bridged and suggests a pathway over those differences. While he proposes a concrete starting place for the project of mutual engagement, he does not enter the clinic as a therapist but argues for the need of the therapist to have an understanding of the person he is treating. In a word, theoretical understanding, whether true or defective, will guide therapeutic practice. Conceding that a direct approach from philosophy may prove too abstract to be immediately useful, he invites the therapist to consider another way, one that has already engaged the therapist: it is to help the patient to act so as to achieve the good of psychological and personal health. Thereby the transcendental good comes into play as the goal toward which the sought-for restoration to health is oriented, that is, toward the true happiness and fulfillment of the person. To determine the overriding good is the theme of this first essay, which engages the cooperation of the true and the good in their relation to understanding and practice.

In the second essay, Matthew Cuddeback coins the suggestive phrase "ontological selfhood" to express the ownership each person exercises over his or her own actions. Here we encounter the transcendental property of unity, which is identified in its core with the substantial form, and specifically in the human being with the soul, as the first principle of that ownership. It is this formal principle from which properly human actions flow as from their unitary source or selfhood, or in another felicitous phrase, from the person's "ontological self-dominion." The appropriate self-possession is, precisely, to possess health. A dynamic self-ownership comes into play in the governance of the emotions, so that an appropriate selfhood in which reason governs the emotions provides a dynamic standard for the remedy of disorder, whether it be the loss of integral unity (as in schizophrenia) or the tyranny of a false unity (as in addiction).

The suggestion that governance of the emotions and appetites should be provided by the nobler power of reason is taken up by John Cuddeback. It is not reason alone, however, that is the appropriate principle of healthy human action, for reason operates as a "principle within a principle," the latter principle being the good, and specifically the good of the human person (*bonum humanum*). It is here that the concept of law enters the discourse, since law is an ordination to the end by providing the norms that ought to govern reason in its practical use, if reason is to reason well. The norms are known from the inclinations of human nature, and these inclinations are rooted in a shared love of the transcendental and the transcendent Good.

With Craig Steven Titus's essay we turn to the strengths or virtues that should operate in the governance of action. The overarching, normative virtue is that of prudence, not however in the vulgar sense of caution but as the guide to creative reasonable action. Indeed, the cultivation of prudence spans the entire range of human action, putting into play the integration of rational, volitional, emotional, and social skills. Titus describes the various types of prudence with delicate nuances. Of particular interest is the discussion of the exceptional case. At the same time, he keeps before us the unitary character of prudent action: it consists in "doing the right thing, for the right reason, with the right choices and emotions, at the right time." Moreover, prudence incorporates both the subjective disposition of the agent as well as the objective norm of action. He acknowledges, too, that time, development, and experience are needed to bring about a realization and actualization of the good in being. Of especial value is the importance given to the temporal conditions in which prudence is to be developed, as well as the complexity of the secondary and supportive skills and virtues that come to be integrated in a fully formed prudential judgment. These include the support of persons and community and of the psychotherapist where needed. Given the need for development through experience and self-discipline, including the variety of factors that enter into a well-formed action, the role of moral wisdom can be initiated and furthered with the help of psychotherapeutic guidance.

The remaining essays take up the topics of freedom and the emotions. Tobias Hoffmann underscores St. Thomas's understanding of freedom as a rational desire that grounds free choice, just as the desire for happiness provides the basis for our free choices. He also addresses the struggle to combat evil and to make the choices that lead to freedom.

Paul Gondreau reflects upon the role of the senses and the emotions in an integrated and healthy life, while he reflects upon the pathologies that require psychotherapy. Most striking is the insistence upon the effect of the movements which the sense powers have upon the soul, as they participate or fail to participate in the goals of the rational soul. It is telling that Thomas gives especial attention to the emotions or passions, not in the context of his treatment of the intellect, but rather in the course of his discussion of the moral virtues. Aquinas's decision to treat the emotions in relation to the practical pursuit of human well-being and happiness points to the role of psychotherapy in their adjustment. There follows a positive discussion of the interplay between the anthropology outlined in the essay and the role of psychotherapy in regard to the emotions. Steering between Kant's rationalism, Hume's empiricism, and Mill's utilitarianism, the synthesis of reason and emotion in Thomas's philosophy fits it well as a ground for modern psychotherapy. The concluding remarks touching on psychopathology lead us to the next essay.

In it Daniel McInerny places the question that is central to the whole project: In what way, if any, can philosophy be of help to the psychotherapist and the client? McInerny replies that the symptoms and conditions of dis-order can be recognized as such only on the basis of a sense of order. For the diagnostic narrative of dis-ease takes its cues from the narrative of what it is to be a healthy and authentic human being. Such a narrative requires a conception of anthropology and the appropriate virtues, and in the broadest and deepest sense it engages the very texture of being itself. Nevertheless, dis-order haunts human existence, and many difficulties arise in the course of daily life. The traditional designation of the strengths or virtues with which we need to face and overcome such difficulties include the virtues of fortitude and hope, virtues that enable us to face fear, despair, and the other irascible emotions. While setting forth an understanding of the virtues, especially those dealing with difficulties to be overcome, the essay reflects upon the contribution the therapist can make to help the client come to a self-understanding of the alteration in practices that are meant to lead to a new and fuller life.

Overarching Considerations

Indeed, it is precisely the desire for health and happiness that brings the client to the therapist, and David Franks addresses the way in which that desire inaugurates a process of healing. The process entails the integration of body and soul, of mind and emotions, and the bringing of the passions under what Pope John Paul II termed "the personalistic norm."[15] At the same time the essay intones a message of concern over the tendency in much of today's society to elevate the sexual drive to an undeserved eminence. What remains positive in his essay is the recurring theme of the underlying reality of the integration of the passions in the whole person.

The collection of essays as a whole urges us to notice that there are several layers of intelligibility and practice underlying the diagnosis and treatment of psychic maladies and the maintenance of mental and emotional health. There is the level of diagnosis that reads in the symptoms the underlying condition. There are the recommended practices for the removal of the symptoms, the eradication of the condition, and the restoration to health. Yet there is also the deeper substratum that needs to become operative in the therapist's and the recovering client's understanding of what constitutes health for the client. This deeper therapy reposes upon an integrated understanding of the human person. Finally, there is the context within which that person comes to live out a free and healthy lifestyle. Since this engages other persons, the things of nature and the very dynamics of existence itself, the deepest and broadest texture of being is available to be drawn upon for support. And through the transcendental properties of being, especially through the unity, the true, and the good, such ontological support is deeply embedded in reality. To be sure, not all of these dimensions need to be raised to the state

---

15 Karol Wojtyła, *Love and Responsibility* (San Francisco: Ignatius, 1981), 40ff.

of explicit consciousness. Habits learned from family, teachers, fellow workers, and society, and from religious sources, may be intuitively grasped and made part of one's values and conduct. The purpose of the essays that follow is to make intellectually explicit those habits and virtues that are truly effective in the pursuit of the good life.

Part II

Basic Elements

Modern psychology has attended less to why people are happy than to why they are not. Contemporary psychological sciences nonetheless have started to change their focus by including in their study what renders persons and communities happy, that is, what makes them flourish. At the same time, the classical tradition (Aristotelian and Thomist) has affirmed that consideration of happiness, including ultimate happiness, is needed to understand human thought, affection, and action, and for nurturing what is best therein.

A problem arises though because of conflicting construals of what makes human persons happy and of the various states of character and virtue that contribute to lasting happiness. A dialogue between the psychologist and the philosopher can start, as Christopher Thompson suggests, at the therapist's door in order to compare the qualities of everyday flourishing and ultimate happiness that come to light in the diverse construals of the human person, interpersonal relationships, and transcendence.

Chapter 3

At the Therapist's Door

Christopher J. Thompson

The time has arrived for a positive psychology. Our message is to remind our field that psychology is not just the study of pathology, weakness, and damage; it is also the study of strength and virtue. Treatment is not just fixing what is broken; it is nurturing what is best.

Martin Seligman[16]

The remarks in the preceding quotation are taken from the introductory essay of a special edition of the *American Psychologist*, the leading journal of the American Psychological Association. The entire issue is dedicated to the special questions of happiness, excellence, and optimal human functioning, and although the work is not particularly sympathetic to a Thomistic approach, it signals one of the more positive developments in the field of psychology and provides Catholic intellectuals with an important

---

[16] Martin Seligman and Mihaly Csikszentmihalyi, "Positive Psychology: An Introduction," *American Psychologist* 55, no. 1 (January 2000): 14. See also Christopher Peterson and Martin E. P. Seligman, eds., *Character Strengths and Virtues: A Handbook and Classification* (London: Oxford University Press, 2005).

opportunity.[17] It is a positive sign because the overall theme of the essays bears upon one of the most important claims of the Thomistic tradition: the desire for happiness. The issue, therefore, represents an opportunity for Thomists to bring to the table their remarkable tradition of reflection and scholarship upon the questions of human flourishing and its challenges.[18] By bringing the insights of St. Thomas into the contemporary conversation, both Thomists and contemporary psychologists can bear much fruit. The challenge immediately presents itself, however, as to how effectively to bring these significant dimensions into dialogue with one another.

Many of the essays in this volume are exegetical in nature and seek to explicate in a useful way important insights of St. Thomas by drawing heavily upon his work directly. They take the primary texts as their point of departure in an effort to bring the best of his insights into a contemporary setting. As an important complement to these efforts, my essay explores a more theoretical approach and seeks to explore more immediately the opportunities for a creative correlation between the fundamental insights of St. Thomas's efforts and those of the contemporary clinician.

Whether exegetical or theoretical, all of the approaches are seeking to establish a relationship and thus have to confront the very real problem of establishing a basis upon which a constructive encounter might begin to emerge. My essay offers an attempt to reflect on the possibility of establishing that context.

---

[17] For a broader evaluation of the merits of positive psychology from a Catholic perspective see, Paul C. Vitz, "Psychology in Recovery," *First Things* 151 (March 2005): 17–22.

[18] For a brief history of Thomism especially in matters of philosophy and theology, see Romanus Cessario, O.P., *A Short History of Thomism* (Washington, DC: The Catholic University of America Press, 2005).

Any exchange of ideas among Catholic philosophers or theologians and contemporary clinical psychologists will have to confront at the beginning a number of difficulties. Perhaps first among them is the difference in the meaning of terms.

In the contemporary academy, *clinical psychology* is employed in any number of ways and does not identify a single method or set of convictions about its modes of inquiry, its procedures for research, or its plan of development and progress. Granted that there may be some common elements across the field concerning the major figures and movements within clinical psychology, most contemporary clinical psychologists would likely confirm the diversity of perspectives and are comfortable in recognizing the vast multiplicity of approaches within the field.[19]

Psychology, on the other hand, when employed by Catholic, Thomistic scholars, emerges from within a much more uniform tradition with a more or less agreed-upon intellectual pedigree, textual tradition, and commentatorial development. There is, to be sure, a long and extensive conversation among Thomistic scholars, but there remains nonetheless, especially when compared with its contemporary counterpart, a more or less fixed tradition of material and formal components.[20] Sign up for a class in "Thomistic Psychology" and most practitioners in the field could name its essential sources and directions for development. Take a course in "clinical psychology" and the adage seems apropos: *as many opinions as heads.*

---

[19] A recent textbook indicates that there are at least 250 approaches to psychological therapy. See David G. Myers, *Psychology*, 5th ed. (Holland, MI: Worth Publishers, 1998), 488.

[20] For a historical overview of some of the leading efforts in the United States to combine the insights of St. Thomas and the discipline of psychology, especially in the late nineteenth and early twentieth century see, Robert W. Kugelman, "Neoscholastic Psychology Revisited," *History of Psychology* 8 (2005): 131–175.

Philosophical Virtues and Psychological Strengths

All of this means, then, that if we are to take up the challenge of entering into an exchange with contemporary psychologists, some working parameters as to what one means will be required. More than likely, some artificial constraints will have to be imposed on the notion of "contemporary psychology" in order at least to get the conversation started. The question is: how to shape it?

One distinction that seems helpful in *beginning* the conversation between psychology and Thomism is to borrow a distinction from the classic Thomistic tradition: namely, the distinction between speculative and practical inquiry. For Thomists, not all inquiry is the same, not all inquiry is ordered toward the same objective. Speculative reasoning aims at the most coherent and comprehensive grasp of the truth of things. Practical reasoning, on the other hand, typically aims at the achievement of some good, doing something well. Speculative reasoning has the truth of things as its proper object and is not immediately concerned with matters of practice or activity. Practical reasoning presupposes that one grasps the truth of things (if only provisionally), before one can engage in practical matters. The distinction articulated here is hardly adequate and is not a hard and fast one, but it nonetheless supplies an important context for any conversation to proceed.

The reason it is important is this: for Thomists, *psychology*, is the study of the *psyche*, the soul and its operations, and it is first and foremost a speculative inquiry. It has as its object the truth of man and his powers and operations. Its principal aim, as opposed to a practical inquiry, is the truth of things, in this instance the truth about man as an embodied soul, endowed with certain powers. It is not, at least in its principal expression, concerned with doing or practice. Thomistic psychology names a kind of speculative, philosophical reasoning, not practical considerations, and has for its object of inquiry man in his essence, not, principally, individual men and women given in empirical experience. Its methods are philosophical and rely upon the common experiences and knowledge open to all. Contemporary psychology, with its emphasis on scientific, experimental data, on the other hand, is a specialized form of investigation, and its conclusions are not generally available to the average reflective man or woman.[21]

All of this means, then, that any interface between clinical psychology and contemporary Thomists will have to recognize three essential problems: confusion concerning the nomenclature of terms, confusion concerning the mode of reasoning employed, and confusion concerning the proper objects of its inquiry. Psychology taken in the sense of "contemporary clinical psychology" names a vast diversity of approaches, a largely practical inquiry, with an almost exclusive reliance upon empirical data in its development and advance. In the other, *psychology* names a fairly uniform tradition of philosophical discourse with authoritative resources and texts, a species of inquiry that is largely speculative and that examines the nature of man in his essence, his nature, not man given in the multiplicity of empirical findings.

Is there, however, a way to bridge the distance? Is there a way of weaving together what appear to be irreconcilable modes of inquiry? Yes, I would propose, and I offer here the outlines of a direction for progress.

It is my conviction that the shortest route to an engaging encounter between Thomism and contemporary psychotherapeutic practice is to focus upon the clinical setting, the environment of counselor and client, for it is here in this very practical setting

---

[21] For a classic presentation of some of the issues mentioned here see Robert Brennan, O.P., *General Psychology: A Study of Man Based on St. Thomas* (New York: MacMillan Company, 1952) 15–26, and, more recently, Chad Ripperger, F.S.S.P., *Introduction to the Science of Mental Health*, Vol. I: *Philosophical Psychology* (Lincoln, Nebraska: 2001), 1–14.

that a productive interface of the two "world views" begins to emerge.

It may seem at first blush to be a mistake to begin here, for earlier I had concluded that *psychology* in the Thomistic tradition names a largely speculative inquiry into the nature of man and his essence and does not immediately lend itself to a mode of practical reasoning. The contemporary clinical setting, by contrast, with its focus on the counselor-client relationship, seems immediately concerned with practical issues and not the more theoretical questions of the nature of man.

But here an opening for engagement actually begins to emerge, and for two reasons, the first more theoretical, the other more mundane, but nonetheless important.

In the first place, the Thomist would argue that any practical inquiry into what an individual man or woman ought to do, especially any practical inquiry of the sort that likely occurs in the psychotherapeutic setting, must first emerge from a thorough grasp of what man is in his nature, or what it means to be a human being. No health professional worthy of the name would embark upon the task of suggesting remedies without first having a working grasp of the essential facets of what it means to be a human being in the first place. For as an exercise of practical reasoning, sound clinical advice must first be rooted in a speculative grasp, a systematic understanding of the nature of man and his activities *qua* man. Anyone interested in securing and nurturing the health of the human being must first grasp what it is to be one.

Clinical psychology, then, if it is to be practiced within a manner consistent with the essential outlines of a Thomistic inquiry, would seem best served if it first recognized and embraced the speculative principles upon which its practical inquiry depends.

But granted the systematic point concerning the relationship of speculative and practical reasoning, a philosophy of the human person and the advice given, there is a more mundane point of entry into a common conversation that does not rely upon what some might take to be a more complicated and theoretical exchange. There is, in other words, another catalyst, one more promising for conversation between the clinical psychologist and the Thomist, and that is the focus of the remainder of this chapter.

The counselor setting

It is my conviction that the best point of entry is not to begin with the speculative facets of the Thomistic philosophy of man. Rather, the best place *to begin* a fruitful dialogue is in the counselor setting, on the home turf of the clinical psychologist. The simple reason for this is that the therapist seems committed to the notion of helping people, of helping people achieve something approximating a good life, lived with some degree of consistency, and it is precisely here, at the question of pursuing a good and satisfying life that the Thomist and the contemporary psychotherapist might find that spark, that catalyst for engaging conversation and exchange for the mutual benefit of each.

For the truth of the matter remains that despite the diversity of terms, the vast differences of histories and methodologies, the theoretical impasses and hurdles, both St. Thomas and the contemporary psychotherapist seem to have one, central conviction in common: all human action, more precisely, all healthy, rational action, proceeds from the desire to achieve a good, from the desire to pursue an end. And both the contemporary psychotherapist and the Thomist share the conviction that health and happiness lie principally in the pursuit, indeed achievement, of goals worthy of the human person.

For St. Thomas, all agents act for an end.[22] Human agents, then, are motivated by the pursuit of an end or good that draws

---

[22] *ST* I-II, Q. 1, art. 2.

the individual in a particular direction. Where there is no goal, there is no movement.[23]

There are, to be sure, activities done by a human being that are not explicitly motivated by any articulated desire but are nonetheless actions "of a man."[24] I am circulating my blood and digesting my last meal as I write this essay, for example, but such actions do not betray, says St. Thomas, anything uniquely human. Such acts do not disclose the uniqueness of my "human" acting. Rather human actions, actions that are properly identified as "human" are actions that proceed from a deliberate will and have at their core a certain reasonableness and rationale about them. Healthy human activity is action ordered toward an end.[25]

To act reasonably, then, *is* to be acting for an end. All rational action is motivated by some *thing* perceived to be good, and while one might not be able always and explicitly to articulate the goal of one's action, it must be the case, St. Thomas suggests, that there be a goal in order for the action to be considered reasonable.

[23] *ST* I-II, Q. 1, art. 1.

[24] St. Thomas distinguishes between the *actus hominis* and the *actus humanus*, between activities of a human being and properly human acts. The former, while purposeful, do not normally fall under the domain of reflective, deliberate intelligence; the latter are expressions of an intellectual awareness. See Tobias Hoffman's chapter on the spiritual nature of our free will. The distinction is not unimportant, for it helps separate out what a biologist specializing in gastrointestinal matters might know and what the dietician or health counselor might consider. Both may consider the human activities surrounding nourishment, the former under the guise of an *actus hominis*, the latter as an *actus humanus*.

[25] A fuller treatment of Thomas's understanding of human action in general can be found in Ralph McInerny, *Aquinas on Human Action: A Theory of Practice* (Washington, DC: The Catholic University Press of America, 1992); see especially chapter 2, "What Does It All Mean?", on the importance of ends for human action.

At the Therapist's Door

One might be able to get a better grasp of this essential Thomistic principle if one were to consider its opposite: action that lacks any particular goal or end. You might run into a friend on campus and ask her, in passing, where she is off to this afternoon. If her response is, "I have no idea," or "Was I going somewhere?" or something else along the lines suggesting no particular end in view, it might be wise to suggest she take a break. Your friend is starting to show the signs of mental duress. Healthy individuals are able to give an account of their actions, and to give an account is to give a rationale of the goals guiding such actions.

Living a healthy human life, living reasonably, then, will be a goal-directed activity. And whether it is the Thomist over coffee or the therapist in a session, assisting others in pursuing the reasonable life will entail a discussion of that life's goals or purposes.

Goals and purposes are plural nouns and as such suggest a variety and plurality of directions for one's life. Such, however, is not a full picture of human action according to St. Thomas. For while rational actions depend on goals, one goal and only one must serve as the anchor in the chain of motives. Some one thing must be understood, even if unreflectively, as the ultimate goal of one's living. There must be one predominant interest that provides the rationale for the decisions we make. Just as a woman might take any number of routes to her office in the morning, so there may be any number of ways to pursue one's purposes in life. But that there is only one dominant end that gives rhyme or reason to one's intermittent decisions is as clear to St. Thomas as the notion that one cannot walk in two directions at once.[26] One can enact a

---

[26] Walter Farrell, O.P., *Companion to the Summa* (New York: Sheed and Ward, 1940), II:3–22. Although perhaps dated in some of its examples, the materials here are invaluable in providing a more accessible portrait for what is happening in St. Thomas's *Summa*. It is available on the web in its entirety at www.op.org/Farrell/companion.

complex series of actions ordered toward intermediate ends, but not two opposing ways at the same time. One can pursue a complex variety of ends, but proceed in only one essential direction. While some of us can multitask, none can serve two masters.

In passing it should be noted that this is in marked contrast to those who perceive of the task of life as a never-ending search for meaning, an infinite unfolding of possibility and becoming. Not so for St. Thomas; there must be an "ultimate" in the chain of motives, or nothing would be desired at all. "To dream the impossible dream" or "to reach for unreachable stars" might make for a good musical, but one ought not to forget that what I am alluding to here is the theme song of a benevolent lunatic.

Nor will just any chain of reasoning suffice for the healthy person, the rational life. The mentally ill, for example, can often provide a complex account of the goals that give shape to their activities: world domination or avoiding alien abduction, for example. It will not be sufficient, in other words, to characterize the reasonable life as one that is goal-driven; rather, certain goals, goods that motivate, will be appropriate for healthy individuals while other goals will not. Living reasonably, living in accordance with reason, then, will not simply be living according to a plan; that may have the appearance of order but still lack reasonableness. Rather, living reasonably in a substantive way means being motivated toward goals that befit the person. It will entail sorting through the myriad of motivations and ordering one's life in accordance with those goals which are perfective of the human person. It will not be enough that one's life be simply ordered; rather, living an authentically reasonable life, a healthy life, will entail ordering one's life around the truth of what it means to be a human being.[27]

---

[27] See Romanus Cessario, O.P., *The Moral Virtues and Theological Ethics* (Notre Dame: University of Notre Dame Press, 2009), and *An Introduction to Catholic Moral Theology: Catholic Moral*

At the Therapist's Door

To begin to ponder what it means to be a human being in order to answer the questions as to which goods one ought to pursue is inadvertently to drift from a practical to a speculative consideration, from a conversation concerning what one ought to do to a conversation concerning who one is. It is to move from a consideration of what is good to a consideration of what is true.

To introduce the notion of the truth of what it means to be a human person supplies a critical methodological element in the discourse. For up to now all we have noted is that human action is end-guided and that rational agents are motivated creatures. A knowledge of the truth of what it means to be a human being, however, supplies us with a critical answer to a problem not yet articulated: namely, if all action is ordered toward the achievement of a good, what makes for evil acts? Whence emerges dysfunction?

For Thomas, an analysis of evil acts will not emerge from a consideration of the end-guided character of human activity alone, for as we have been saying all along: *all* human acts, even wicked acts, are for the sake of some end. Something more, then, is needed to complete the analysis; indeed, much more.

St. Thomas argues that while all actions proceed under the banner of some alluring ultimacy, only those actions which are ordered to our true end (namely, God) are candidates for authentically rational behavior and contribute to truly happy living. Desiring, in other words, even desiring for some thing ultimately, will not constitute a healthy human act; rather, desiring in accordance with the truth of who we are as persons ordered toward union with God will be the measure by which actions are judged to be authentically reasonable, befitting our dignity as persons, praiseworthy, healthy.[28]

Thought I (Washington, DC: The Catholic University of America Press, 2001).

[28] For more on the interrelationship between the will and the intellect, see the essays by Craig Titus and Tobias Hoffman.

Philosophical Virtues and Psychological Strengths

Man is, by nature, made for union with God and finds his true perfection in life, his authentic happiness only in an everlasting friendship with the God who created him. There is no escaping this fact for St. Thomas; even the sinful man is made for this. He remains a creature made for union with God and always works for something he considers to be perfecting, but he misjudges where his authentic satisfaction lies, where authentic fulfillment is to be found. Assuming he is not mentally ill, he is acting for ends and coordinates them under the guiding principle of something ultimate. The problem emerges in just what that something is. Often the fault lies in investing a kind of ultimacy in objects that cannot bear the load. If the ultimate end is not friendship with God, or if his proximate goals are not ordered to such an end, misery, dysfunction, or — to the extent to which the disorder is result of deliberate choices — sin results.

The completely perfected life, beatitude, is enjoyed fully, St. Thomas argues, only in the next life. We can nonetheless enjoy such a state, albeit in imperfect ways, in partial ways, in this life. And it is the degree to which we enjoy such a beatifying state that the actions of our life are to be judged as reasonable or not, healthy or not, praiseworthy or not.

Of course, practically speaking, not all of our actions are to be explicitly cast in terms of such dramatic ultimacy. We are directed to God above, not God alone. We live, in other words, in a world of proximate goals, interim ends, and while it is true that reasoned action betrays ultimate directions in the long run, we need not always be explicitly referring to such a feature to be acting reasonably.[29]

Pleasure, wealth, health, friendship, honor, the joy of marital intimacy can all serve as proximate ends, interim goals for healthy, rational action, and for so many people, for so much of

[29] *ST* I-II, Q. 1, art. 6, ad. 3.

their lives, such ends provide the threads of life's dramatic narrative. As created by God, such ends are in themselves good. Difficulties emerge, dysfunction likely ensues (for the therapist), unhappiness follows (for the Thomist therapist) when we invest ultimate significance in things of mere interim value, when we place our confidence in things in excessive ways. The soul, being made for the vision of God, is often inclined to set its sights on lower objects of concern.

Fallen human beings remain ordered to beatitude, it must be said, as the invitation to divine friendship is given to us as those who are loved by God, not as flawless. Sinful men and women are no less made for beatitude, and to dwell in sin is to dwell in contradiction with reality. Thus, while beatitude remains the goal of all striving in principle, in practice we direct ourselves toward other goods. More fully, we ascribe to partial goods an esteem that ought to be reserved to God alone.

All of us as creatures, then, remain directed toward beatitude, but because we are fallen, we no longer spontaneously order our lives in accordance with such a goal. Achieving our perfected state takes effort and deliberate thought, advice and the counsel of friends, conversion and the life of graced renewal. The Thomistic therapist has to confront the very real fact that while all of us by nature may be made for the perfected, complete life, none of us knows instinctively where it is to be found. As Paul Wadell says, "It is natural for us to want to be happy, but none of us naturally knows where happiness is to be found."[30]

Human activity in this context, then, belies a more complex relationship of goal-directed activity, of actions directed in various ways toward competing and partial goods, some pursued properly within the overall truth of beatitude, others only apparently

---

30 Paul Wadell, *The Primacy of Love: An Introduction to the Ethics of Aquinas* (Notre Dame: University of Notre Dame Press, 1992), 43.

so. The human person, as fallen, is habitually inclined to be mistaken in his judgments and must therefore regularly reflect on the direction of his or her life. All plans of an authentically rational sort aim at some good to be achieved; what makes such planning the object of praise, however, is not that they are desired, but the extent to which they fit within the overall order of the person's relationship to God.

The good of sexual union, for example, is rightly considered as a reasonable motive for marriage. It can provide the ordering end of a rational person's decisions. But it is only properly pursued in a manner consistent with the rational nature and dignity of the human person, when it is ordered in accordance with the truth of the human being as created by God. As a created good, it is capable of serving as the goal of our reasonable action. As a created good it is to be enjoyed, however, only as a partial or interim good and is not, then, to be pursued at all costs or in all circumstances. The single man must order his life choices in a manner that excludes the real good of sexual union. The married man must order his choices in a manner that includes sexual union within the overall vocation to beatitude. In both cases, sexual union is a noble candidate for goal-directed, rational action. In both cases it is rightly esteemed within the context of beatitude.

All human activity, then, while directed toward goals or ends, will become evaluated not simply on those terms (although it helps distinguish the action as reasonable as opposed to irrational). Rather, human activity in any substantive sense will be activity directed in commensuration with the truth of things—the truth of the person and the truth of the situation. There will, then, be better and worse forms of human action precisely insofar as such actions more or less conform to the truth of what it means to be a human being. All action is directed toward some good; some action is directed toward apparent goods, others to authentic ones.

At the Therapist's Door

Discerning the differences between apparent and authentic goods is a complex affair but is nonetheless incumbent upon any human being who wishes to live the reasonable life in any substantive way. It will require, among other things, not just keen analysis of the active life; but rather, at its core, a keen analysis of the human person at the center of that life. Moreover, such an analysis will provide not only insights into what it means to be a human being, but rather, which ends or goals an authentic human being ought to pursue.

For both the Thomist and therapist interested in helping people live reasonable lives with consistency, it will be necessary that a thorough, albeit working, grasp of what it means to be a human being is essential. At the center of all authentic help of another is a keen grasp of what the other, in truth, is.

Therapists working within this Thomistic tradition, then, will have to begin to develop a profound sense of the invitation to beatitude given to each individual human person, as well as a keen grasp of the deep, although partial, possession of such happiness that can be possible in this life. Only then are they able to exercise the practical guidance that would facilitate an integral response to the universal invitation to fullness of life, to nurture what is best.

What underlies human psychology is the basic unity and vitality that we call the person. The human person cannot be fully understood simply by referring to a list of particular functions, behaviors, or genetic coding. All of these qualities, when studied in a non-reductionist manner, give indications that something more is needed in order to explain the human agent and the human psyche or soul.

In face of different notions of the self and even of "no self," philosophical and theological reflection on the person can clarify the unified and personal basis (ontological self or personhood) that underlies diverse manifestations of thought, choice, action, and emotion. Matthew Cuddeback identifies how the principle of identity (the soul) accounts not only for the unity of the person, but also for the dominion that the person has in action and well-being. The therapist and the philosopher are keenly interested in how in the midst of conflicting inclinations the human person expresses responsibility and reaches out to other persons.

Chapter 4

Personal Unity

Matthew Cuddeback

Man is meant for seeing.

Josef Pieper

The methods and language of cognitive behavioral therapy presuppose that the human person is ontologically one, a lived unity. After a brief exposition of this point, I shall attempt to show that this ontological unity can be elucidated by the philosophical anthropology of Thomas Aquinas. Despite the challenge of translating Aquinas's language for our day, the attempt to do so rewards the effort.

I take it as one of the central principles of cognitive therapy that the person undergoing therapy should be encouraged to look at, or examine, his or her thoughts. Cognitive therapy helps patients to understand the relationship among their thoughts, behaviors, and feelings. There are two important *philosophical* presuppositions at play here. The first presupposition may seem too patent to enunciate: a person's thoughts, actions, and feelings are *already his or her own* before he or she examines or influences or changes them; that is, these thoughts, actions, and feelings are the patient's own on a level that may be called ontological. Treatment of a person's thoughts, actions, and feelings through cognitive therapy presupposes ontological ownership of one's thoughts, feelings, and actions. We may call this situation in which a person owns his or her thoughts ontological selfhood. The second philosophical presupposition at work in this case study is that the human person has the ability to "look at" his own thoughts, actions, and feelings, and to exercise some control over them.

The same philosophical presuppositions are at play in the treatment through dialectical behavior therapy of, for example, Borderline Personality Disorder. In this disorder, the patient is unable to reconcile a tendency to overreact emotionally with the social consequences of these reactions, and so he or she vacillates between over-controlling and under-controlling his or her impulses and emotions. Through dialectical behavior therapy, a patient can be taught to observe emotional reactions without a need to react. Here again we have the philosophical presuppositions mentioned above. The patient's ontological selfhood is already there, apart from his or her making or unmaking of it. His thoughts, actions, and feelings are ontologically his own, whether or not they are well-controlled. In addition, the patient's ability to "look at" herself, to have reflexive knowledge of herself or some part of herself, with the eventual aim of exercising some self-dominion, is presupposed.

Cognitive therapy's effort to help a patient toward a successful outcome of the therapy assumes some ontology of human nature and its abilities. A therapy's suppositions about this ontology, explicit or implicit, will affect what is deemed a successful outcome of the therapy.

I shall now examine the two ontological presuppositions mentioned above—ontological selfhood and reflexive knowledge—using principles from the philosophical anthropology of Thomas Aquinas. My aim in doing so is to provide an ontological and anthropological ground for psychological methods such

Personal Unity

as those just mentioned, as well as to suggest criteria on which the soundness or unsoundness of psychological methods might be judged.

Ontological selfhood

For Aquinas, a self in the fullest and richest sense is a person: human, angelic, or divine. Our concern here is the human person. But for Aquinas, the selfhood of a person is rooted not in any self-aware or free decision or action, but in an ontological principle that is there prior to any self-aware or free action. In keeping with a long tradition, he calls this ontological principle the soul. The human soul is the first principle of human ontological selfhood.

One of Aquinas's most impressive achievements was effectively to bring an Aristotelian language about the soul as the substantial form and first act of the human body to which it is united into the philosophical and theological anthropology of the Western Christian tradition. About this work of synthesis Anton Pegis says: "To fill the Aristotelian bottle of matter and form with the life of the Augustinian wayfarer was certainly to create a new reality, the notion of man as an incarnated intelligence."[31] The Aristotelian language of soul as form of the body may stir the emotions less, but still today it has tremendous value for those who look to grasp the unity of the human person.

Questions 75–77 of the first part of the *Summa Theologica* contain one of Aquinas's mature treatments of the ontological unity of human nature. In these questions Aquinas directs us to see the soul, understood as the substantial form of the human person, as the all-else-foreclosing first principle of his or her unity.

Some explanation of this vocabulary may be helpful. A substance, for Aquinas, is something that can exist in itself; a cat, a

---

31 Anton Pegis, *At the Origins of the Thomistic Notion of Man* (New York: Macmillan, 1963), 59.

tree, and a human being can each exist in itself. Beige, irritable, and "waving in the breeze," cannot exist in themselves: a *horse* is beige, *Jones* is irritable, *grass* is waving in the breeze. For Aquinas, beige, irritable, and waving in the breeze are not substances, but accidents. Substances, such as a horse and Jones and grass, are the original unities with which the world is populated: everything is either a substance, or something that depends on a substance for its existence. A substantial form is a philosophical principle of explanation of the identity and unity of these original unities called substances. It is not obervable with the eyes of the body, but is arrived at as the conclusion of an argument.

The soul as a principle of identity and unity

The *Summa Theologica's* treatment of the nature of the human person begins, in question 75, article 1, with a consideration of the soul as the first cause of life in any living body. The fact that Aquinas begins his so-called treatise on man with such a broad ontological consideration shows how much ontology forms his account of the human person. He will move from a general ontology of the soul to an ontology of the human soul in particular.

For Aquinas, the fact that a body is alive rather than not stands in need of explanation. The explanatory cause, however, cannot itself be a body, for not all bodies are alive. There must be some deeper cause of a living thing's life, a cause that is not a body, but a cause that makes the body to be such a body, organized in this way so as to be a living whole. That cause he calls the "act" of the body, or its "soul." The soul is the first principle of life in a living body. It gives the body its particular structure and determination, making it to be this kind of body.[32]

---

[32] Aquinas argues that the soul plays this role as a subsistent part of the whole man (*ST* I, Q. 75, art. 2), and so is not man himself (*ST* I, Q. 75, art. 4).

Personal Unity

In the fifth article of question 75 Aquinas insists on what could be called the "unmixed absoluteness" of the soul as act.[33] He argues as follows: Soul is form, and form is act, and act repulses potency. When Aquinas argues that the soul as act repulses potency, he is arguing that it is *itself* without mixture — that is, not a mere collection of parts. As such, it is fit to be the principle of the identity and unity of a living thing. The soul as act stands forth from flux and allows a living thing to "say," in some basic way, "I." The soul, understood as act, makes the thing it ensouls a *self*, gives it an identity. It is the first principle of ontological selfhood.

So the human soul, the first act of the human person, is the principle of a human person's ontological selfhood. For Aquinas, all that is in a human person (thoughts, actions, feelings), no matter how hidden or inaccessible (subconscious, automatic, instinctive) will fall within the "field" of the soul as act, that is, will fall within the field of the one ontological human self. These thoughts, actions, and feelings already have something to do with each other at a level that is real and deep.

33 "It is the definition (*ratio*) of soul that it be the form of some body. But it is either form according to the whole of itself or according to some part of itself. If according to the whole of itself then it is impossible that a part of it be matter, if by matter we understand something purely potential. For form as form is act [*form inquantum forma est actus*]; that which is purely potential may not be a part of act, since potentiality is repugnant to act [*repugnet actui*] as being divided from act" (ST I, Q. 75, art. 5). Cf. ST 1, Q. 76, art. 7: "Now the form, through itself, makes a thing to be actual since it is itself essentially an act; nor does it give existence by means of something else. Wherefore the unity of a thing composed of matter and form, is by virtue of the form itself, which by reason of its very nature is united to matter as its act. Nor is there any other cause of union except the agent, which causes matter to be in act, as the Philosopher says, in *Metaphysics* 8."

Philosophical Virtues and Psychological Strengths

The first article of question 76 gives us another avenue toward grasping the soul as the first act of a living thing. It is an approach in which we reason from our attribution of actions to a thing, to the unitary source of those actions. By this attribution Aquinas means something as simple a saying, "The tree flowers," or, "Cindy sings," where flowering is attributed to the tree and singing to Cindy. The principle Aquinas gives us is the following:

> That by which a thing first acts is the form of that to which the action is attributed . . . The reason for this is that nothing acts except so far as it is in act; and so, a thing acts by that whereby it is in act. (*ST* I, Q. 76, art. 1)

This is a compact statement of a broad teaching on form as act and so form as principle of identity. Aquinas applies it to the human person, but we should take a moment to understand the broader teaching. According to this principle, my attribution of diverse actions to same agent ("The tree is flowering," "Cindy is singing") leads me to get through the diversity and multiplicity of those actions, so as to arrive at the *one source* of those actions. The one source of those actions is the act whereby an agent is *in act*, standing forth, whereby it expresses its "self" in the most fundamental way. This grasp of the unifying act is one in which unity is grasped as dominating the multiplicity of parts and the multiplicity of temporal succession.[34] The root of this unity of a thing's actions—a unity that makes its actions to be its own—is "that whereby a thing is in act," or act.

Let us apply this to the human person. We attribute diverse actions to the same individual: "Jane digests her dinner," "Jane

---

[34] For a fuller exposition of this point see Lawrence Dewan, O.P., "The Importance of Substance," in *Form and Being: Studies in Thomistic Metaphysics*, vol. 45 of the series Studies in Philosophy and the History of Philosophy (Washington: Te Catholic University of America Press, 2006).

tastes the carrot cake," "Jane understands music theory." Our attribution of these diverse actions to the same agent shows that despite their diversity the actions have same source: Jane. If we seek a philosophical explanation of Jane's ability to be the one source of these diverse actions, we must come, Aquinas would argue, to the root act or actuality that makes her one. In the case of the human person, this root act or actuality is called the soul, or better, the "intellectual soul," since understanding is the action that distinguishes this soul from any other soul.

From unity to dominion

Later in this same article, we find a compelling passage in which Aquinas makes us *imagine* the firstness of man's soul-act or soul-form as a "dominion" that it has over man's body:

> The more noble a form is, the more it has dominion over bodily matter, and the less it is immersed in it, and the more does it exceed it in its operation and power [*virtute*] . . . The human soul is the highest and noblest of forms. And so it exceeds bodily matter in its power in that it has an operation and a power in which bodily matter has no share whatever. This power is called the intellect. (*ST* I, Q. 76, art. 1)

This passage takes the classical notion of the great chain of being and reads it according to the optic of the dominion a thing's form has over its body. As we ascend the chain of being, we find increasingly rich ways in which the body is put at the service of the form, and so actions and purposes, of a thing. For example, a marigold has a more noble form than does a mineral, and a tiger has a more noble soul than a marigold. In the latter case, the greater nobility, and so its greater dominion over the body, is shown in the tiger's self-motion and in the fact that many of its body parts are at the service of the life of sensation (both the sensing and the pursuit and avoidance that come with sensation).

But the human soul is the most noble of earthly forms and has a dominion over the body to which it is united greater than that exercised by other forms over their corresponding bodies. We might call this an "ontological self-dominion," for we possess it by being human, and not as the fruit of a self-aware action. We come into the world with it. It is manifested in the peculiar complex structure of the human body, in its preparedness to serve the widely varied actions and purposes that constitute human life, from digestion and growth to friendship, speech, and the pursuit of truth.[35] For example, Aquinas, as many before and after him, takes the human person's upright posture as an example of the soul's dominion over the body and as evidence that the body is "for the sake of," made to serve, the soul and its purposes. With his head on high, and with the refinement of his senses, the human person is fitted for drawing what is true from the knowledge of bodies and for fixing his or her gaze upward, toward God.[36]

Aquinas's account of this inner liberty and dominion of form as act reaches a high expression in the eighth and last article of question 76, when he asks whether the soul is whole in each body

[35] See the hierarchy described at the end of ST I-II, Q. 94, art. 2. This teaching on self-dominion harks back to the teaching in Q. 75, art. 5 on form as "unmixed act": only if act is unmixed and itself is it up to ruling the body. Indeed, only then is it up to acting at all. For Aquinas, all talk of human selfhood, personality, freedom, and virtue must be rooted in the actuality of the soul. All of those things proper to the life of the spirit — knowledge of ideals and universals, free will — are rooted in the inner liberty of the soul as act.

[36] See Thomas Aquinas, *Disputed Question on the Soul*, 8. See also the discussion of the upright posture in Leon R. Kass, M.D., *The Hungry Soul: Eating and the Perfection of Our Nature* (Chicago: University of Chicago Press, 1999), ch. 2, "The Human Form: Omnivorosus Erectus."

part and argues that, basically, it is. Repeatedly in this article he appeals to the role of the soul as form and act.

> If the soul were united to the body only as its mover, then it could be said that it is not in each of the body's parts, but in only one [part], by which it moves the others. But since the soul is united to the body as form, it must be in the whole [body] and in each of the body's parts. (ST I, Q. 76, art. 8)

And a bit further on: "Act is *in* that of which it is the act [*actus autem est in eo cuius est actus*]. Hence, the soul is *in* the whole body, and *in* each of its parts" (ST I, Q. 76, art. 8; emphasis added).

From this, Aquinas concludes that the soul is in the whole body and in each of its parts, "according to the whole of its perfection and essence, but not according to the whole of its power." The soul's various powers are in the requisite body part (sight in the eye, hearing in the ear), but not in the whole body. Still, the soul is compared "to the whole [body] first and *per se*, as to that which it properly and proportionately perfects; and [it is compared] to the [body's] parts secondarily, according as these parts have an ordering to the whole" (ST I, Q. 76, a. 8).

This article is a strong expression of the all-dominating, integrative power of the soul as act. Act is *in* a thing. It is present to all that is in a thing. Only so is it up to making a thing to be "everywhere itself." A principal concern of this article is to show that man is everywhere *himself* or *herself*. Aquinas is arguing that we cannot explain either that any part of man is *what* it is (a hand, an eye) or that any part has an ordering to the whole, unless the soul is whole in each body part. Or again, we cannot explain these things unless there is something in us that is not bodily, unless there is in us an *act*, in our case the soul, that unifies us. This is the ground for my ownership of my parts, and not merely bodily parts: my thoughts, my actions, my feelings, my instincts.

Philosophical Virtues and Psychological Strengths

An important element of Aquinas's broader teaching on form is that every being, insofar as it is a being, tends to conserve its own unity: "A thing has being in the manner it possesses unity. Hence, each thing fights off [repugnat] its own division as much as it can, lest thereby it tend toward nonbeing" (SCG I, ch. 42).

This inclination to be and stay one could not be more original. For Aquinas it is the inclination of a thing's *form* to conserve its own being (ST I, Q. 59, a. 2). Without this actively conserved unity a thing could not be. This conservation is not self-conscious, but deeper than that: it is the inner life of an existing substance in which it "returns to itself" (ST I, Q. 14, art. 2 *ad* 1) in a primally performed self-consonance—a "selving" at the deepest level.[37] For Aquinas, the identity of the existing substance is in fact actively preserved identity and unity. We are touching a first law of being (ST I-II, Q. 94, art. 2).

The unity of man's powers of action: form and flow

In articles 6 and 7 of question 77 of the treatise on man, Aquinas argues that a substantial form productively *causes* those things which inhere in it—powers, properties, accidents—in such a way that these *flow* from the substantial form as effect from cause. In fact the substantial form causes according to a certain order: first the higher, more "essential" powers and properties, and therefrom the lower and more accidental. In man, for example, the intellectual powers flow first (not temporally, but in the sense of causal priority) from the substantial form, and the sense powers flow from the intellectual powers. Aquinas also speaks of these powers as *rooted* in the substantial form.

This teaching about flow is essential for Aquinas's account of the ontological unity of man and of human action. Question 77

[37] See Kenneth L. Schmitz on this point in his "Immateriality Past and Present," in *Proceedings of the American Catholic Philosophical Association* 52 (1978): 1-15.

shows that to capture man's unity, the Aristotelian language of form and matter must be quickened by a Neoplatonic language of causal flow: the flow of powers from the soul. So yes, the intellect inheres in the soul as proper accident in substantial form, but there is more: the intellect flows from the soul. Yes, sense is united to intellect, but there is more: sense "participates" in intellect as flowing from it and ordered back to it.

In the *Summa Theologica's* treatment of the human person, this teaching on the *participation* of the lower powers in the higher powers is one of the first things that Aquinas unfolds from his teaching on the soul as first act of man. This teaching in Aquinas, I would add, is in a significant way the ground for what the following chapters in this volume will say. For example, the life of virtue is the human life in which reason governs our desires and emotions. But we might ask, *why* should reason be what governs? Plato and Aristotle would say: reason is what is the most noble thing in us, and what is most noble should rule. But in question 77, articles 6 and 7, on the flow of powers from the substantial form of the soul, Aquinas endeavors to provide another metaphysical grounding for the nobility of reason and for the fittingness of its rule over and guidance of all else in the human person: the intellect *causes* the lower powers as both their active cause and the cause to which the lower powers are ordered (*per modum finis et activi principii*) (Q. 77, art. 7). This utterance fills out the picture of the dominion of the soul as first act (Q. 76, art. 1) and the ordering of the parts of man to the whole (Q. 76, art. 8).

Notice how the teaching on the flow of powers from the soul effects our grasp of the human feelings, desires, and emotions that are described in the examples of therapy mentioned at the start of this essay. On Aquinas's account, human feelings are already, ontologically, under the influence of intellect, insofar as these feelings have intellect as their productive principle and final cause. This makes sense of the assumption that the patient's feelings are his or her own. But more than that, it also makes sense of the assumption that it is *good* for the patient to have mastery over his or her feelings. Human feelings are *meant* to be under the guidance of human reason, for reason is the productive and final cause of the powers with which one experiences feelings and emotions.[38]

Although human desires and emotions may be called by Aquinas "animal," insofar as all animals share them, they are not merely animal desire and emotions. Aquinas's teaching on the flow of powers from the soul shows us why. Human desires and emotions are always already susceptible to the rule of reason, for they are always under its attraction, so to speak.

Putting ontology in conversation with psychological therapy

It makes a significant difference to psychological therapy whether it assumes that the human person is ontologically one, where what is deepmost in the person is something like the "act" of which Aquinas speaks, or assumes that the human being is some kind of play of drives, pulls, and pushes. If it assumes the latter, or something like it, the definition of *psychological wholeness* runs the risk of being arbitrary: something the therapist or the therapeutic community determines, especially in a postmodern view of psychology. At stake is a standard of human wholeness or wellness, and that standard must find its deepest roots in something ontological. It is first at the level of ontology that it must be determined that both our mental acts and our emotions are our own, and that we can and should inspect and control our emotions through mental acts, to use the language mentioned at the start of this essay.

---

[38] An example of the way that human sense desires and powers are meant to be brought under and even serve reason can be found in the human act of eating, as Leon Kass shows in *The Hungry Soul*.

Personal Unity

If ontological unity is a kind of standard, is psychological pathology a case of mere dispersal or disunity? Not necessarily. Though a pathology may involve dispersal or disunity, it may also involve a kind of pseudo-unity, a hardened and misguided self-preservation. There seems to me to be two things to say here. First, if a pathology is characterized by a pseudo-unity, this seems to point to something fundamental about the human being, namely, that unity is a concern that runs down to the ontological level. The concern is always there because of its deep roots in our human ontology. This opens the door for Aquinas's ontological considerations as a basis for psychotherapy.

The search for the difference between true and false unity comes down to a search for a standard according to which to *order* our capacities, desires, emotions, and actions. Authentic human wholeness or unity needs a standard for order. Here Aquinas can help, especially in his teaching on the primacy of soul over body and on the flow of our human powers from the soul. The emotion of anger, the bodily pleasures of food, drink, and sex are already operating under the ontological attraction of the rational powers to which they are ordered. And so they *ought* to be ordered to the genuine good of those higher powers. Of course, it is only through a discussion of natural law that we begin to account for the ultimate good, beyond us, at which we are aimed.

A full explanation of human happiness considers the ordering of human inclinations and their relationship with human prosocial action. The psychologist seeks to understand the developmental and the therapeutic pathways toward responsible and flourishing action. Nonetheless, mechanistic and deterministic visions of animal instinct and desires do not do full justice to human nature or prosocial action. Rather, human beings express a specific potential toward the mature reasoning and committed love that transcend reductionist explanations. Philosophical reflection and theological sources help to explain this ordering of human nature that can be understood as a participation in a larger order or law. John Cuddeback explains the particular interest for understanding human psychology and society of the human ordering that manifests itself in the basic human inclinations for self-preservation, family, society, truth, and goodness. Overcoming conflicts between these inclinations involves finding the order between their different ends as parts of a prosocial personal life and, forthmostly, of finding their ordering to the ultimate end of human life. A realist notion recognizes that the source of ordering is deeper than human animality or desire, but finds its footing in human nature and natural law and ultimately in the source of them both, in a divine ordering.

Chapter 5

Ordered Inclinations

John A. Cuddeback

Friends have the same likes and dislikes.

Thomas Aquinas[39]

In his great work *After Virtue*, Alasdair MacIntyre gives what I take to be a devastating critique of "Enlightenment morality," a critique that encompasses many if not most contemporary moral theories.[40] The heart of his critique seems to be the assertion that Enlightenment morality fails by its own criteria since it fails to achieve what it purports to achieve: a rational justification of moral norms regarding human action. The main reason it fails, McIntyre asseverates, is that it lacks a conception of the human end. In explanation of this point MacIntyre offers a simple tripartite conception of traditional morality. There is (a) human nature in its "untutored state," (b) the precepts of rational ethics, and (c) the conception of human-nature-as-it-could-be-if-it-realized-its *telos* (end, state of fulfillment and flourishing). Each

---

[39] *ST* II-II, Q. 104, art. 3 and Q. 29, art. 3, where he cites Cicero's *De Amicitia* and Sallust.

[40] Alasdair MacIntyre, *After Virtue*, 2nd ed. (Notre Dame, Indiana: University of Notre Dame Press, 1984). See especially chapter 5, "Why the Enlightenment Had to Fail."

of these three parts of the traditional conception of morality "re-quires reference to the other two if its status and function [is] to be intelligible."[41]

But by the Enlightenment conception of reason and its pow-ers, reason can "supply no genuine comprehension of man's true end." Thus one of the key parts, indeed the central one—the understanding of the end—drops out of the schema, and En-lightenment thinkers are left with the "impossible and quixotic"[42] project of trying to justify norms of practical reason without a real conception of the end.

Leaving aside the particulars of MacIntyre's historical and philosophical arguments, we can focus on what I take to be the central and pivotal insight of his position. It is a philosophical point with a closely connected historical corollary. We might put it this simply: the *telos* of man is the key to ethics, and when thinkers within the Western tradition rejected the tradition's un-derstanding of the end, their justification of morality withered as a vine with no root.

I begin this chapter with the assertion that a proper under-standing of natural law is necessary for a proper understanding of the moral life. In this chapter I will give a brief sketch of some fundamental principles of the moral life, through focusing on key elements of the Thomistic conception of natural law, particularly the notion of the end, and the order of actions that are for the sake of the end. To do this I will consider in turn each of the fol-lowing three points:

1) Reason, the measure of human action, measures human action well when it measures by the true end of man.
2) The moral order is promulgated by natural law, and nat-urally knowable through natural law.

[41] MacIntyre, *After Virtue*, 53.
[42] Ibid., 55.

3) Man's happiness consists in freely living according to the moral order established by law, both natural and supernatural.

Reason measures human action well when it measures by the true end of man

The first point in this proposition is that reason is the measure of human action. Actions are *human* precisely inasmuch as they proceed from reason and will.[43] Reason is thus called the "proper principle" of human actions,[44] and it is also their "measure." In other words, it is in relation to reason that human actions are constituted in their kind or species, and that they are good or evil.[45] Aquinas says: "Now human acts are called good and evil in relation to reason because, as Dionysius says, the good of man is 'to live according to reason,' whereas evil is to live apart from reason."[46] The good life, then, for a human person is *secundum rationem esse*, literally *to be* according to reason.

But what does it mean to be, or to live, according to reason? Or more specifically, when Aquinas says that the object of an action is good or evil according to whether it is "in accord with"

---

[43] See ST I-II, Q. 1, art. 1. Here Aquinas argues that man differs from other creatures precisely in being "lord of his own actions," which he is by virtue of reason and will. That which sets man apart from other creatures is said to be "proper" to him, or belonging to him inasmuch as he is human. Central to Plato and Aristotle's understanding of human nature and ethics is their assertion that rational activity is the "function" or "proper function" of man. Cf. Plato, *Republic*, 352–353, and Aristotle, *NE* 1097b22 ff.

[44] Ibid, ad. 3.

[45] See ST I-II, Q. 18, art. 5.

[46] Ibid. Again, that the good life is one according to reason is a central theme in Plato and Aristotle. Cf. *Republic*, 442c and 586e-587a, and *NE* 1098a7–18.

reason, what does this mean? Aquinas is very clear: there is a principle within a principle here.[47] At one point he says that reason is the principle of human actions "*since* it belongs to reason to order to the end, which is the first principle in all matters of action, according to the Philosopher."[48] The *end*, then, is the principle within the principle of reason. Thus, to be in accord with reason means for Aquinas nothing other than to be in accord with the order to the end.[49] If moral goodness, then, consists in acting in accord with reason, we can also say that moral goodness consists in acting in accord with the order to the end.

Order to the end is a somewhat tricky phrase, in part because *order* can be a noun or a verb. When we speak of *the* order to the end (using *order* as a noun), we mean a real set of *relations*, both of actions to the end and of actions to one another. An example might be helpful. In the art of medicine there is an end (health) and an order to this end. A doctor prescribes some change in diet, understanding that there is a specific relation between the recommended diet and health. He also prescribes a regimen of exercise, which is related to health, as well as to the diet. Health, the rich, complex, and proper functioning of the human body, is the root, the determining principle of the art of medicine. Good medical practice is precisely that practice which is in accord with the order to the end of medicine. Similarly, good human actions are those in accord with the order to the end of man.

The *verb to order* means to put order into something. It is used as a verb when, for instance, Aquinas says, "it belongs to reason to order to the end." Reason "orders to the end" by putting some

---

[47] See *ST* I-II, Q. 90, art. 2 for the language of principle within a principle.

[48] *ST* I-II, Q. 90, art. 1, emphasis added.

[49] We see here just how right MacIntyre is in his assertion that without the true end, there cannot be a true justification of morality.

order into human actions. It is in this way that reason is also said to measure human action. Now, it is critical here that we make explicit a distinction implied above. While human reason can be said to give measure in any truly human act, it does not always measure (or order) *well*. Again, there is a real, objective order of actions to the end of man. We certainly do not always act in accord with this order.[50] Moral philosophy, or ethics, is all about the true order to the end, which reason *should* put into voluntary human action.[51]

Thus we say that *good* human actions are those that are measured *well* by reason. And human reason measures *well* when we act in accord with the objective order, to the *true* end of man. To speak of a *true* end of man is to imply that all human persons, by their human nature, have an end — in the sense of a completion or fulfillment that *should* come to be — that is given in reality, and not determined by them.[52] The great Western tradition's understanding of what constitutes this end was well expressed by Aristotle: the life of virtue, lived among friends, culminating in a loving contemplation of the highest things.[53] This is the

---

[50] We can put this another way: to act by reason is not necessarily to act by right reason.

[51] See *Commentary on Aristotle's Nicomachean Ethics*, nos. 2–3. If post-Enlightenment ethics has for the most part set aside the end of man as something knowable by reason, or if it has set up false ends, this should not be separated from the fact that as individuals men turn away from their true end. Indeed, the dominant forms of ethics in a community are surely reflections of a communal stance toward the end; this communal stance has a direct correlation to the stance of at least a significant number of individuals in the community.

[52] Of course, as free agents persons are a real determinant of whether the true end is actually achieved.

[53] This is a necessarily brief statement of how to conceive the end of man. Christianity further develops this notion, particularly in its understanding of a supernatural end in the next life.

perfection of the human person; this is what life is about. It is in reference to this great good that we understand the distinction between what is morally good and what is morally evil. To put this point in stronger, and more technical, terms: the very goodness of a human action is caused by its relation (order) to the ultimate end.[54] Pope John Paul II expressed this point in the encyclical *Vertitatis Splendor*, when he said:

> Activity is morally good when it attests to and expresses the voluntary ordering of the person to his ultimate end and the conformity of a concrete action with the human good as it is acknowledged in its truth by reason.[55]

We can consider an example. Why is an act of rendering what is due to another—that is, an act of the cardinal virtue of justice—a morally good action? While it is important to avoid oversimplification, it is possible to answer: just action is good because it leads to, and participates in, the goodness of the end of man. The most fully just actions are those that spring from a firm disposition or habit, or in other words, from the virtue of justice.[56]

---

[54] Here is a more technical defense of this point. Aquinas asks whether there is an ultimate end of human life (*ST* I-II, Q. 1, art. 4). To answer the question he begins by making a point about a "per se order" of causes. In a per se order of causes there must be a first cause, from which all the other causes receive their very causality. We need not concern ourselves with the argument for this point but should focus on the import of his application of it to the realm of final causes. There must be some first or ultimate end, which is the cause of all final causality (in the moral realm) and thus of the very desirability of all that a man desires. Two articles later Aquinas says: "Hence secondary desirable things move the appetite only as ordered to a primary desirable thing, which is the ultimate end."

[55] John Paul II, *Veritatis Splendor* (1993), no. 72.

[56] See Aristotle, *NE* 1104a30–b12 on the importance of acting from a firmly established disposition. Here he distinguishes

Ordered Inclinations

Without the virtue of justice, man cannot achieve the greatness to which he is called. Indeed justice is a *part* of that greatness, and its (justice's) greatness cannot be understood apart from the whole of which it is a part.[57] A just action is one kind of action that is ordered to, for the sake of, the true end of man.

It is worth noting that right order to the end is the standard and measure both of the object of the action (which constitutes the action as a certain kind of action), and of the intention of the action. Aquinas holds that for a concrete individual action to be morally good, both the object and the intention of the action must be good.[58] The Pope explains the goodness of the object of an action as follows:

> The primary and decisive element for moral judgment is the object of the human act, which establishes whether it is capable of being ordered to the good and to the ultimate end, which is God.[59]

Individual good actions are actions that are good (or morally indifferent) in their object or kind, that are done from a good intention, that is, an intention that is itself rooted in a willing of the true ultimate end. We should note that some kinds of actions can never be good. The reason for this is in how these kinds of actions stand in relation to the human end. John Paul II explains:

---

between simply doing the kind of action a just man does, and actually doing it as a just man (i.e., one with the habitual disposition or virtue) does it.

[57] Aquinas holds that justice, one of the four cardinal virtues, is preeminent among moral virtues, both because it has the noblest subject—the will—and because it is a good not only of the just person himself but also of others, to whom justice always looks. See *ST* II-II, Q. 58, art. 12.

[58] See, e.g., *ST* I-II, Q. 18, art. 4, corp. and ad. 3. Note: the object can be indifferent; see *ST* I-II, Q. 18, art. 8.

[59] John Paul II, *Veritatis Splendor*, no. 79.

Philosophical Virtues and Psychological Strengths

Reason attests that there are objects of the human act which are by their nature "incapable of being ordered" to God, because they radically contradict the good of the person made in his image. These are the acts which, in the church's moral tradition, have been termed "intrinsically evil" (*intrinsece malum*): They are such always and per se, in other words, on account of their very object and quite apart from the ulterior intentions of the one acting and the circumstances.[60]

This passage raises an issue that should be addressed briefly before we go on: moral evil. If human reason measures *well* when we act in accord with the objective order, to the *true* end of man, what does moral evil look like? It is important here to bear in mind the scholastic maxim that goodness is in a fullness or completeness in being, and evil is in a lack—a lack that can come in many forms and that can be considered from many angles. Moral goodness and evil pertain to the fullness or completeness of human action. What is most due in human willing and action is the order of reason, and thus moral goodness and moral evil can be identified with the presence or the lack of the order of reason in human action.[61]

One way, and perhaps the most important one, to understand the privation that constitutes moral evil is as an abandonment of reason's ruling role to a lower power—especially the sense appetite. The sense appetite of itself, or in other words apart from being properly ordered by reason, does not tend toward the ultimate end of man.[62] A life lived more or less according to the dictates of

---

[60] Ibid, no. 80.

[61] See *ST* I-II, Q. 18, art. 1, corp. and ad. 3.

[62] See Aquinas, *On Evil*, trans. R. Regan (Oxford: Oxford University Press, 2003), IV.2, p. 205: "[T]he lower powers by their own impulse are turned toward lower things."

the sense appetite would thus be disordered.[63] Moral evil always implies that an action is not in accord with the true end, whether it be an action actually fitted to a false ultimate end or simply one unfitted to the true ultimate end.[64]

The moral order is promulgated by and naturally knowable through natural law

We stated earlier that the order to the end is something given in reality. In fact it exists first of all in the mind of God, as the eternal law, and is impressed upon creatures in their very creation.[65] Aquinas refers to the eternal law as "an understanding (type) of the *order* of those things which are to be done by those who are subject to his governance."[66] He further says that it is

---

63 "Disorder" as constitutive of moral evil is not interchangeable with, but is related to the "disorder" normally referred to in mental or psychological sickness. The connection is in the truth that mental health can itself be properly understood only within the context of a true notion of the end of man. Put otherwise, mental health can be understood in terms of the conditions required for free human action; but free human action itself demands to be understood first and primarily in terms of its ultimate end: the truly good life. We might also note that some disorders in the psychological realm are themselves also moral disorders.

64 This last distinction is an approximation of Aquinas's distinction between mortal and venial sin, respectively. See On Evil, Q. 7, art. 1. Here Aquinas notes that "sin consists of a disorder of the soul, just as physical disease consists of a disorder of the body. And so sin is a disease of the soul, as it were, and pardon is for sin what healing is for disease."

65 See ST I-II, Q. 91, art. 1 and Q. 93, art. 1.

66 ST I-II, Q. 93, art. 1. We should perhaps note here an ambiguity in the meaning of the term *law*. For Aquinas and the tradition, law is always first and foremost an affair of reason as directing action to some end, as is evident in the above definition of the eternal law. Another meaning, prevalent especially in modern science, is law as an unchanging or regular pattern

Philosophical Virtues and Psychological Strengths

from an "impress" of this eternal law that creatures receive their natural inclinations.[67] Now, the eternal law is impressed upon *human* creatures in a unique way. Aquinas explains in a much-quoted passage:

> Now among all others, the rational creature is subject to Divine providence in the most excellent way, in so far as it partakes of a share of providence, by being provident both for itself and for others. Wherefore it has a share of the Eternal Reason, whereby it has a natural inclination to its proper act and end: and this participation of the eternal law in the rational creature is called the natural law.[68]

In the *natural* law, then, God shares with the human creature insight into God's own understanding of the moral order, the order of things to the end. It should always be remembered that natural law is first of all an instruction, an instruction about the true human good.[69] Aquinas says: "Accordingly the first direction of our acts to their end must needs be *through* the natural law."[70]

We turn now to consider how the natural law is known, or perhaps more precisely how, through the natural law, man naturally knows fundamental aspects of the moral order, or the order

---

of action, e.g., the law of gravity. This latter usage is derivative from and not to be confused with the primary meaning. *Natural law* for Aquinas is not a description of how men will act; it is a prescription, and a direction, for how they should act.

[67] See *ST* I-II, Q. 91, art. 2.

[68] *ST* I-II, Q. 91, art. 2.

[69] See *ST* I-II, Q. 90, prologue.

[70] *ST* I-II, Q. 91, art. 2, ad. 2, emphasis added. For a further consideration of natural law and its place in ethics, see Russell Hittinger, *The First Grace: Rediscovering the Natural Law in a Post-Christian World* (Wilmington, Delaware: ISI, 2003), especially the first two chapters.

of actions to the end. Natural law is indeed natural first of all in the fact that the precepts or principles of natural law are *naturally* known. *Synderesis* is the name of a habit natural to all men that contains the first principles or precepts of the natural law.[71] Just how this habit is actualized and perfected is a complex issue. Here we can focus on two key aspects of how the natural law is known: through our natural inclinations and through the traditions of human communities.

In perhaps his most famous article on natural law, Aquinas says that

all those things to which man has a natural inclination, are naturally apprehended by reason as being good, and consequently as objects of pursuit, and their contraries as evil, and objects of avoidance. Wherefore according to the order of natural inclinations, is the order of the precepts of the natural law.[72]

It is clear here that for Aquinas the order of precepts of the natural law and the order of natural inclinations are parallel—they correspond one to the other. This text should not be taken as meaning that man discovers the precepts of the natural law simply and firstly by observing his own inclinations. The inclinations themselves spring from some kind of original knowledge that is the fruit of the instruction of natural law.[73] But it is also the case that having natural inclinations toward certain objects tends to yield the judgment that those objects are good

---

71 ST I, Q. 79, art. 12. On synderesis see also ST I-II, Q. 94, art. 1, ad. 2, and *DM* Q. 3, art. 12, ad, 13.

72 ST I-II, Q. 94, art. 2.

73 On this point see L. Dewan, "Jacques Maritain and the Philosophy of Cooperation" in *L'alterite. Vivere ensemble differents*, M. Gourgues and G. D. Mailhiot, eds. (Montreal: Bellarmin, 1986), 109–117.

and to be pursued.[74] Indeed, observation of and attentiveness to these inclinations aids in the conceptualization and articulation of the natural law precepts. Aquinas enumerates different levels of precepts of the natural law precisely by enumerating levels of natural inclinations in man.

One example that Aquinas uses is man's natural inclination to live in society. It should be clear from experience that this is an inclination natural to man. The natural inclination to live in society must itself arise from some primordial and preconscious insight into the goodness of living in society. The very inclination itself then tends to yield an actual judgment of the goodness of living in society.

It is, of course, not always obvious just what is or is not a natural inclination. Acquired inclinations that are good, or virtuous, are a "natural" extension or fulfillment of natural inclination. In other words, it is in virtue that natural inclinations reach their fitting completion. It is for this reason that the virtuous woman is most able to recognize natural inclinations themselves. At the same time, since vice is contrary to natural inclination, the vicious woman is least able to recognize natural inclinations, since the natural inclinations in her are obfuscated by acquired habit.

---

[74] What Aquinas calls judgment through inclination can also be called connatural knowledge. See ST I-II, Q. 58, art. 5. Such knowledge follows upon both natural inclinations, yielding a natural knowledge of natural law, and acquired inclinations, yielding the moral knowledge an agent has according to his own moral character. (Of course, these should be distinguished without being separated.) See Aquinas's *Commentary on Nicomachean Ethics*, nos. 517–523 for his explanation of how having inclinations of various kinds yields judgments about the goodness of the objects of the inclinations. Yves Simon treats some of these points in *The Tradition of Natural Law: A Philosopher's Reflections*, Vukan Kuic, ed. (New York: Fordham University Press, 1992), 125ff.

Ordered Inclinations

We might say that the "second nature" of habit either amplifies or obfuscates the inclinations of human nature itself.

In *Veritatis Splendor*, John Paul II refers to how the natural law is known when, following the quotation given earlier about the object of the human act as being capable of being ordered to the ultimate end, he says:

> This capability is grasped by reason in the very being of man, considered in his integral truth, and therefore in his natural inclinations, his motivations and his finalities, which always have a spiritual dimension as well. It is precisely these which are the contents of the natural law and hence that ordered complex of "personal goods" which serve the "good of the person"; the good which is the person himself and his perfection.[75]

Our second point about how the natural law is known points to the social nature of man, and the corresponding social aspect of the pursuit of truth. It is clear in human experience that in the realm of speculative or theoretical truth, individual men achieve wisdom only as members of a community, indeed a multigenerational community. It is not otherwise in the realm of practical knowledge. *Knowledge* of natural law arises, develops, and is passed on within communities and societies—such as the family, civil society, and the Church. Jacques Maritain says:

> Those inclinations *were really genuine* which in the immensity of the human past have guided reason in becoming aware, little by little, of the regulations that have been most definitely and most generally recognized by the human race, starting from the most ancient communities. For the knowledge of the primordial aspects of natural law was first expressed in social patterns rather than in personal

---

75 John Paul II, *Veritatis Splendor*, no. 79.

judgments: so that we might say that that knowledge has developed within the double protecting tissue of human inclinations and human society.[76]

This is a point of great importance. It sheds more light on the problem of how we are to recognize a true natural inclination of man. Part of the answer to this question is that it is natural that the recognition of natural inclinations occurs within a community. No individual, unless he is of perfect moral disposition, could be trusted always to judge properly of what is a natural inclination.

An example of a person's knowledge of natural law being developed "within the double protecting tissue of human inclinations and human society" is the understanding of the goodness and importance of monogamous marriage between a man and a woman. Surely we can speak of a person's natural inclination to monogamous marriage between man and woman. At the same time, a person's inclinations and attendant practical judgments regarding this subject are obviously and profoundly influenced by examples of married life, and attitudes toward married life, found in his own family and in his community. We might add, particularly as regards this example, that positions enshrined in the positive law of civil society play a unique role in the recognition of natural inclinations and the consequent understanding of natural law.

Earlier we commented on the connection between disorder in the individual and disorder in the community. In concluding this section on knowledge of the natural law, we can advert to this connection again. Given the formative influence a community has on moral character through its culture and customs, and the ever-present possibility of the perversion of inclination at the

---

[76] Jacques Maritain, *Man and the State* (Chicago: University of Chicago Press, 1951), 92.

community and personal level, it is no wonder that knowledge of the natural law varies greatly, both from community to community and within communities. [77]

Man's happiness consists in
freely living according to the moral order

The heart of this third and final proposition is implied in what we have seen already: that natural law is an instruction in the true human good. Through natural law man comes to an understanding of his own end, and how it is to be achieved. Even if natural law were conceived merely as a statement of what is necessary in order to achieve a state of flourishing, and not also as something commanded by a divine lawgiver, it could still be seen as pointing to that way of acting which truly fulfills human nature and man's natural desires. In reality, an adequate notion of natural law (even from a purely philosophical perspective) sees it as the command of a divine governor who orders all things to the common good of the universe and ultimately to himself. [78]

The viewpoint of sacred theology, of course, opens horizons beyond the causality of natural law. Under the New Law of grace, the human person is ordered to a life of supernatural virtue, and

[77] As an example of the judgment of an entire community becoming perverted, Aquinas refers to "the Germans" as not understanding stealing to be evil. See ST I-II, Q. 94, art. 4.

[78] It is possible to consider natural law as an objective order discovered by natural reason, without imputing to it the character of being an instruction and a command from a divine lawgiver. I would argue, however, that this view is necessarily incomplete; the incompleteness is especially apparent when an account is to be given for moral obligation. For at the root of moral obligation, there must be an authority that intends the end; otherwise, why would the end be *due*? Cf. John Paul II, *Veritatis Splendor*, no. 11: "Acknowledging the Lord as God is the very core, the heart of the law, from which the particular precepts flow and toward which they are ordered."

ultimately to the Beatific Vision of God in heaven. Yet in *Veritatis Splendor*, while the Pope is careful to distinguish between different laws, he does not wish to separate them:

> Even if moral/theological reflection usually distinguishes between the positive or revealed law of God and the natural law, and within the economy of salvation between the "old" and the "new" law, it must not be forgotten that these and other useful distinctions always refer to that law whose author is the one and the same God and which is always meant for man. The different ways in which God, acting in history, cares for the world and for mankind are not mutually exclusive; on the contrary, they support each other and intersect. They have their origin and goal in the eternal, wise and loving counsel whereby God predestines men and women "to be conformed to the image of his Son" (Rom. 8:29). God's plan poses no threat to man's genuine freedom; on the contrary, the acceptance of God's plan is the only way to affirm that freedom.[79]

In the tradition of Aquinas, the Pope would have us see the divine governance as a rich whole, contained in the eternal law, of which the natural law is a part. Governance, as Aquinas tells us in the clearest terms, is "nothing but the directing of the things governed to the end; which consists in some good."[80] The actual ultimate end of man transcends, and also fulfills, the direction given in the natural law. Thus a higher law is necessary to direct man to his actual, supernatural end. Aquinas states:

> By the natural law the eternal law is participated proportionately to the capacity of human nature. But to his supernatural end man needs to be directed in a yet higher

---

[79] John Paul II, *Veritatis Splendor*, no. 45.
[80] *ST* I, Q. 103, art. 3.

way. Hence the additional law given by God [i.e., the New Law, or the Law of the Gospel], whereby man shares more perfectly in the eternal law.[81]

Seeing law as an instruction from God as regards man's perfection and happiness is further clarified in seeing law as a gift rooted in, and for the sake of, *friendship*. We cannot understand the ultimate reason for God's giving law to man, if we do not understand that friendship requires it. In this vein Aquinas uses the simple yet striking words of Aristotle: "Friends have the same likes and dislikes."[82] The laws of God are an expression of his "likes and dislikes"—which we *must* share, *if* we are to be his friends. In the end, it is that simple.

The moral life, indeed human life itself, is perhaps best understood, then, as the drama of man's free response to a call *of* love, and a call *to* love—in friendship. In emphasizing the central role of law in the moral life, Aquinas, unlike Kant, does not focus on duty as most fundamental, but on the love of true goodness. Law, again, is an instruction, the conferring of knowledge of what is truly good, an instruction rooted in the intention that those subject to it achieve that good. It is worth recalling here that law is always ordered to the *common good* of a community of some kind.[83] If the moral order is in some sense established by law, this means that the moral order is ultimately about a common good. This common good, while transcending the private good of individuals, is nevertheless the good that is the greatest proper good

---

[81] *ST* I-II, Q. 91, art. 4, ad. 1.

[82] See *ST* II-II, Q. 104, art. 3. He uses this phrase to explain the meaning of 1 John 2:4–5: "He who says 'I know him' but disobeys his commandments is a liar, and the truth is not in him; but whoever keeps his word, in him truly love for God is perfected."

[83] *ST* I-II, Q. 90, art. 2.

of individuals. Law is about the greatest perfection and fulfillment of those under it, the common good.[84]

I conclude with a final quotation from *Veritatis Splendor*. Here John Paul II is unfolding the meaning of Christ's response to the rich young man who asked, "Teacher, what good must I do to have eternal life?" The pope makes clear that the most fundamental moral questions can be adequately answered only through an understanding of natural law as a part of the loving plan of the Creator, who has made us for himself.

> To ask about the good, in fact, ultimately means to turn toward God, the fullness of goodness. Jesus shows that the young man's question is really a religious question and that the goodness that attracts and at the same time obliges man has its source in God, and indeed is God himself. God alone is worthy of being loved "with all one's heart and with all one's soul and with all one's mind" (Mt. 22:37). He is the source of man's happiness. Jesus brings the question about morally good action back to its religious foundations, to the acknowledgment of God, who alone is goodness, fullness of life, the final end of human activity and perfect happiness.[85]

---

[84] To be properly ordered to, or related to, the true end of man implies having a stance toward common goods (of the family, the society, the church) that is not self-centered. The ultimate human good is not a private good, but one that belongs to a whole community. On this point see, for instance, *ST* I-II, Q. 90, art. 2; Q. 92, art. 1, ad. 3; and I, Q. 65, art. 2.

[85] John Paul II, *Veritatis Splendor*, no. 9.

Neither failure nor cruelty nor oppression is the last word on human action. Nonetheless, human history is scarred by unreasonable deeds. While inevitably in need of facing up to error and social injustice, a person's ethical bearing continually calls for further progress. As psychologists, educators, and parents know, human persons become able to pose reasonable acts by gaining mastery of their capacities to deliberate and take counsel about ethical norms and practices. As Craig Steven Titus demonstrates, reasonable action also requires pro-social and emotional skills in any practical decision-making. While developmental and therapeutic approaches can highlight reasons for outright failures, the psychologist observes that progress requires both fidelity to reason and creativity in application to realize wise goals. In one way or another, families, law, and therapy appeal to fitting experience and skills, social attachments and practices, and spiritual resources and divine assistance in order to attain or regain right practical reason in action.

Chapter 6

Reasonable Acts

Craig Steven Titus

It is thought that a young man of
practical wisdom cannot be found
Aristotle[86]

Prudence is one of the most misunderstood and maligned of virtues. It has been unjustly tagged as synonymous with its opposites. The injunction "Be prudent!" has come to mean the

---

[86] Aristotle, *Nicomachean Ethics*, in *The Complete Works of Aristotle*, ed. Jonathan Barnes (Princeton: Princeton University Press, 1984), bk. 6, 1142a13. The context of this statement is found in Aristotle's distinguishing practical and political forms of wisdom. He argues that practical wisdom is neither as isolated nor as easily acquired as one might think. He says: "[P]erhaps one's own good cannot exist without household management, nor without a form of government. Further, how one should order one's own affairs is not clear and needs inquiry. What has been said is confirmed by the fact that while young men become geometricians and mathematicians and wise in matters like these, it is thought that a young man of practical wisdom cannot be found. The cause is that such wisdom is concerned not only with universals but with particulars, which become familiar from experience, but a young man has no experience, for it is length of time that gives experience."

promotion of either overly cautious inactivity ("Be careful!"), or debilitating self-restraint ("Wait and see!"), or cold economic calculation ("Be frugal!"). Its association with reason and reasonable acts has also spelled ill for it in emotivist, voluntarist, and postmodern critiques that equate virtue with sentiment or with the will.[87] Contemporary language and ideology have expressed distrust concerning the potential reasonableness of human acts and concerning the virtue of prudence understood as right practical reason in action. An efficacious defense of prudence, on the contrary, comes from a perspective that construes it as the cognitive strength for human intelligence at three levels: first, speculative discernment of the real, normative, and optimal pathways toward a person's goal of ultimate flourishing;[88] second, the practical decisions that advance one intelligently along those pathways, including toward mental health; and lastly, the personal and socially supported acts that bring one's plans to life.

Right reason or prudence, as a practical affair, puts counsel and thought to work, but not without the will and the emotions, nor without other people. For human reason without good choices, emotional stability, and social support spirals out of control. Human volition without rational direction loves carelessly. Human emotion without intelligently chosen goals tears one apart. And a human person without a community will soon run dry of counsel and support.

---

[87] See David Hume, *A Treatise of Human Nature* (Oxford: Clarendon Press, 1960) bk. 3, pt. 3, sect. 1, p. 574, and Judith Butler, *Subjects of Desire: Hegelian Reflections in Twentieth-Century France* (New York: Columbia University Press, 1999).

[88] When discussing speculative and practical reasoning, it is necessary to refer to true flourishing (happiness or beatitude) as the human *telos* in order to understand human motivation and action (cf. *ST* I-II, Q. 1, art. 2; and Alasdair MacIntyre, *Dependent Rational Animals: Why Human Beings Need the Virtues* (Chicago: Open Court, 1999), 111–112.

Reasonable Acts

This essay's treatment of practical reason in action (prudence or practical wisdom) neither presupposes ready-made psychological and moral "perfection" nor jettisons moral norms. Rather it explores aspects of moral and psychological progress, taking into consideration underdevelopment (situations of overprotection and ignorance), deformity (addictions and phobias), and more standard conditions of growth (common challenges to individual progress and social relationships). From a philosophical perspective, it addresses psychosocial difficulties in relation to the cognitive processes and normative goals that contribute to prudent or imprudent thought and behavior, as well as their bio-emotional conditions. While the first part of this essay refers to psychosocial dysfunction, the last two parts focus on more typical cognitive development and functioning that underlie reasonable acts.

Cognitive Strength

Contemporary treatments of character strengths and virtues, such as that found in the Positive Psychology movement, have recoiled from the terms *prudence* and *rationality*, preferring others such as *creativity, curiosity, open-mindedness, love of learning,* and *perspective*.[89] In effect, the psychological (theoretical, empirical, clinical, and neurological) sciences offer observational input about practical reason, which concerns, for example, decision-making and problem-solving models, the nature of bounded rationality, and reasoning biases.[90] Specialists use related terms

[89] Christopher Peterson and Martin E. P. Seligman, *Character Strengths and Virtues: A Handbook and Classification* (Oxford: Oxford University Press, 2004), 95–196. Moreover, see Peterson and Seligman's attempt to create a social-science equivalent of virtue ethics by employing "the scientific method to inform philosophical pronouncements about the traits of a good person" (p. 89).

[90] Major areas of cognitive research and theory include the psychology of human judgment and decision making—see

either in diagnosis of psychological health and disorder (cognitive competencies and emotional intelligence, on the one hand, personality disorders, neuroses, or psychoses, on the other) and in therapies (cognitive strategies of reframing and reinforcement, and so on). Psychotherapies, moreover, involve a direct concern for various intellectual and practical aspects of the virtue of prudence, although they may claim to situate themselves in a value-free stance, distanced from its normative moral and spiritual aspects and aspirations.

Admittedly human cognitive strengths extend over a wide sensate and intellectual range. They interact with affective and interpersonal capacities in ways that resist simplistic divisions. A renaissance of virtue theory, with input from the philosophical and theological disciplines, has brought to light a revitalized approach that is open to the study of the human person and psychology, as well as moral theory, spirituality, and theology. In this line of thought, a renewed Aristotelian-Augustinian-Thomist treatment of the virtues seeks to trace a global approach that dialogues with psychosocial sciences and resists the reductionist tendency beleaguering some contemporary treatments of cognition.[91]

Growth and Failure in Right Practical Reason

At personal and interpersonal levels, we face numerous potential psychosocial short circuits to right practical reason and action. Prudential judgment entails a global undertaking that transforms a person in his disposition to act. When people

---

D. Kahneman, P. Slovic, and A. Tversky, eds., *Judgment under Uncertainty: Heuristics and Biases* (Cambridge: Cambridge University Press, 1982) —and human problem solving.

[91] A marked potential for dialogue exists with cognitive theory and particular psychotherapies, such as Cognitive Therapy (Aaron Beck), Forgiveness Therapy (Robert Enright), Rational Emotive Behavioral Therapy (Albert Ellis), and Parent Management Therapy.

repeatedly succeed in prudent deliberation about significant projects, in the judgment about the way to achieve it, and in the acts to realize it, they effectively modify their capacities to do similarly in the future.

A virtuous disposition of prudence develops, which disposes us to use our practical reason to attain our goals through free personal action in concrete circumstances. Aquinas's most basic philosophical definition of virtue thus asserts that it "denotes a determinate perfection of a power."[92] Prudence, as a complete disposition to act, brings understanding and reason to loving and felt fruition with promptness, ease, and joy.[93] On the contrary, imprudence, as a disposition to act, disposes us to do misplaced (and maladapted) acts with promptness, ease, and pleasure. But in either case, a disposition does not spell an automatic act. As long as compulsion or psychosis has not overrun our reason and will, dispositions set us on a course that we will not complete without further personal reflection and choice.

Prudence or right practical reason has a directive role in the development of every virtue inasmuch as they are within the purview of reason. At the same time, to act prudently requires other virtues (such as justice, love, self-mastery, courage, hope, and patience) and practices (such as pardon and caring) that involve

---

[92] ST I-II, Q. 56, art. 1. In his fuller discussion of virtue, however, Aquinas uses a customary definition of theological (infused) virtue, which has been attributed to Augustine: "[V]irtue is a good quality of the mind, by which we live righteously, of which no one can make bad use, which God works in us, without us" (ST I-II, Q. 55, art. 4; cf. I-II, Q. 65, art. 1).

[93] See Aquinas's De vertutibus in communi, art. 1; De vertutibus 20.2; Summa contra Gentiles 3.150, no. 7; ST I-II, Q. 65, art. 3, ad 2. See also the spontaneity of the virtue of justice (ST II-II, Q. 58, art. 3, ad. 1). See Romanus Cessario, The Moral Virtues and Theological Ethics (Notre Dame: University of Notre Dame Press, 2009), especially 47–57.

the good use of reason as well as that of the will and the emotions. For example, the development of prudence demands interaction with other virtuous dispositions: pardon (a disposition to forgive past wrongs; for example, pardoning errors committed by parents can allow us to deliberate more clearly about other relationships), temperance (a growing mastery of self regarding pleasure), courage (self-knowledge of and mastery over our emotions of fear and daring, including fears of failure and desires of excellence), hope (optimistic motivation for constructive outcomes, for example, in the face of a difficult therapy), and patience (managing the suffering that cannot be avoided). This approach involves a vast vision of the human person and psychology. It also suggests inroads for developmental and therapeutic projects.

The effort needed to develop virtuous dispositions in practical reason and action in the midst of uncertainty should cause us (1) neither to discredit stable moral principles and norms, (2) nor to deny that there are intrinsically evil acts, (3) nor to promote moral relativism. Rather, a study of how morality unfolds through time and in social context indicates that principles remain true in substance while needing specification in the light of historical circumstances, as John Paul II explains in The Splendor of Truth.[94] At the level of common human experience involving psychological health and dysfunction, however, both philosophers and psychotherapists must ask how best to promote and to develop speculative and practical prudence, as a disposition and in action. In what follows, I will ask: which uncertainties, errors, and distractions typically influence the use of our rational capacities? And how do human beings need experience, employ mentors (including psychotherapists), and engage sources of wisdom in order to develop practical reasoning skills and correct faulty judgments or destructive tendencies?

[94] See John Paul II, Veritatis Splendor, nos. 53, 56.

Reasonable Acts

Uncertainty, Errors, and Distractions

Different causes—the more difficult of which are the special concern of psychotherapeutic ministrations—inhibit the complete and consistent development and exercise of intellectual potential: such as cognitive and affective distractions and compulsions, pathology and addiction, ignorance and error, structural evils, and personal sin. Uncertainty, errors, and distractions complicate the pursuit of a good life. Such disruptive pressures on practical reason can negatively influence our relationship with its center (our knowledge of truth and goodness) or its affective support (our emotions and will). Aquinas explains that the dispositions of bodily sensory powers and emotions can either aid or hinder the rational powers that they serve. Negative pressures take the form of (1) biophysical incapacities such as neurological problems with perception or memory,[95] (2) lack of practice because of inexperience, indoctrination, or laziness, or (3) psychosocial and spiritual pathologies. Such pressures, when minor or neurotic, can limit our responsibility to think and to act and, when serious or psychotic, can diminish or even efface our responsibility. Furthermore, other pressures limit prudent reflection and action from the outside—through violence, lack of education or opportunity, and other social influences.

Acquiring a disposition of prudent reasoning and behavior is uncertain, moreover, because of the nature of practical judgment and action. Even in favorable biopsychosocial situations, humans are neither infallible judges nor always prudent in applying appropriate principles and pursuing their good plans when faced with cognitive and affective complexity or the unforeseen. Practical reason involves contingent matters, which all humans do not discern with the same facility. Even a well-formed disposition to prudence does not dispel all incertitude or actual error in behavior.

[95] Cf. *ST* I-II, Q. 63, art. 1.

Philosophical Virtues and Psychological Strengths

Our inability to comprehend the particularity of singular events renders the prudential judgment less sure than speculative truth. We risk miscalculations and errors when seeking a pathway through the forest of practical details. We make mistakes due to ignorance, lack of good counsel, the deformation of conscience, or even because of ignorance that is in no way our fault. We even become almost blind by being accustomed to compromises or sin, often because of certain social customs and family practices. In most every case, the future is precarious.

Prudence relies upon the cooperation of the will and its virtues, in our desires, intentions, consents, choices, and so on. Through volitional distractions, conflicting desires, and weakness of will, we attend to lesser problems instead of the more important ones that we have intelligently intuited and discerned. In effect, we follow disordered loves and apparent goods. Negative types of stress dissipate the volitional focus we need to complete a difficult task reasonably. Dispositional distractibility can have its cause (1) in a biophysical condition, such as attention deficit disorder, which makes concentration difficult, if not impossible, (2) in the lack of practiced self-discipline, or (3) in an acquired disorder of affections, addiction, or vice.

Prudence not only requires the support of other cognitive and volitional virtues, but also demands virtues that strengthen and direct human emotions. Ordered emotions can serve practical plans, while unruly ones can undermine them. Mastering the focus of our affections and fears is of utmost importance when we are seeking to act prudently. According to Aristotle, temperance disposes one to protect the goods of reason against disordered attractions of pleasure and repulsions of pain by keeping hold of one's intellectual or cognitive attention.[96] Without the self-mastery earned by discipline, inordinate desires for not only pleasure,

[96] *NE* 6.5.1140b12.

but also for knowledge, can take a person off track.[97] For example, moderated and well-founded fear can be especially helpful in promoting a rational investigation of its source and focusing one's attention in order to find a solution. Immoderate fear however is problematic for cognitive processes inasmuch as it: disturbs reasoning, deliberation, and judgment; upsets imagination and undercuts concentration-demanding efforts; and deflates motivation through fear of toil, failure, or loss. Moreover, fear influences counsel when it makes things seem greater or smaller—and thus more dreadful—than they really are. According to Aquinas, a certain type of fear even unravels reason, insofar as it "drives away all thought and dislocates the mind."[98] In extreme cases of fear, even though we seek counsel, we are unable to deliberate and to use it appropriately. Fear is prevalent in a patient who feels threatened, abandoned, or isolated.

Of special interest for the psychotherapist are different ways in which a person acquires vicious dispositions that contradict prudence. Types of imprudence and false prudence can resemble prudence in psychological function. They can resemble each other in their capacity to handle cognitive complexity[99] and to put a chosen plan into action. Nonetheless, the difference in effect on the well-being of the person is marked. When

---

[97] On control of intellectual desire and attention, see Aquinas on *studiositas* and its opposite, *curiositas* (*ST* II-II, Q. 166, 167) and an excellent article by Gregory Reichberg, "Studiositas, The Virtue of Attention," in D. McInerny, ed., *The Common Things: Essays on Thomism and Education* (Washington, DC: Maritain Association, 1999), 143–152. On control of sensual desire, see Aquinas on *prudentia carnis* (*ST* II-II, Q. 55, arts. 1, 2) as well as the virtues related to temperance (II-II, Q. 141ff.).

[98] *ST* I-II, Q. 44, art. 2, corp. and ad. 2.

[99] Such cognitive complexity, for example, will exhibit nonexclusive adjudication between seemingly competing notions such as the pairs: justice and mercy, autonomy and heteronomy, nature and grace.

someone forms imprudent dispositions, he employs (1) memory to accomplish egotistical and evil ends, (2) intelligence to rationalize his pursuit of partial versus ultimate truth, (3) lessons from others for wrongheaded solutions, (4) acumen for unjust self-advantage, and (5) quick judgment, foresight, and circumspection in order to arrive at the means that suit his own purposes, but that disserve justice and the common good. He even uses caution about the things that might hinder his self-serving power and pleasures.[100] Human beings can form stable, vicious patterns of precipitation, thoughtlessness, inconstancy, selfish pleasure-seeking, negligence, and various types of false prudence, such as cunning, deceit, fraud, needless fears, and covetousness. An often-neglected question for philosophers, theologians, and psychotherapists alike concerns how psychosocial therapies and spiritual practices might undo such learned patterns of thought, choice, and behavior.

Personal Experience and the Therapist

Age and theory do not necessarily yield enriched thought and acquired prudence. The elderly do not unavoidably exhibit sage lives or perceptive counsel. Nonetheless, there are internal and external resources that help people to act reasonably and to acquire a disposition to do so. As described later, people internalize the first principles of practical reason through experience. Not to seek good and not to avoid evil relative to oneself or to others in a coherent manner is a sign of pathology. While the first practical principles become evident to all, first principles alone do not suffice for mature dispositions and responsible action. Personal experience is cultivated through the influence of extrinsic

---

[100] See Aquinas's discussion of imprudence (ST II-II, Q. 53, arts. 1, 2) in comparison with his analysis of the integral parts of prudence (ST II-II, Q. 49, arts. 1–8).

principles of reasonable action, such as teachers, mentors, and psychotherapists. It is also guided by intelligent custom and just law. We internalize principles, knowledge, and virtue through personal reflection with the help of such external sources.

To demonstrate the correlation between personal growth and guidance, Aquinas uses two principal images — the arts and disciple-master interaction. In particular, he borrows from, yet renews, insights from the Greek philosophical tradition of *paideia* through his Christian treatment of the relationship between master and disciple. For Aquinas, the master or teacher par excellence is Christ.[101]

In order to understand profoundly the array of reasonable practices that are born of moral theory, wisdom, and prudence, people first need experience.[102] Aristotle avers: "The cause

---

[101] Cf. *ST* III, Q. 7, art. 7. Christ is seconded in this role by the Apostles, bishops, and the masters of theology who teach and comment on Sacred Scripture. In this perspective, Aquinas regroups the gifts of the Holy Spirit (cf. 1 Cor. 12) around the teacher, since through instruction one human being can act upon another on the spiritual level. Cf. *ST* I-II, Q. 111, art. 4; Servais-Théodore Pinckaers, *A l'école de l'admiration* (Versailles: Ed. St. Paul, 2000); Servais Pinckaers Pinckaers, *The Sources of Christian Ethics*, trans. M. T. Noble (Washington, DC: The Catholic University Press, 1995), 359–374; and Gerard Verbeke, "L'éducation morale et les arts chez Aristote et Thomas d'Aquin," in *Scientia und ars im Hoch- und Spätmittelarter* (Berlin: De Gruyter, 1994), 449–467.

[102] In his general discussion of science, Aquinas notes that, in order to elaborate a moral science, we need related personal experience. This view was not uncommon. Aristotle states it in his *Nicomachean Ethics* (1.3.1095a2-11). In his commentary *In Librum de Causis* (lect. 1, ed. Saffrey, pp. 1–2; in Mauer, 1963, 91), Aquinas lists the order of learning the sciences as follows: firST logic; second, mathematics; third, natural sciences; fourth, moral science; and fifth, metaphysics and divine science.

is that such wisdom is concerned not only with universals but with particulars, which become familiar from experience, but a young man has no experience, for it is length of time that gives experience."[103] Aquinas corroborates this view, explaining that moral wisdom's "natural principles, which are not abstracted from sensible things, are known through experience, for which a long time is required."[104] Second, prudence brings to reason not only indispensable knowledge, but also efficacy in action. Aristotle says: "We see that the experienced are more effective than those who have reason, but lack experience."[105]

Prudent action nonetheless is not achieved by raw experience, knowledge, or reasoning alone. Cognitive experience is insufficient, as is the knowledge of the sage, unless we also acquire consequent efficacy of will and mastery over our emotions. For intellectual inexperience as well as volitional and emotional disorder or immaturity can waylay right action, as has been mentioned. To understand human action, one cannot be a slave of passion or continually seeking the pleasures of disordered passion.[106] Hence, to study reasonable acts and to put them into practice, we need the experience that constitutes the moral character involved in a range of virtue strengths.

The shared cognitive competency of teachers, mentors, and psychotherapists (as sources of authority, knowledge, and wisdom) helps a person develop prudence, conscience, and responsible action.[107] These outside resources are needed especially during

---

[103] NE 6.8.1142a12–15.

[104] Cf. In Ethic., bk. 6, lect. 7, no. 1209; NE 1.3.1095a2–11 and In Ethic., bk. 1, lect. 3.38–40.

[105] Metaphysics, A.981a14–15; cf. Aquinas, In duodecim libros Metaphysicorum Aristotelis A.981a14–15.

[106] Cf. In Ethic., bk. 1, lect. 3 no. 40; cf. NE 1.3.1095a2–11; In Ethic., bk. 6, lect. 7 no. 1211.

[107] See Gladys Sweeney, Craig S. Titus, and Bill Nordling, "Training Psychologists and Christian Anthropology," in

the first phase of growth, where one struggles with fitting discernment, adjudication, and acts, and where one needs to establish basic skills or to reestablish them, for example, by overcoming disordered or compulsive cognitions, affections, and practices.[108] Moreover, relationships and culture transmit a heritage of understanding, wisdom, or revelation that supports prudent behavior as well.

The master, mentor, or therapist (as exterior principle and light) leads the disciple or patient-client (interior principle) to acquire personal knowledge and understanding.[109] A person employs the light of the intellect (personal intelligence) and other sources of light (both teachers and God) to acquire knowledge and virtue. An external teacher does not directly cause us to learn or to develop. We must directly engage ourselves. Yet, to appropriate human experience personally, we depend upon a teacher's aid. For example, commitment to psychological treatment is a first step toward personal change, which is completed only if the patient-client seeks appropriate behavior modification (perhaps through role-taking therapies) and further growth by applying throughout life the self-knowledge, skills, and wisdom acquired

Edification: The Journal of the Society of Christian Psychology 3 (2009): 51–56.

108 Aquinas (ST II-II, Q. 24, art. 9) identifies three stages of development: the beginner, the proficient, and the advanced. Discussions of the three stages are found in Servais Pinckaers, The Sources of Christian Ethics, trans. M. T. Noble (Washington, DC: The Catholic University of America Press, 1995), 354–378; and C. S. Titus, "Moral Development and Making All Things New in Christ," The Thomist 72 (2008): 233–258.

109 Cf. ST I, Q. 117, art. 1; II-II, Q. 181, art. 3, corp. and ad. 2, and parallel places: Sent., bk. 2, d. 9.2, ad. 4; d. 28.5, ad. 3; SCG II, Q. 75; DV Q. 11, art. 1; Opusc. XVI, De unitate intellectus contra Averroistas, 5.

in therapy. An appropriate attachment to such a figure can aid in learning and stabilizing a person's affections and reasoning.[110]

Learning can also result from informal interactions with unlikely sources: the poor and weak, young and old alike. Such interactions lead us from things unknown by us to things experienced by another person, in a twofold way. First, the person provides instructive aids to help us acquire knowledge, sometimes simply through his example of defusing a potentially violent situation. A therapy might seek to diffuse a particular crisis or more chronic conditions through prudent instruction and recommendations for behavioral changes or by narrative engagement. Secondly, the person instructs by proposing formal or informal exercises that proceed from experience through principles to cognitive conclusions and concrete actions. For example, a dialectic discussion about conflict resolution between spouses based on principles of commitment and forgiveness can lead to acts of pardon, caring, and love. Such demonstrations strengthen our rational competencies, train our wills, and aid us in better integrating our emotions.[111] The exercise of defusing symptoms is only one of the ways in which intelligent cognition can involve progress in prudence and in psychological health.

The therapist or counselor, moreover, might be seen as a type of guide that aids the client to understand himself. She might structure the opportunity for him to reflect upon his life and dreams, his emotions and behavior. She may ask questions that lead the client further and encourage him to address life in a more responsible manner. The client then has the opportunity to change his life and even to have hope for further positive developments in the future.

---

[110] See works on attachment theory by John Bowlby, Mary Ainsworth, Mary Main, and Peter Fonagy.

[111] Cf. ST I, Q. 117, art. 1.

Right Practical Reason

From a virtue perspective and with more technical precision, prudence or right practical reason concerns intellectual and practical deliberative and agentive capacities that are informed with age and influenced by the social entourage. The seeds of prudent action are found in the natural inclinations to what is good, true, and just for the person, family, and society (ST I-II, Q. 94, art. 2). These seeds are manifest in naturally known first practical principles (such as "Do good and avoid evil"). The disposition to prudent action is refined through the use of one's discernment and judgment to realize goals and apply principles. We exert extensive cognitive effort in order to make personal progress, to educate children, and to build communities. After things have gone wrong, we multiply efforts to reeducate ourselves through self-guided reframing exercises or to counsel others in reinforcement therapies.

To understand the virtue perspective and its application to pathways of development and therapy, we need to recognize that the terms *virtue* and *prudence* have three aspects inasmuch as they refer to a practice (act), a norm, and a disposition to act. A philosophical perspective distinguishes these three uses of the virtue of prudence: as *a practical rational act* or practice itself, involving deliberation, judgment, and a command to act; as *an ethical norm for action*, based in the reality of human nature and its finality; and as a *disposition to act in a rational and principled way*, at speculative and practical levels.

Deliberative Capacities of the Virtue of Prudence

According to Aristotle, the practical virtue of prudence or practical wisdom (*phronesis*) concerns an intermediate choice that discerns "the mean relative to us, this being determined by a rational principle, and by that principle by which the man of practical wisdom would determine it" (*NE* 1107a1–3). Such practical exigency involves a concrete application fitted to the person at hand. When we see a prudent person do an appropriate deed, we have a basis for understanding the goal and the adaptive functioning of prudence. In prudential acts, an intelligent person acts for a good and true goal in a good manner. Optimally such practical virtue involves not only doing something well but also expressing appropriate emotions "at the right time, with reference to the right objects, towards the right people, with the right motive, and in the right ways" (*NE* 1106b20–22). Acting rightly for a good and true end involves adaptive creativity as well as normative fidelity. With innovative intuition, imagination, and reason, one discovers ways to serve faithfully the foreseen ends, even in less than optimal situations.

The virtue of prudence proper, defined by Aquinas as right practical reason, requires the development of human potential in order to apply our cognitive capacities to particular speculative and practical issues and to put our reasoned decisions into practice.[112] It involves an effort to develop intellectual and sensate, cognitive, and appetitive capacities according to human nature's potential for intelligent excellence. Aquinas calls this development, acquired *connaturality*, which is a type of second nature. Concerning the acquired virtue of prudence, he says that "in order that one be rightly disposed with regard to particular principles of action, namely, their ends, one needs to be perfected by certain dispositions, whereby it becomes, as it were, connatural to him to judge rightly about an end."[113] The moral virtue of prudence entails that the virtuous person judges aright about the means to these ends.

---

[112] Aquinas says that prudence is *recta ratio agibilium*. Cf. *ST* I-II, Q. 57, art. 4; I-II, Q. 56, art. 4; II-II, Q. 47, arts. 2, 8; I-II, Q. 57, art. 5 ad. 1; I-II, Q. 65, art. 1; *SCG* I, Q. 93.

[113] *ST* II-II, Q. 58, art. 5.

Aquinas goes further than Aristotle in affirming that the norm for human actions is found not only through human reason (that is, the judgment of the prudent person), but in eternal law. Regarding both human and divine normative sources, prudence involves not only the understanding of a plan that will bring us flourishing, nor merely an intuition of first practical (ethical) principles, nor even a judgment about the application of such principles, although all of these express human intelligence and are important. It requires putting the plan into action as well. An architect's blueprints alone will not keep a family warm and dry, nor will a simple abstract understanding of the good life necessarily make the person act for his or her own good, or that of others.

Cognitive Speculation and Praxis

Some persons excel in abstract thought. They master speculative adjudication about general principles and theories. Others shine in problem-solving and practical matters. They sagely apply principle to concrete action. A person needs predilections, education, and experience to acquire cognitive skills in any of these areas. Accordingly, we distinguish right reason as speculative (intellectual prudence) or practical (moral prudence) and by its field of application, such as family, business, political, and military prudence. Classical virtue theory has analyzed cognitive strengths in terms of intellectual virtues—namely, understanding, science-knowledge, wisdom, art, prudence, and their auxiliary virtues such as integrity or honesty (*honestas*) and inquisitiveness or attentive observation (*studiositas*, which is much more than scholarly attention). It also has treated cognitive weaknesses, failures, and vices. The virtue approach has, moreover, a rich vocabulary and conceptual repertoire for the spiritual domain.[114]

114 This essay does not intend to enter into the spiritual domain
of cognition. However, a simple typology will serve those who
are interested. According to Aquinas, the grace of God builds

Philosophical Virtues and Psychological Strengths

Aristotle's understanding of practical wisdom involves both intellectual excellence (*arête*) and applied or practical character (*hexis*). As an intellectual virtue, it seeks the excellent means toward a good life in general. "It is a true and reasoned state of capacity to act with regard to the things that are good or bad for man," concerning practical judgments about what is to be done according to right reason.[115] It does not concern things of universal necessity, laws of physics, or making artifacts, as do the virtues of philosophical wisdom, science, and art respectively. Rather, it concerns the course of reasoning and responsibility about what is variable in human acts, that is, about practical judgments and customs concerning the means to human goals. As an intellectual virtue, prudence thus involves speculative judgments about uncertain human deeds. Such an act is good and right; another is evil and wrongheaded. *"This principle of justice — 'you must return things to their proper owner' — applies in this situation."* We reason practically about how to act in a given situation.[116] This is

---

up cognitive — as well as volitional and emotional — areas of human nature, through the infused moral virtues. This focused unfolding of natural virtues stems from the foundation set in place by the theological virtues of faith, hope, and charity. It applies especially to acts that are needed for salvation. Faith, in particular, is the theological virtue that strengthens the intellect to believe in what is revealed by God (for example, about Jesus Christ, the resurrection, and eternal life). Specific gifts of the Holy Spirit perfect the intellect in different ways: understanding, knowledge, counsel, and wisdom. See *ST* I-II, Q. 55–62, 68.

[115] *NE* 6.5.1140b5 and 1114b15.

[116] Cf. *ST* I-II, Q. 79, art. 11; II-II, Q. 47, art. 1, art. 4, 5. Aquinas says that prudence "requires that one be rightly disposed with regards to ends; and this depends on the rightness of appetite [the will and emotion]" (*ST* I-II, Q. 57, art. 4). Prudence as a moral virtue's seat is "practical intellect charged with good will" (*ST* I-II, Q. 56, art. 3).

necessary since we can have general knowledge about such principles and not understand its particular application.

Inasmuch as we have acquired prudence as a moral virtue, we are disposed to act in accordance with right reason about how to achieve a goal, affecting right desire and doing quickly what is decided. *"I now return the lawn mower that you lent me."* Such a judgment and corresponding action are based not merely on an abstract principle. Rather, they first and foremost are based in reality, in relationships, and in commitments with the involved persons and things. Each person needs to develop these cognitive skills—this moral virtue of prudence—because one can have general knowledge, and even understand particular applications, but not perform the needed deed, because of cognitive failures due to conflicts of desire, weakness of will, negligence, a disordered cognitive fascination with power, an emotive addiction to pleasure, a lack of understanding or imagining the good of other people, or other influences. In this sense, "moral" involves the practical as well as the normative—doing or not doing something that you judge good to do. In these matters, a person employs both natural inclinations (and instincts) and acquired dispositions to act reasonably.

Another distinction concerns the types of prudence: personal prudence, domestic prudence, military prudence, political prudence, and so on. These species of prudence do not develop in each person in exactly the same way. For example, President J. F. Kennedy had a good deal of political prudence, while lacking certain aspects of personal prudence (temperance and marital fidelity).[117] Even with natural capacities such as a prudent

---

117 On problems related to the unequal development of virtue and to the divided self or the flawed saint, see C. S. Titus, "Moral Development and the Connection of the Virtues: Aquinas, Porter, and the Flawed Saint," in *Ressourcement Thomism: Sacred Doctrine, the Sacraments, and the Moral Life,*

or political temperament and inquisitive tendencies, we need experience to exercise these potential skills in order to develop prudence in particular domains such as family matters, business, and politics. The experiences of temperance, sexual identity, and culture influence the way in which people make decisions, individuals make progress, and psychotherapists recommend particular strategies.

In the midst of its assorted types, there is a common core to human prudence. We act intellectually and morally by employing intuition, reason, and right judgment in the application of operative principles. A sound judgment supposes that through inclination, experience, or grace we are moved by reality and principles appropriate for the concrete situation.[118] Prudence, however, does not require only acts of discernment, judgment, and self-directive command, nor only an accurate appraisal of a situation, but it requires an underlying disposition to act reasonably as well. By either acquired or infused inclinations, the virtuous disposition brings about such a unity with the goal that it enables discernment and right judgment about the means to the end and the mean between extremes. Moreover, in order to form and guard the virtue of prudence, we must act upon the disposition (toward ethical principles, inclinations, and ends) with some consistency and rectitude. Particular acts of careful and accurate reasoning

---

eds. R. Hütter and M. Levering (Washington, DC: The Catholic University of America Press, 2010).

[118] Aquinas thus writes: "The fact that a cognitive power is well disposed to receive things as they are at root is from nature, but its flowering is from practice or from the gift of grace" (*ST* II-II, Q. 51, art. 3, ad. 1). There is another level of connaturality that we find in infused prudence and the gift of counsel. According to Aquinas, in addition to acquired prudence, grace can properly dispose a cognitive power to perceive the truth and goodness of things.

lead to established dispositions that engender further thoughtful acts and intellectual spontaneity.[119]

When we attain new positions, however, such as those with family responsibility and political influence, we may well need to develop other aspects of our cognitive and affective capacities. For example, the cognitively competent parent needs to verify that his competency applies to another domain, such as that of psychotherapy, without presuming that related skills will transfer straightaway to a new terrain. An acquired disposition of personal prudence will serve in the future, but mistakes are possible, especially when one thinks that a past solution will necessarily serve without attending to the novelty of the reality at hand. Moreover, new types of complexity (such as the therapist's responsibility for a suicidal patient) challenge one to develop further aspects of cognitive and relational skills.

Prudence thus has two interrelated dimensions: (1) personally acquired knowledge and a developed disposition to act rationally in concrete situations and (2) theory about ethical practice. As a human being with a particular genetic makeup and with interpersonal experience gathered from the first moments of existence, a person has a basis for prudence, which develops further with personal reflection and action. On the one hand, through experience, one develops rational, volitional, emotional and social capacities. That is, as a parent, a teacher, or a therapist, a person acquires practical knowledge, patterns of judgments about practical matters, and dispositions to act. On the other hand, through study and academic illustrations, one acquires abstract knowledge

---

[119] On the relationship between morality and spontaneity, see Servais-Théodore Pinckaers, "Morality and the Movement of the Holy Spirit: Aquinas's Doctrine of *Instinctus*," in *The Pinckaers Reader: Renewing Thomistic Moral Theology*, eds. J. Berkman and C.S. Titus (Washington, DC: The Catholic University of America Press, 2005).

of principles and practical judgments; for instance, how to use them in therapeutic techniques. The twofold nature of prudence functions with conscious precision due to practical knowledge, which one will not consistently use unless a person is also sympathetically affected by the goal and animated by practical knowledge about how to achieve it.

I have highlighted the human disposition (involving reason and will, perception and affection) that facilitates the movement from speculative knowledge to practical action. For his part, Jacques Maritain distinguishes three types of knowledge and their application.[120] First, speculative sciences, such as speculative philosophy, which seeks knowledge for the sake of knowing, are purely speculative. Second, speculatively practical sciences, such as moral philosophy, theoretical medicine, and philosophical psychology, involve knowledge of operations and acts, with the purpose of directing action. Third, practically practical science, such as practical moral sciences, practical medicine, and psychotherapy involves more direct and practical application of theory. The exercise of the latter sciences is practical in the highest degree. Someone immediately applies practical theory in a concrete action: prudence that seeks to instill intelligence in handling a conflict; medicine that must effectuate actual medical procedures; or a session of psychotherapy that employs reinforcement strategies to instill practical knowledge and facilitate constructive practice.

Conscience and Prudence:
Good and Evil in Principles and Knowledge

First principles and final goals constitute the cognitive-affective motor for human acts. To understand a person's moral act,

---

[120] See J. Maritain, *Distinguish to Unite: or the Degrees of Knowledge* (New York: Charles Scribner's Sons, 1959), 458–464.

one needs to find the principle(s) and goal(s) that motivate it. Even in more spontaneous deeds, we are moved to seek some good thing or to shun something that is evil or wrongheaded. This first principle of morality is the foundation for derivative principles of action, of which each person is more or less conscious, and which one comes to understand through experience, admonition, and reflection. Aquinas formulates this practical foundation of natural law as: "good is to be done and pursued, and evil is to be avoided" (*ST* I-II, Q. 94, art. 2). This principle holds true even when we find our motivation in a good that is merely an apparent one (that is, that we discover later to be evil).

According to realist ethics, practical reason does not create basic practical principles for rational judgment. Rather humans discover them through a basic human disposition of practical reason that has been classically called synderesis, which comes from St. Paul's use of the term syneidesis (cf. Rom. 2:15). St. Jerome calls the disposition of first practical principles the pure spark of conscience.121 No adequate English term covers this disposition itself, which is often simply identified with conscience. Aquinas interrelates, but differentiates synderesis from conscience itself.122 He metaphorically distinguishes the pure spark of conscience—knowledge of good and evil that cannot be effaced—from the fire of conscience itself—which as a particular judgment can be erroneous for various reasons.123

---

121 See St. Jerome, *Commentary on Ezekiel* 1:6, 7 (ML 25, 22). Aquinas cites Jerome in his discussion on the distinction of *synderesis* and conscience in *DV* Q. 16 and 17, and in *ST* I, Q. 79, arts. 12, 13.

122 Aquinas avers: "*Synderesis* is said to incite us to good and to deter us from evil in that through first principles we both begin investigation and judge what we find" (*ST* I, Q. 79, art. 12). See also: *DV* Q. 17, art. 2, ad. 3; cf. *ST* I-II, Q. 62, art. 1.

123 St. Thomas, *DV* Q. 17, art. 2, ad. 3. By conscience, we intend more than the content of superego in a Freudian sense, which

Philosophical Virtues and Psychological Strengths

For his part, Joseph Cardinal Ratzinger (the present Pope Benedict XVI) has identified the close relationship of *synderesis* to conscience.[124] He finds their separation an infelicitous effect of a certain medieval Scholasticism. Furthermore, he argues that "*anamnesis*" (a Platonic and biblical concept) can replace the untranslatable *synderesis*. Anamnesis is "linguistically clearer and philosophically deeper and purer, but above all [it] also harmonizes with key motifs of biblical thought and the anthropology derived therefrom." With this said, we should recall that the term *conscience* has often replaced larger notions of practical reason in moral theology (with the advent of Nominalism and the moral handbooks that shaped a Catholic casuistic approach to moral issues for use in the ministry of the sacrament of confession or reconciliation). Regrettably, in the process, moral judgment has often lost its deeper and fuller developmental, social, and spiritual dimensions. This issue is best understood when interrelating the range of conscience as an act, the disposition of first moral principles (*synderesis*), and prudence as a disposition to rational action, as Servais Pinckaers suggests.[125]

Through experiential contact with reality, including through natural inclinations, a person acquires an instinctive understanding (intuitive grasp) of these first practical principles, which govern our practice just as others govern our speculative thought. It is at this level that we grasp pure and inviolable practical principles ("do not kill," "do not lie"). Originally we only potentially know principles and the actions toward which these principles direct

---

tends to flatten and limit the content, the source, and the finality of conscience.

[124] See, J. Ratzinger, "Conscience and Truth," in *Catholic Conscience. Foundation and Formation* (Braintree, Massachusetts: The Pope John Center, 1999), 19.

[125] See Servais-Théodore Pinckaers, "Conscience and the Virtue of Prudence," *The Pinckaers Reader*, 253–266.

us. We need experience, through which we are brought to sense and intellectual knowledge "by the action of sensible objects on the senses, and to the actuality of understanding by teaching or discovery," as Aquinas explains (*ST* I, Q. 84, art. 3). The human person as knower only at first potentially knows principles of sense and understanding. These normative principles involve our knowledge of the natural law, which is confirmed and clarified in the Decalogue, which is concretized in the life of virtue (through the New Law of grace).[126] First normative principles are the common basis for understanding morality and behavior in general. They also serve therapeutic work (reframing and reinforcement strategies, and so on), especially when a patient realizes that his behavior is running counter to his deeper life aspirations, faith, and commitments.

The first level of moral science and prudent action, however, is not yet prudence per se. Experiential knowledge of practical principles forms the basis for free moral action and constitutes the seeds of virtues that are developed in turn and that interact with other dimensions of custom, law, and grace. These starting points direct reason to truth, will to goodness, and each of them away from error and evil.[127] Without the corresponding particular right judgment and action, however, the knowledge of these basic principles falls short, lacking the fullness of prudence and of the

---

126 See Servais-Théodore Pinckaers, "The Return of the New Law to Moral Theology," *The Pinckaers Reader*, 369–384.

127 Even in the post-lapsus human condition—with all the disordered effects on human individuals and society—Aquinas claims that, "the seeds of virtue, which are in us, are an ordering of the will and reason to the good connatural to us" (*Sent.*, bk. 3, d. 33, question 1, article 2, solution 3, corpus; cf. *ST* I-II, Q. 51, art. 1; I-II, Q. 63, art. 1; I-II, Q. 27, art. 3). He states also that "not to want something evil seems to be connatural, since evils are against nature" (*Sent.*, bk. 4 d. 49, Q. 5, art. 5, sol. 3, ex.).

freedom of excellence. While knowledge of the law (natural and divine) is necessary, it is not sufficient. John Paul II says:

> what is essential is a sort of "connaturality" between man and the true good [*ST* II-II, Q. 45, art. 2]. Such connaturality is rooted in and develops through the virtuous attitudes of the individual himself: prudence and the other cardinal virtues, and even before these the theological virtues of faith, hope and charity. This is the meaning of Jesus' saying: "He who does what is true comes to the light" (Jn 3:21).[128]

To the chagrin of relativists, the seeking of good and the avoidance of evil are central to the human person. They are founded upon the natural inclinations to know and love the good. Even fear and anger relate to the more basic aspirations of love and desire for persons and things that one esteems as good and beautiful, useful and worthwhile, and more or less fulfilling of personal aspirations and social goals. However, practical patterns of love and desire are shaped throughout life. When they develop into disordered emotional dispositions, we tend to experience extreme forms of fear, aggressiveness, attachment, and self-love. In such cases, one will need to acquire further skills that reframe misguided conceptions of the good in the context of larger social and moral principles and goals.

Psychosocial Context and Tripartite Structure of Practical Reason

This last section offers a more technical analysis of the psychological context and tripartite structure of prudence. Human acts unfold in rather unpredictable ways and in the midst of a host of social influences. Some acts are spontaneous. Others take months

---

[128] *Veritatis Splendor*, no. 64.

to develop fully, involving slow progress, occasional regression, and labored resolutions. Each person—not only those with serious psychopathology or substance-dependence—has something unique about the way in which he has come to his present state of life, one in the midst of life as father and carpenter, another as mother and teacher, in every case with distinct social input. Moreover, every person has particular attractions, repulsions, fascinations, and embodied commitments. Even in the midst of such diversity, however, there is something common. Aquinas's tripartite philosophical overview of the basic psychosocial structure of the virtue of prudence aids in understanding the developmental progress of the human intellect from intuitive plan and desire to complete action through three phases:[129] (1) personal deliberation

129 To be more complete, Aquinas offers a structural and causal explanation of twelve intellectual (speculative and practical, rational and volitional) steps involved in moral action. This analysis of moral action has received much commentary, although a good part of it has not appropriated Aquinas's synthetic vision—in particular concerning interaction with the sensate powers (cognition and emotion) and with natural and spiritual inclinations. Aquinas's account of the moral act (ST I-II, Q. 6–21) is not so much a phenomenology of conscious or unconscious psychological events (or partial acts) that compose moral agency, nor of conscientiousness, which Peterson and Seligman (*Character Strengths and Virtues*, 484) identify as a key personality trait descriptor for prudence. Rather, Thomas's structural study offers a tool to explore the human person in its depths and in its spontaneous experience. His approach offers insights that we can apply to understand the temporal unfolding of a variety of acts, even when they appear unruly and unsynchronized. He follows a vertical plan boring to the center and first cause found in the ultimate end that enables every truly voluntary act. In particular, understanding this approach to the dialectical dynamics of human actions requires attention to sensate affections and cognitions (external and internal) and the natural and spiritual inclinations as well.

and taking counsel, (2) right judgment and conscience, and (3) self-direction and practical action.

Deliberation and Taking Counsel

How can one render justice to a friend, who, in a state of blind rage, requests that I return his axe so that he can take vengeance on a neighbor? When there are several ways to achieve a goal, we need to deliberate about them, specify the viable ones, and consent to a truly good one.[130] Since we cannot comprehend with certainty the truth of conditional things through simple insight, we must engage our imagination and social support. I ask myself what I can do about my friend's request. When possible, I seek advice from trusted and competent people. By force of will, searching intelligence, or seeming luck, I eventually discover what to do. Such efforts at personal deliberation and taking counsel involve both a virtuous act and a disposition that support prudence as a larger process.[131]

Counsel—considered as deliberation and as taking good counsel—is directed to prudent action. For its part, prudence (which principally concerns self-motivated action) must elicit counsel in order to discover what has to be done. Moreover, beyond our natural inclinations and grasp of basic principles, we seek to acquire dispositions to take good counsel and to move quickly once we have taken it.[132] Building upon deliberation, our consent involves a volitional engagement. We affirm that the means proposed through the act of deliberation is good and fitting.[133]

On the psychological level, a person may tend to express an inability to deliberate prudently. For example, a compulsive behavior

---

[130] Cf. *ST* I-II, Q. 14.
[131] Cf. *ST* II-II, Q. 51, art. 1 and Q. 51, art. 2.
[132] Cf. *ST* II-II, Q. 51, art. 1, ad. 2; and I-II, Q. 44, art. 2 sc.
[133] Cf. *ST* I-II, Q. 15.

influences her capacity to reason in accord with her engagements and relationships. Personal and therapeutic interventions help to heal and correct a compulsive disposition. In effect, even the commitment to start a therapy involves openness to counsel, which can help someone to understand herself, to recognize ways to modify her behavior (such as through reframing strategies), and to continue more consistent personal growth (through prevention and development strategies). The counsel of therapists (like that of family and friends) may well bring prudent correctives to personal deliberation that has been marked by compulsion, hatred, or other negative influences.

On another level of analysis, in the case of good deliberation and counsel through the gift of counsel (the gift of the Holy Spirit), we adjudicate about divine things through a spiritual instinct, which firmly and surely establishes moral judgment, and manifests itself in spontaneity of action.[134] The Holy Spirit directs those who seek guidance according to the nature of human freedom, reason, and will, affirming our use of them. At the most basic level, we are passive in the face of such a spiritual event, but concomitantly, at a practical level, we actively seek it and affirm our reception of it. Thus, the gift of counsel instructs human reason in what to do. It aids one's rectitude of reason. It also allays anxiety about human action and removes hesitation that precedes decisions to act reasonably.

Right Practical Judgment

After deliberation and counsel, we verify how adequate the plan is. *Does the particular deed that I have selected—refusing to return the axe to my enraged friend—fulfill my intended goal in a reasonable way? Is it just?* A practical judgment concerns whether

---

134 Cf. *ST* II-II, Q. 52, arts. 1–4; Pinckaers, "Morality and the Movement of the Holy Spirit," 396–406.

the envisaged action conforms to the sought-after goal.[135] To say "practical judgment," therefore, does not necessarily mean a simple judgment. Reality, imagination, and emotions influence us. We might have to overcome past injury with pardon or present fear with confidence. While there may be agreement concerning counsel—as a speculative (psycho-social-spiritual) search employing common principles and therapies—the next speculative effort of personal practical reason does not always allow a straightforward judgment. Indeed, practical adjudication involves knowledge of particular reality, specific principles, and practical applications, which can be erroneous due to cognitive mistakes and emotional disturbances.

Ordinary and extraordinary situations affect judgment. Some people tend to judge well in run-of-the-mill conditions, while making disastrous judgments when faced with situations beyond common occurrence or under pressure. Practical judgment thus is supported by two virtuous dispositions that Aquinas distinguishes as (1) right judgment (*synesis*) according to common rules of action in the familiar course of events and (2) a discriminating judgment (*gnome*) that appeals to higher principles, in extraordinary and complex situations.[136] He says:

> Right judgment [*synesis*] and a discriminating judgment [*gnome*] differ in respect of the different rules on which judgment is based: for the first judges of actions according to the common law; while the second bases its judgment on the natural law, in those cases where the common law fails to apply.[137]

---

[135] On practical judgment (*judicium practicum*) see *ST* I-II, Q. 57, art. 6, corp. and ad. 3.

[136] See *ST* II-II, Q. 51, art. 3 concerning *synesis*, and II-II, Q. 51, art. 4 concerning *gnome*.

[137] *ST* I-II, Q. 57, art. 6. Furthermore, Aquinas explains: "The potential parts of a virtue are the virtues connected with it,

Reasonable Acts

On the one hand, human beings judge aright about reality and intended plans that concern the common course of events, such as feeding one's family, taking the subway, or being fair in the workplace. Ordinary situations involve judging reality rightly according to common rules of action and our daily routines. We have the most experience at this level. Without hesitation I return the axe to my neighbor who intends to chop firewood.

In extraordinary and complex situations, on the other hand, we need a discriminating judgment that appeals to higher principles. Sometimes appeal to and application of the pertinent principle will not be evident to others — certainly not to my enraged friend, if I refuse him his axe. We employ perspicacious judgment to identify that the customary practice or common rule is not fitting, that another principle applies for a good reason. This may happen even with only an intuitive grasp of the supporting reason. Even though beyond the common course of events only God's providence is absolutely complete, perspicacious people, through reason, make more discriminating judgments about reality.[138] *I decide to keep my neighbor's axe hidden (at the present time)*

which are directed to certain secondary acts or matters, not having, as it were, the whole power of the principal virtue. In this way the parts of prudence are 'good counsel (*eubulia*),' which concerns counsel, '*synesis*,' which concerns judgment in matters of ordinary occurrence, and 'gnome,' which concerns judgment in matters of exception to the common law: while 'prudence' is about the chief act, viz. that of commanding" (*ST* II-II, Q. 48, art. 1; cf. II-II, Q. 51). For example, a common rule does not apply when a circumstance is so extreme that it substitutes itself for the object of the act (cf. I-II, Q. 18, art. 10, corp. and ad. 2), thus changing the nature of the act; for example, in self-defense.

138 Through the light of higher principles and a genomic judgment, Aquinas affirms that there is only one command that is prudent (*ST* II-II, Q. 51, art. 4, ad. 2; I-II, Q. 14, art. 1; II-II, Q. 51, art. 4, ad. 3).

and to attempt to defuse his murderous rage. I intend neither to assist him in his deed nor to steal his axe. Rather, I intend to resist the evil he announced. At this time, the operative principle is to protect innocent life. I also intend to prevent my friend from committing an egregious error and crime that he would commit more easily with the axe. My friend's state of emotions does not forfeit the ownership of his property. The object of my act is not theft, for I will gladly return the axe when my neighbor regains his habitual composure. I am not obliged, however, to return borrowed property to its rightful owner under such circumstances. I would even be an accomplice to murder, if I did. Faced with such a practical decision to take, we choose a practical plan as the way to attain the end.[139]

At this level, a judgment of conscience and the virtue of prudence coincide. Conscience is the knowledge about the good or evil nature of past or future events (*DV* Q. 17, art. 1). It condemns past evils, affirms past good deeds and learns from them both, while inciting one to do good and avoid evil deeds in the future. Although conscience and right practical judgment have parallel functions, the virtue of prudence is more comprehensive in scope; it also demands action and involves a host of virtues that require a correct apprehension of the person and reality.[140]

---

[139] This choice (*electio*) is a volitional act (cf. *ST* I-II, Q. 13, especially art. 6). This is the affective movement needed, since man is not determined by lesser ends, but only by the ultimate beatitude that alone will fulfill him.

[140] Aquinas notes that the virtue of sound practical judgment requires support in the sensate cognitive powers through not only the external but also the internal senses. Moreover, this virtue finds perfection through practice or grace either (1) directly through the cognitive power and the reception of true and correct perceptions and conceptions or (2) indirectly through the good moral disposition of the appetitive power (cf. *ST* II-II, Q. 51, art. 3 and Q. 51, art. 3, ad. 1).

Practical Acts

*I actually tell my neighbor that I will not give him back his axe in
the present situation, and I actually take other appropriate steps to
defuse the dangerous situation* (such as engaging the help of other
friends or even the police, if necessary). Prudence goes further
than practical knowledge, deliberation, and judgment in a cogni-
tive-affective effort to put them into act. Right practical reason
requires that a person do something—that he actually perform
a fitting act. Indeed without self-directed commands, one does
nothing.

Furthermore, without a measured act, prudence is incomplete
as a moral virtue and ineffective of the good imagined. In this
third stage of the act of the virtue of prudence, the person moves
himself from theory through decision into practice. Through a
complete range of cognitions and affections—which may take a
brief moment or laborious years—the person accomplishes what
he desired, planned, and decided in order to attain his goal. This
self-command, self-motivation, or internal pressure on the per-
son to act utilizes the means acquired by practical reason.[141] This
complete act requires that the prudent person call upon his dis-
positions of memory, understanding, docility, acumen, reasoned
judgment, foresight, circumspection, and caution as integral ele-
ments of such reasonable acts.[142] He does this in a social context,
at times aided by family and friends. When a difficulty in prac-
tically facing reality is persistent and debilitating—for instance
due to fear, compulsion, or addiction—therapeutic behavioral
strategies and professional assistance may be needed.

---

[141] Cf. *ST* I-II, Q. 1; II-II, Q. 47, art. 8; I-II, Q. 57, art. 6; II-II, Q. 51.

[142] Aquinas thus identifies the integral parts of prudence (cf. *ST* II-II, Q. 48 and II-II, Q. 49, arts. 1–8). He says that prudence needs solicitude and vigilance as well (cf. I-II, Q. 47, art. 9).

Philosophical Virtues and Psychological Strengths

Conclusion

Right practical reason employs philosophical virtues and psychological strengths. This essay has illustrated that a developmental view of the virtue of prudence (right practical reason in action) bridges part of the gap between human nature's origin and finality, in terms of prudence as disposition to act, as norm, and as practice. The twin sources of intelligence—origin and flourishing—provide the context for discussing the formal development of human cognitive skills and related therapeutic efforts. In prudential action and therapy, we do not simply seek what is normatively permitted and avoid what is forbidden. In personal and interpersonal relations (including with God), we employ reason and affections to address actively and contemplate lovingly truth, goodness, unity, and beauty. Therein, we participate in the ultimate source of intelligibility and flourishing. Acts of imprudence produce the contrary. They compound problems such as depression, addiction, and marital discord. Engendering a practical creativity and normative uprightness in reasonable action throughout life—including with the support of psychotherapy—requires connecting four levels of philosophical virtue, psychological strength, and everyday practice: the volitional, which addresses the ordering of love and faces distractions from the environment; the emotional, which manages affective attractions and repulsions; the social, which deals with the beneficial and nefarious influences of family, peers, and culture; and the rational, which faces cognitive complexity and adjudicates between competing versions of truth and goodness. At personal, social, and spiritual levels, people employ these resources to perform reasonable acts that are both creative and faithful.

Contemporary psychological and philosophical theories of action often either exaggerate or denigrate human freedom and choice. Admittedly, the influence of mechanistic determinism seems to make nonsense of freedom, while nonessentialist relativism tends to obscure any criteria for choice, except choice itself. A large part of misunderstandings about human action revolves around the lack of distinguishing the "freedom of indifference" from the "freedom for excellence," that is, the freedom from unjust oppression and intrusion from the freedom that involves voluntarily moving toward a positive goal that will bring about human flourishing. Tobias Hoffmann explains how each of these two types of freedom has a place to play in human action and helps to explain the diverse movements of human reason and affection. Moreover, a constructive middle ground between mechanistic determinism and non-essentialist relativism identifies both the universality due to human nature and the diversity that comes through human history and personal growth.

Chapter 7

Free Choices

Tobias Hoffmann

*Since what characterizes a human being is to
live in accord with reason, one is truly a slave
when one is misguided by something foreign
from that which belongs to reason.*

Thomas Aquinas[143]

In common discourse, it is often thought that to be free means to have a choice. The will is accordingly understood as the capacity to make choices. Yet sometimes we have several options, and not one of them is attractive. Having to choose among bad alternatives can hardly be identified with freedom. Conversely, it may happen that only one option is available, but we would not have chosen differently even if there had been alternatives.

We make choices to fulfill a desire, and we are satisfied—that is, free—when something fulfills our desire. Accordingly, we are free when we attain something that fulfills a desire. That which corresponds to a desire of ours we consider "good." The pursuit of some goods may prevent us from obtaining higher goods, and hence, considered from a broader perspective, our freedom does

---

[143] St. Thomas Aquinas, *Super Romanos*, ch. 6, lect. 4.

not consist in discriminately pursuing just any goods, but only those that contribute to our flourishing in life.

Thomas understands freedom in these terms, and likewise he conceives of the will above all as characterized by desire, and more specifically as a capacity to desire what one rationally assesses as good. Thomas does, of course, admit that human beings are endowed with the capacity for free choice. But the point of free choice is not simply to choose, but to choose according to what we understand to be good, or to be preferable if there are several alternatives. The existential conditions of life, however, make it difficult to exercise free choice coherently with our own desires, because we may be unaware of what we most intimately desire, or by acting in accord with a certain desire we may act against a more profound desire, one that we are either unaware of or that we find too costly to fulfill or one that at a given time is not very strong. Hence, to flourish in life does not simply depend on a decision to do so. We may well know what is good, make good resolutions and desire to be coherent in acting accordingly, but when it comes to concrete decisions, we may act contrary to our own resolutions.

The goal of this chapter is to present the essential features of Thomas's account of the human will as the basis of our quest for fulfillment.[144] Special focus will be on the possibility to achieve

---

[144] The human will and the philosophical problems implied in Thomas's notion of the will are the object of numerous articles. For studies that illustrate the chronological progression of Thomas's doctrine of the human will, see D.M. Gallagher, "Thomas Aquinas on the Will as a Rational Appetite," in *Journal for the History of Philosophy* 29 (1991): 559–584. For Thomas's teaching in comparison to that of his contemporaries, see B. Kent, *Virtues of the Will: The Transformation of Ethics in the Late Thirteenth Century* (Washington, DC: The Catholic University of America Press, 1995). For a presentation of Thomas's doctrine of the will in comparison with contemporary

or to fail to attain true freedom, understood as flourishing. First, I will expound Thomas's account of the will's rational desire for the good, next I will discuss the capacity for free choice, and lastly I will examine the possibility of unfreedom—that is, of failing to do what truly satisfies of our desires—and the need of virtues to achieve and sustain our freedom.

The Will as Rational Appetite

A basic experience of human existence is that we have desires. Concrete desires may arise in us suddenly, without being solicited and prior to rational reflection. Thus we do not decide to be hungry or thirsty, and normally we do not decide to fall in love. In addition to desires for particular things that we can articulate to ourselves or to others, we oftentimes feel a need for something without having a clear idea of what that something is. A certain longing when listening to music or reading good poetry reveals to us that we are lacking something, without telling us how we can satisfy our desire. Although we may distract ourselves from such desires, we cannot evade them entirely. In other cases, desires follow upon rational reflection, such as the desire for a good college education or even the desire for a hammer when we want to hang up a picture.

Thomas offers us a classification of desires that helps to shed light on these different experiences of desires: of uncontrolled and controlled desires, and of specific and nonspecific desires. He distinguishes between three kinds of "appetites" (*appetitus*), a term that indicates either desire itself or the capacity to have desires. By making this distinction, Thomas lays the basis for his notion of the human will, which he defines as "rational appetite."

---

debates, see, for example, E.S. Stump, "Aquinas's Account of Freedom: Intellect and Will," in *The Monist* 80 (1997): 576–597.

Philosophical Virtues and Psychological Strengths

For Thomas, as for his contemporaries, the notion of appetite extends both to animate and inanimate nature. Everything, whether material or immaterial, is ordered to something else by way of some type of appetite (*DV* Q. 23, art. 1). Thus Thomas describes also the forces of nature as kinds of appetite or desire. The typical example is gravitation: a stone has an "appetite" to fall down. The interrelation of things extends, of course, beyond matter and beyond gravitational or other natural forces. Following Aristotle, Thomas claims that everything strives for the good, that is, for something that accomplishes it.[145] For example, a dog has a desire for food and for regenerative activity. Food perfects or satisfies the individual dog by allowing it to live; regeneration guarantees the continuance of the species.

Thomas explains the working of the human will in analogy to natural forces and to desires of animals. Just as stones are naturally inclined to fall, and just as brute animals desire food and the like, so also the activity of the human will consists in the pursuit of something and in the adhesion to it once it is attained. Yet there is a fundamental difference between inclinations of inanimate nature, animal desires, and human willing. The difference is marked by the way in which desire or inclination relates to apprehension. A drop of water falls without knowing where it is headed or why it is falling. This inclination follows upon what medieval thinkers called a *natural appetite* or *natural inclination*. When a dog feels hungry, it seeks food, and when it finds some food within its reach, it will eat it. A new quality is added, which was lacking in the drop of water: the behavior originates in the dog upon *apprehension*. What moves the dog is not only a "natural appetite"—as when the dog falls down from the sofa—, but also a "sense appetite," an inclination that follows upon sense perception

---

[145] See, e.g., Thomas Aquinas, *DV* Q. 22, art. 1, and *ST* I, Q. 59, art. 1.

(*ST* III, Q. 6, art. 1; *ST* I, Q. 80, arts. 1–2). The dog acts upon apprehension, but—as will be argued in the next section—it has no reflective knowledge of why it acts in one way or the other.

Like animals, human beings have a sense appetite; both animals and humans desire what is pleasant to the senses and shun what is painful. Yet human beings not only perceive reality with their senses; they also dispose of a mode of knowledge that is qualitatively different from animal apprehension. Thanks to intellectual knowledge, our apprehension of reality is not restricted to sense perception by which we perceive particular things as particulars, but we form general notions that allow us to compare a general idea with different particular instances that correspond to it. When an architect is planning a house, the general notion of "house" allows her or him to think of a variety of designs, not just a particular one, and from these various possibilities, she or he can choose a particular design (cf. *DM* Q. 6, art. 1). As human beings, we can judge how a particular thing or action is conducive to a goal that we have in mind, and thus we can also give the reason we act in a specific way. Thanks to our capacity for rational judgment, we have a rational appetite, which for Thomas is nothing other than the will. As a rational appetite, the will is inclined to everything that reason apprehends as good and suitable, no matter whether it is truly good or only seemingly so (*ST* III, Q. 8, art. 1).

As will be shown in the next section, Thomas holds that the rational appetite has the capacity of free choice, because something desired under a general notion can be achieved through a variety of particular actions. Yet not every inclination of the rational appetite is an expression of free choice. That which is understood as good and suitable from every possible point of view is desired necessarily; such is happiness.[146] Note that the word

---

[146] *ST* III, Q. 10, art. 2; *DM* Q. 6.

happiness describes above all the objective state of one who flourishes, and only secondarily the good feelings that accompany such flourishing. We do not decide to desire happiness, nor can we decide not to desire it. Although the will is a rational appetite, its basic inclination to happiness is, as it were, a natural appetite; Thomas speaks of it as "natural inclination" (see, e.g., *DV* Q. 22, art. 5). Every more particular desire of the will is based upon this general desire for happiness; through every particular object of our desire, we expect to attain some share of happiness. Happiness, however, is not itself subordinate to a further end, as though someone desired happiness in order to achieve something beyond happiness. Accordingly, Thomas considers happiness as the ultimate end of the human person, understanding by happiness that which completely fulfills all human desire (*ST* III, Q. 1, arts. 5–8).

The distinction between the three kinds of appetites allows us to account for the different experiences of desire mentioned earlier. Those desires that arise in us often apart from our control and that regard the pursuit of what is pleasurable to our senses and the avoidance of what is painful belong to what Thomas calls the *sense appetite*.[147] The inescapable desire for something fulfilling without necessarily having a clear understanding of what this fulfillment consists in is what Thomas describes in terms of the *natural inclination* of the will to happiness. Although imperfect happiness is possible in the present life, Thomas argues that the complete fulfillment of our desire for happiness cannot be attained in this life (*ST* III, Q. 3, art. 8; Q. 5, art. 3). Desires that are consequent upon reflection on our needs—that is, desires that follow upon deliberation about how they can best be met—coincide with our free choices (*ST* III, Q. 13, art. 1). To choose to take a specific action in order to apply for a job is to desire that action as the means

---

[147] *ST* Ia, Q. 81, art. 2; cf. *ST* Ia-IIae, Q. 23, art. 1.

by which we hope to attain the job. Both the necessary desire for happiness and the reflected and free desire for specific things that promote happiness belong to the *rational appetite*.

For Thomas, desire characterizes the human will more fundamentally than choice. We make choices because we desire something, and thus desire is prior to choice. For this reason, Thomas and other medieval authors did not identify freedom with free choice. Freedom extends further than free choice: the desire for the ultimate end, happiness, is a matter of *free will*, but not of *free choice* (DV Q. 24, art. 2, ad. 20). We cannot help desiring happiness, and yet this desire is free, because it is not coerced—that is, violently imposed on our will—but rather lies in our very nature. Nobody would perceive the satisfaction of his desires as violence (DV Q. 22, art. 5; ST I, Q. 82, art. 1). The ultimate perfection of the will does not consist in an act of free choice, but rather in the attainment of the ultimate end of the human person and in the loving rest in it (see, e.g., ST III, Q. 11, art. 1).

Free Choice

Whether our actions are conducive to attaining happiness or separate us from that end depends on whether the choices we make are good or bad. How is it possible to make consistently good choices? This problem will be discussed in the following section.

First we must further examine the very capacity of choosing. In particular, we must ask whether our choices are free—in other words, whether we have control of our choices and thus of our actions or whether we act by necessity. To deny free choice, Thomas argues, would undermine the principles of moral philosophy, since then "deliberation, exhortation, precept, and punishment and praise and blame, with which moral philosophy is concerned, is nullified" (DM Q. 6). To this consideration we may add that the meaning of the entire moral vocabulary essentially depends on whether our actions are in our control. If to love someone is nothing more than a biological state, and not at all a free expression of the person, the meaning of love is manifestly diminished. Or to use Thomas's own example, to have pity for someone as a compulsory passion is less meaningful than feeling pity upon a rational judgment as a free expression of oneself.[148]

For Thomas, the possibility of making free choices springs from the intellectual nature of the human soul. To illustrate the peculiar nature of free choice, Thomas compares human agency with animal behavior.[149] What brute animals and human beings have in common, Thomas tells us (*DV* Q. 24, arts. 1–2), is that they act and move themselves following a cognitive act, which Thomas qualifies as judgment. It is a judgment that determines the animal's desire, and this desire is followed by action, unless an obstacle prevents the action from occurring. Whether there is free choice depends on whether it is possible to control the judgment that leads to action.

Thomas makes two related points to show that animals do not have control of the judgments that determine their movements. He observes that entire animal species have equal patterns of action: all swallows build their nests alike, bees invariably make honeycombs, and spiders always make their webs in the same way.[150] In addition, he remarks that certain perceptions of animals move them to determinate actions. When a dog is infuriated, it will bark; sheep that see a wolf approaching will flee (*DV* Q. 24, art. 2). Animals have no control of their desires, Thomas

[148] *ST* III, Q. 24, art. 3; *DM* Q. 3, art. 11.

[149] For Thomas's philosophical discussion of animals, see J. Barad, *Aquinas on the Nature and Treatment of Animals* (San Francisco and London: International Scholars Publication, 1995). For the topic here discussed, see in particular pp. 95–112.

[150] *DV* Q. 24, art. 1; *SCG* II, ch. 82; Aquinas, *De virtutibus in communi*, Q. 1, art. 6.

specifies; for example, when an animal sees something delightful, it cannot avoid craving it.[151]

Thomas argues that judgment, desire, and action are as consequent upon each other in human beings as they are in animals. Hence, to argue that as human beings we have control of our actions implies for Thomas to show that we have mastery of our desires, which in turn presupposes the demonstration that we have control of our judgments.

Do we have freedom of judgment? And is it true that animals have no control of their judgment? For Thomas, the answer to this question hinges on a fundamentally different manner of knowledge in humans and in animals. The apprehension of animals is restricted to sense perception, which operates by way of a bodily organ and hence is bound to the conditions of matter. For this reason, sense perception is restricted to the apprehension of something particular as particular (DV Q. 22, art. 4, corp. and ad. 4). Animals lack the capacity to distance themselves from the particular. They cannot form universal concepts, and thus they cannot conceptualize what is desirable here and now as an instance of what is desirable in general. Accordingly, they cannot distinguish between immediate goals and superior goals, and thus they cannot conceive of ends as ends and of means as means. Why cannot a swallow decide to build a nest different from one that hangs from something, such as the roof of a barn? If the swallow understood the goal of the nest—namely, to breed its offspring—and if it had insight into the way in which different means may allow it to attain this goal—a nest of this type rather than of a different type as suited for the goal of breeding the offspring—it could choose to build the nest in many different ways. But it lacks precisely this insight into the intelligible character of the end (ratio finis), the end as end, and it also lacks

---

[151] DV Q. 22, art. 4; cf. ST III, Q. 6, art. 2.

the understanding of how different possible means relate to this end. Lacking this insight, Thomas tells us, the swallow and all other animals act from what he calls *natural judgment*, which is a judgment that is immediately consequent upon the perception of the environment and not in control of the animal. Thomas contrasts the natural judgment of animals with the judgment of human beings that he calls *free judgment*, about which more will be said below (*DV* Q. 24, art. 1; cf. *DV* Q. 22, art. 4). Since animals do not control their judgment, they do not freely choose between alternatives. Thomas admits that certain animals may act cleverly, and he gives the example of the ability of a hunting dog to conclude by exclusion that a deer must have taken a specific path if the other possibilities have been ruled out. Yet he explains such ability entirely in terms of animal instinct, saying that animals "have a natural inclination to certain well-ordered processes" (*ST* I-II, Q. 13, art. 1, ad 3).

Thomas draws a sharp line between the entire class of brute animals and human beings. He does not distinguish between levels of intelligence in different animal species. His examples of animals that show equal patterns of behavior include bees, spiders, and swallows, but not dogs, chimpanzees, and dolphins. Modern research has brought to light surprising facts about the capacities of dolphins, for example, such as their ability to employ certain means toward specific ends and to try new means if a previous one is found to be unsuccessful. Dolphins even demonstrate rudimentary linguistic comprehension.[152] Thomas's account of animal behavior certainly needs to be adjusted in light of modern biological

---

[152] For a discussion of the intelligence of dolphins and of other higher animals in comparison with human intelligence in view of its relevance for practical rationality, see A. MacIntyre, *Dependent Rational Animals: Why Human Beings Need the Virtues* (Chicago and La Salle, Illinois: Open Court, 1999), 21–61.

research. Yet the fundamental insight of his account remains untouched by such amendment. The point is that although animals have cognitive acts by which they relate to their environment and which can display a certain level of intelligence—cognitive acts that Thomas calls *natural judgments*—animals do not have control of these cognitive acts and consequently do not control their inclinations and the actions that follow them. Human beings, conversely, do have control of their judgments:

> Human beings judge about what actions to do by the power of reason, and hence, they can also judge their own judgment, because they know the intelligible character of the end (*ratio finis*) and the rational aspect of that which is ordered to the end, and also the relationship and connection between the two. Thus human beings are not only their own cause with regard to motion, but also to judging.[153]

Why does the ability to form such a meta-judgment entail free choice? If we did not have the capacity to evaluate our own perceptions, we could not rank our desires and renounce something attractive for the sake of something more valuable. Animals cannot distance themselves from what they judge as pleasant or harmful. A sheep has good reason to flee the wolf, but it cannot conceive why it may be better to resist the drive to flee. Likewise, although it may follow the instructions of a trainer, a hungry dog in the presence of tasty dog food does not refrain from eating for a higher reason, as human beings do when they fast or when they are on a hunger strike.

The root of human freedom, conversely, is the ability to compare a number of possible actions in view of achieving an end. Which action we decide for does not necessarily follow our

---

[153] *De veritate*, Q. 24, art. 1. The translation is mine. Cf. SCG II, ch. 48.

immediate desires. Reconsidering the reasons one thing is preferable to something else, we may in fact shape our desires according to what we understand to be more reasonable.

We can distance ourselves from what is perceived as good and suitable prior to reflection, because we understand how different things are related to higher goals. Thus we understand why the pursuit of one thing may be preferable to another. The comparison between several available means to attain the desired end leads us to conclude which is the best means and hence which course of action to take. Our decision to start acting accordingly follows upon this conclusion (see, e.g., *DM* Q. 6). Consider a woman who, after graduation, needs to be financially independent and therefore searches for a job. Her freedom regarding the method of the job search is consequent upon her capacity to apprehend the goal of making a living under a general notion that allows for different jobs to fit her understanding of the desired end. Which position she will choose to apply for depends on the way in which she deliberates about different available means to attain this goal. The deliberation itself is not determined to one result, since the means available, that is, the different possible jobs, can be thought of from different perspectives. One job may pay well but require night work; another may involve moving to another town; a third may not be challenging enough. Which of these conditions is prevalent for her depends on her own evaluation, and according to this evaluation she determines the course her deliberation takes. The result of the deliberation is her practical judgment about which job to apply for, and her desire to take the concrete required action follows this judgment. To the extent that she determines her own deliberation, she has free choice.

Freedom and Unfreedom

The desire to flourish is so basic that it cannot be entirely eliminated, even though it may be felt at times less strongly than at other times. That we want to flourish means that we seek not only particular goods that satisfy certain limited desires, but a state in which we experience complete satisfaction of our desires and needs, a state that Thomas calls *beatitudo* (happiness). Our aspiration to happiness motivates every one of our actions, whether we are aware of it or not. Either we hope for happiness as included in the actions themselves, as when we see something beautiful, when we play a game, when we taste something delightful; or we expect our actions to be instrumental to happiness, as when we drive downtown in order to see the art gallery (cf. *ST* III, Q. 1, art. 6). For Thomas, the point of all human actions is the perfection of happiness, and moral science (ethics) is the study of how happiness can be attained. In his view, that which truly promotes happiness is ethical, and conversely only that which is ethical is truly conducive to happiness (cf. *ST* I-II, Q. 4, art. 4). Hence, the question of how one can achieve happiness coincides with the problem of morality.

Although we expect our actions to promote our happiness, they may in truth remove us from it and make us "unfree."[154] The cause of unfreedom may be that we have an inadequate idea of what our happiness consists in, so that the general shape we want to give to our lives may turn out to be something not ultimately satisfying. The general desire for happiness, however, is only the remote, not the proximate basis for our concrete choices. For this reason, unfreedom may also result from that which determines

---

154 Aquinas does not speak of unfreedom. He rather opposes freedom (*libertas*) and servitude (*servitus*) (*ST* II-II, Q. 183, art. 4; *Super Romanos*, ch. 6, lect. 4): "[T]his state [of sin] involves true servitude, no true freedom however, but only apparent freedom. Since what characterizes a human being is to live in accord with reason, one is truly a slave when one is misguided by something foreign from that which belongs to reason.... The works of sin are in fact fruitless, because they do not help one to attain happiness."

our choices in a more immediate way. We choose our actions with particular short- or long-term goals in mind, aiming at something we perceive as good and suitable and from which we explicitly or tacitly expect a share in happiness. Hence, our freedom to attain something good depends no less on what we set as our goals than on what particular actions we do. Sometimes we may also simply act from routine, that is, without bringing the goals of our actions explicitly to our awareness. Routine as such is neither negative nor positive. Yet when one does bad actions from routine, it may be an additional source of unfreedom.

In what follows, I will briefly discuss different moral states that cause unfreedom. One such condition is what Aquinas calls *precipitation*, which is impulsive behavior due to the lack of the habit to reflect upon one's own motives of action. Two other moral states that cause unfreedom, which may or may not include precipitous behavior, are vice and incontinence. *Vices* are habits that incline us to evil and that distort our understanding of what is good. *Incontinence* is the incapacity to act according to one's own better judgment. The common feature of these states is that they give rise to a mistaken idea of what is good to do in a specific situation. I will then discuss in outline two moral states that are conducive to the human good and hence to happiness: *continence*, which is the state of those who do what is good despite temptation to do evil, and *moral virtue*, which allows a person to do what is good with ease and pleasure and which makes a person truly free.

As mentioned in the previous section, the various things that solicit our senses in daily life constantly lead us to make judgments regarding what would be good to attain and hence what would be good to do in view of these things. For example, when we are hungry or thirsty, we immediately think it would be good to eat or drink. This judgment is sufficient to lead us to act, but it is not sufficient to lead us to a completely free, reflected action, and it does not guarantee that such action promotes our good (or the good of others). Sometimes a hungry person should wait to eat, or should avoid eating whatever spontaneously comes to mind and is within reach. Failing to reflect sufficiently before acting is called *precipitation*, and although such action is done voluntarily, it cannot be regarded as done by free choice in the full sense of the term. For free choice requires reflection upon one's practical judgment. This involves taking time to deliberate, that is, pondering different possible courses of action and acting only after sufficient consideration of the various factors that are relevant for the decision: "memory of the past, insight into the present, shrewdness in attending future results, reasoning in connecting one thing to another, docility in accepting the judgments of those more experienced."[155] Thomas anticipates here what will later become a cornerstone of cognitive therapy: the need to acquire the capacity to reflect about what otherwise would be unconscious patterns of judgment and behavior.

Yet the self-awareness regarding one's motives is by itself insufficient for leading a satisfactory life, because even when we act after sufficient deliberation, we may act for motives that are not conducive to flourishing. We may also know and desire in principle what is good and virtuous, but fail to act accordingly. Although nobody wants to pursue illusionary goals, and no one wants to act foolishly, it is not easy to attain the clarity of mind and strength of will that allow one to act consistently with the desire for the good. When doing evil, we mistakenly think that our acts promote the good (our good or the good of others) (see, e.g., *ST* III, Q. 77, art. 2). This false belief may be due to deception or to self-deception. If we were aware that the goal we strive for or the action we are about to do is making us wretched, we would

---

155 *ST* II-II, Q. 53, art. 3, trans. Blackfriars (New York and London: Cambridge University Press, 1974), vol. 36, p. 129; cf. Q. 53, art. 4.

abandon the goal and refrain from the act. Thieves and adulterers consider that which they aim at as something good, because they see their actions as useful or as pleasant. Yet in truth their actions hinder their true well-being and flourishing. The tension between the true good and the apparent good is what underlies the possibility of moral failure.

Does this mean that good action is merely a matter of correct knowledge, so that morality is a matter of intellectual talent and not of moral character? Unmistaken awareness of the true good here and now does, in fact, result in morally good action, but in order to have such practical knowledge, character rather than mere intellectual ability is required. Theoretical knowledge of what is good does not move a person to act according to it. A teacher of ethics may teach the students an impeccable moral theory, yet his actions may contradict his teaching if, deep in his heart, he is not convinced of what he says (cf. *DM* Q. 3, art. 9, ad 8). Only practical knowledge that is applied to a specific case truly moves one to act in accord with one's moral judgment (*Sententia libri de anima* 3 lect. 16). The ability to apply right practical knowledge to a specific situation constitutes a virtue in itself, the virtue of prudence or practical wisdom. It requires that something is perceived not only as good, but also as good here and now, *bonum et conveniens*.[156]

Hence, what someone deems worthy of being pursued depends less on intellectual insight than on one's moral disposition: a temperate person considers the harm and disorder of adultery and hence wants to avoid it, whereas a habitual adulterer considers adultery pleasant and seeks occasions for it. To the extent that evil habits are dominant, it is more difficult to understand what is good or bad, that is, what is worthy of being pursued or avoided.

---

[156] *ST* I-II, Q. 9, art. 2; *DM* Q. 6, art. 1, Leon. 23, 149b, lines 420–422.

Even if one knows generally what is best, he may act contrary to this knowledge when affected by strong emotions. Thus one who thinks that adultery is bad may act contrary to this knowledge when desire and emotion abound, making him or her momentarily believe that this particular act of adultery is good because it is pleasant. This lapse is an indication that the general moral knowledge was not sufficiently internalized in order to resist temptation. The scholastics call habitual evildoing *malice* or *vice*, and they name momentary weakness caused by passion *incontinence*.[157] Vice distorts the understanding of what goals are worthy of being pursued. An incontinent person, conversely, tends in general to the good, but her or his good intention is momentarily corrupted by strong opposing passions (*ST* Ia-IIae, Q. 78, art. 4).

According to our understanding of unfreedom as the inability to attain genuine personal accomplishment, we can say that not only persons with vices, but also incontinent persons are unfree, yet in different respects. Those who have vices do not act contrary to what they consider best, but their conception of what is good is altogether mistaken. They are unfree in the sense that they are pursuing things that do not contribute to their true good, such as pleasure at all cost. The problem is that they may not even perceive themselves as unfree.

Alcoholics, for example, do not easily let themselves be convinced that they must give up drinking. They more readily see the positive effects of drinking and the negative effects of being abstinent, rather than the contrary. Their freedom is impaired: they are marked by self-deception, which makes it difficult for them to see why they should change. Even if they do understand that

---

[157] The account of late medieval thinkers regarding vice, incontinence, continence, and virtue is based upon Aristotle, *Nicomachean Ethics*, 7.1–10, but integrates also elements from Augustine's teaching on the will and on the need to be sustained by grace in order fully to attain the human good.

they should give up drinking, their capacity to change is severely impaired by strong habits.

Incontinent persons, conversely, have in general the right understanding of what is good and the desire to act accordingly, but insofar as they act contrary to their own moral judgment, they are unfree to do what they would generally rather do. Someone who has sought help to overcome alcoholism may again and again give in to the temptation to drink, and at the moment of temptation he may say to himself that this one drink won't really make a difference.

Speaking of the conditions of vicious and incontinent persons as unfree does not imply that they are acting involuntarily. In Thomas's view, they act voluntarily because they have control of their actions and could have acted otherwise (ST IIa-IIae, Q. 156, art. 3).

According to Thomas, a human person is never so entangled with evil that she or he cannot change. Incontinent persons change more easily, because they already have the correct understanding of what is good. Those who are inclined to evil by habits improve with more difficulty, but change is possible for them as well.[158]

How can a person be motivated to change? Ethical reflections will fall on deaf ears if offered to those whose perception of the good is distorted by vices and will be insufficient for the incontinent, because what they lack is not ethical awareness but the capacity to act accordingly. External coercion, as employed by the legal system, may lead a person to avoid living out certain vices,

---

[158] For a more detailed discussion of the difficulties and possibilties of the incontinent to overcome their weakness, see my "Aquinas on the Moral Progress of the Weak Willed," in *The Problem of Weakness of Will in Medieval Philosophy*, eds. T. Hoffmann, J. Müller, and M. Perkams (Leuven: Peeters Publishers, 2006).

but it does not by itself induce a change of mind. It is rather because of some attraction that a person may want to improve. The love for wife and children may motivate an alcoholic to make efforts to reduce consumption or to become abstinent. The role of educators or therapists is to present the better alternative, not abstractly, but in its attractiveness and beauty.[159]

Once motivated to improve, the person's resources that are least affected by vices may be instrumental in overcoming bad habits, as Aquinas suggests. For example, someone's concupiscible appetite may be corrupted by intemperance. Yet the irascible appetite may help to strengthen the force of resistance against such softness by striving for something arduous (DV Q. 24, art. 10). This idea is in fact employed in some rehabilitation centers, where addicts are made to perform physically strenuous and challenging activities.

In the process of overcoming vice, the bad inclinations continue to persist for a long time. Incontinence and continence are the moral states in which people still feel an attraction to what is not good, although in their rational awareness they do not want to give in to their bad desires. Incontinent persons fail to do so when passions abound. By contrast, those who are able to resist temptation are called continent (ST IIII, Q. 155, art. 3).

Achieving continence, and thus the ability to withstand what draws us to act badly in virtue of the desire for a higher good, is an important step toward overcoming evil. But the ideal is to attain the capacity of doing what is good easily, promptly, and with pleasure. This ideal is attained when one has acquired moral virtues (De virtutibus in communi, Q. 1, art. 9, ad. 13). As vice is a habitual disposition that disposes a person to act badly, so virtue is a habit that disposes a person to act well. The moral virtues

---

[159] Cf. A. Ramos, "Moral Beauty and Affective Knowledge in Aquinas" in Acta Philosophica 13 (2004): 321–337.

have the effect of ordering the emotions and the will so that one follows more promptly the dictate of right reason (*ST* III, Q. 56, art. 4; Q. 56, art. 6).

For example, temperate persons not only act according to the dictate of right reason, but their emotions also conform to right reason. Far from eliminating emotions, virtues order them according to right reason (*ST* III, Q. 56, art. 4; *ST* II-II, Q. 141, art. 7, ad. 1; Q. 155, art. 4). Whereas vices distort our understanding of the good and make us aim at what is evil under the aspect of good, virtues rectify; they allow us to discern what goods to strive for (*ST* III, Q. 58, arts. 4–5). The temperate person believes deep in his heart that alcohol should not be drunk immoderately.

To be just, temperate, or courageous in a particular situation, it is not only important to be rightly disposed by way of the moral virtues. It is moreover crucial to understand concretely which actions one must perform in order to act according to these virtues. It is prudence that enables one to have the understanding of what action the case at hand requires (see, e.g., *ST* III, Q. 57, art. 5; Q. 58, art. 4).

The freedom that consists in doing what is good is not attained simply by willpower, but by a long path toward virtue so that our desires may conform to what is conducive to the true good and ultimately to happiness. Virtuous persons not only have the understanding of what is good, but it is also easier for them to act accordingly.

Conclusion

The human will as rational appetite unfailingly desires the good universally, but it does not of necessity desire this rather than that particular good. With every action we aim at something we perceive as good. How we act and to which particular aims we give preference is up to us: we can freely choose our actions according to what we consider best. Knowledge and affection are tied together in free choice: our inclinations follow our understanding of what is best. Conversely, our conception of what is best depends on our character, which in turn has been shaped by previous choices.

The general inclination to the good and to happiness does not warrant that our choices are always good. The will as rational appetite aims at what we think is good, but it does not provide us with the understanding of what is good. We may search for fulfillment where it cannot be found. We do not pursue illusionary goals in full awareness of their empty promise, and we are not easily convinced that we are wrong when we aim at what is bad. Also in this regard, knowledge and affection are closely connected: when we do evil habitually, we are inclined to think that the evil we are seeking is good. In order to abstain from doing evil, we must be convinced in our heart that we should avoid it.

If we are to be free to do what is conducive to happiness, our actions and desires must be conform to right reason. This freedom is attained by means of moral virtues and prudence, which not only facilitate doing what is good, but also provide us with the practical knowledge of what is worthwhile to pursue and what concretely must be done to act accordingly. To attain these virtues is only in part a matter of the personal effort of the individual. According to Thomas, moral progress requires good upbringing and the assistance of others. As a theologian, Aquinas holds that divine grace is instrumental in moral progress, and he recommends praying for divine assistance (ST I-II, Q. 109, arts. 9–10).

Different approaches to psychology, philosophy, and the Christian tradition recognize the positive potential of emotions at psychological, moral, and spiritual levels. Human emotions involve an interactive dialogue with will and reason where each has its own voice, while being reliant on the others according to their competencies, as Paul Gondreau says. Emotions communicate a pre-rational judgment of the compatibility of the object (or the person) with human flourishing. They come to a further type of participation in the life of reason when they are receptive to rational adjudication and desires. The challenge for psychology and philosophy involves identifying the specificity and interplay of emotional intelligence, on the one hand, and intellectual intuition and rational discourse, on the other. The psychotherapist, philosophical adviser, and spiritual counselor, for their own parts, find that psychological strengths and virtues (acquired and infused by divine grace) can lead to the further humanizing and shaping of emotions that become more balanced in their own expression and more responsive to reason, will, and true flourishing.

Chapter 8

Balanced Emotions

Paul Gondreau

The soul's "appetitive and in general desiring element in a sense shares in [reason], in so far as it listens to and obeys it; this is the sense in which we speak of paying heed to one's father or one's friends, not that in which we speak of 'the rational' in mathematics."

Aristotle[160]

The ancient Greek drama *Oresteia* recounts the story of how the young Orestes, after avenging his father's murder by slaying the killer, Orestes's own mother, must flee from the relentless pursuit of the dreadful Furies. These latter are the older pre-Olympian earth goddesses who avenge the killing of one's kin. Eventually, the Olympian goddess Athena convinces the Furies to suspend momentarily the pursuit of blood vengeance and allow a trial by jury to settle Orestes's fate.

During the trial, the Furies, not without due cause, make their case for just retribution. After a tie vote results in a hung jury, Athena, mindful that blood vengeance leads to unending carnage, intervenes and casts the deciding vote in favor of Orestes, thereby acquitting him.

[160] *NE* I.13.1102b30–34.

Philosophical Virtues and Psychological Strengths

Pointing out that the tie vote legitimates the Furies' case, Athena follows by offering the Furies a place, albeit a subservient one, among the Olympian gods, where they will serve no longer as goddesses of blood vengeance but as protectors of households. They accept and become transformed into the Eumenides—"the friendly ones"—that is, they take their place as earth goddesses who subordinate their lower instinctive desires for blood vengeance to the wise judgment of the higher gods, such as Athena. Dwelling in the sky on the top of Mount Olympus, these higher gods follow the guidance of reason and enlightened wisdom.

Of the many lessons to be gleaned from this ancient Greek drama written by the famous playwright Aeschylus, chief among them, I think, is the invaluable insight it imparts into the nature of human emotion and its relation to reason. The lower instinctual drives, the emotions, exemplified in the *Oresteia* by the desire for just retribution on the part of the earth goddesses, the Furies, are not bad in themselves and might be quite legitimate. For this reason, they should not be eradicated from human life. Movements of the lower appetites, the emotions play an integral and essential role in our lives, paralleling the way the Furies, once transformed into the kindly Eumenides, go on to play an integral and essential role in the Olympic pantheon as protectors of households. But because the emotions belong to the lower impulsive dimension of the human person, they are by nature subordinate to our higher faculties and ought to be subservient to the commanding role of human reason, of our higher cognitive power, represented in the *Oresteia* by Athena and the other Olympian gods. Reason's role, as Aeschylus understands it, is to integrate harmoniously the lower drives, the emotions, into human life in a balanced way neither by suppressing the emotions outright nor by giving them free reign over our actions.

Aeschylus provides us with a view of human emotion and its relation to our overall good that resonates well, it seems to me, with modern clinical psychology (and thus with a view, we should add, that helps offset the one-sided interpretation of Greek tragedy offered by Freud). Clinical therapists almost uniformly concur that emotion plays a vital role in the life of psychological health, or, conversely, of psychological imbalance. Our affective dispositions, our emotional reactions to persons and events around us, represent a gateway into the general state of our psyches. Almost all agree that psychological well-being walks hand in hand with, indeed, is consequent upon, the sustained experience of well-regulated or properly balanced emotion. Most clinicians want their patients to integrate their feelings and emotions in a properly balanced way so that they may live happy lives.

At the same time, an imbalance in emotion almost always indicates some type of psychopathology. To diagnose depression, for example, therapists look for extreme mood swings and irritability in a patient, coupled with emotional deprivation, or with feelings of excessive sadness. Extreme mood swings and emotional overreaction (or underreaction) might also indicate the presence of borderline personality disorder. Persons prone to alcohol abuse and addiction invariably suffer from some kind of emotional deficiency, such as emotional withdrawal or instability. Marital problems almost always include the mismanagement of emotions, especially anger. Cognitive therapy, in particular, affirms that the presence of a high degree of emotion or affect indicates that a schema (or underlying maladaptive pattern of behavior) has been triggered.[161] In practically every therapeutic setting, from depression to marital counseling to alcohol abuse and addiction, the therapist, knowing that psychological disorders almost always impact the emotions, seeks to establish a link between the patient's behavior and his emotions.

---

[161] Aaron T. Beck, the founder of cognitive therapy, first lays this out in his seminal work, *Cognitive Therapy and the Emotional Disorders* (New York: International Universities Press, 1976).

Philosophical Virtues and Psychological Strengths

With this in mind, the field of clinical psychology would stand to benefit from gaining a fuller, deeper understanding of human emotion. This present study aims at providing the beginnings of one. Written from a predominantly philosophical perspective, yet always with an eye on the clinical setting, this study will note points of pertinence for the therapist wherever appropriate. This will include occasional references to anonymous clinical examples in order to underscore, by way of concrete illustration, such pertinence.[162]

Fundamental Goods and Human Emotion

The relation of first or fundamental goods to genuine human happiness and to psychological wholeness sets the larger backdrop of this study. Thomas Aquinas, who reflected deeply on the relation of emotional health to overall human happiness and who speaks for the Catholic view on this issue, offers us the key to situating the emotions against this larger backdrop of fundamental goods.[163] With Aquinas, we can say the fundamental good

[162] These examples were kindly provided to the author by Dr. Gladys Sweeney of the Institute for the Psychological Sciences, Arlington, Virginia.

[163] Aquinas gave emotional balance and its relation to our overall well-being more consideration than did any ancient or medieval thinker and more than most modern thinkers. Evidence for this is found in the simple fact that the largest treatise in Aquinas's most important and best-known work, the *Summa Theologica* (*ST*), is the treatise on the passions. Despite this, René Descartes, the seventeenth-century father of modern philosophy, has this to say about his ancient and medieval predecessors' regard for the emotions: "The defects of the sciences we have from the ancients are nowhere more apparent than in their writings on the passions.... [T]he teachings of the ancients about the passions are so meagre and for the most part so implausible (*si peu croyable*) that I cannot hope to approach the truth except by departing from the paths they have followed" (*The Passions of the Soul*, pt. 1,

that concerns emotion is that of sense goods, or the enjoyment of bodily goods (such as pleasures gained through eating and drinking). These are goods in the most immediate and tangible sense of the term and which first come to most people's minds when they think of the word *good*.

Aquinas follows by defining the emotions as instinctive inclinations toward, or aversions to, some physical good or evil cognitively perceived as such by the senses. He calls them *sensory appetitive movements*, that is, movements of the lower, animal-like inclination in the human being (the internal inclination we share in common with the animals). The sensory (or sensitive) appetite accounts for our inclination to, or our internal motion toward, bodily goods or evils perceived by the senses, and to the eventual procurement or evasion of these sense goods or evils. Emotion pertains to the actual internal movement itself of this lower appetite or inclination.

The Twofold Appetitive Ordering in the Human Person

The first point to underscore here is that we share our internal affective ordering to sense goods, to goods of the body, in common with the animals. Yet human beings are not mere animals. We experience emotion in a unique fashion.[164] The interplay that our

---

art. 1, in *The Philosophical Writings of Descartes*, trans. Robert Stoothoff [Cambridge: Cambridge University Press, 1985], I:328). Yet Descartes himself gives scanty attention to the morality of the passions in his lengthy *Passions of the Soul*, since he separates the passions from virtuous action. Servais Pinckaers offers a detailed comparison of Descartes's teaching on the passions to Aquinas's in "Reappropriating Aquinas's Account of the Passions," in *The Pinckaers Reader*, 273–287, 279–282.

164 "Considered in themselves the passions are common to both man and animal, but as commanded by reason (*a ratione imperantur*), they are proper to man" (*ST* I-II, Q. 24, art. 1, ad. 1). For more on this, cf. Stephen Loughlin, "Similarities

lower sensitive inclination (or appetite) enjoys with reason (or our higher cognitive power) and will, our highest faculties, casts an entirely new dynamic on the human experience of emotion. This dynamic encompasses the entire psychological dimension of human life and explains why emotional states are so intimately related to the life of the mind. Take, for instance, the case of a patient diagnosed with severe depressive disorder who had experienced feeling abandoned and unloved by her father when she was a child. Later, after getting married, she often became powerless in the face of crippling fears that her husband would leave her. Here feelings and emotions originating from her childhood resurfaced later and infected a relationship unique to mature, rational human adults; in short, such feelings and emotions cast a pall over her entire psyche.

More specifically, the unique experience of emotion in the human person is explained by the fact that, in addition to our internal affective ordering to created bodily goods, from which arise the emotions, we enjoy a higher appetitive ordering. This higher appetitive ordering concerns the will, the faculty that works with reason (our cognitive power), to equip the human being to choose freely.[165] The will orders us internally to the universal good, to the *summum bonum*.

The Human Person Is Not a Disintegrated Self

That human beings have a twofold appetitive inclination does not mean that their internal ordering lacks integrity. For Aquinas

---

and Differences between Human and Animal Emotion in Aquinas's Thought," in *The Thomist* 65 (2001): 45–65.

[165] For more on the freedom of the human person by means of the will, see the earlier study in this book by Tobias Hoffmann as well David M. Gallagher, "Thomas Aquinas on the Will as a Rational Appetite," in *Journal for the History of Philosophy* 29 (1991): 559–584.

in particular, the human person is not a disintegrated self. Our enjoyment of higher goods should not exclude our affective enjoyment of sense goods. Although subordinate to the higher, the lower affective ordering to bodily goods shares actively and integrally in our higher rational ordering to ultimate goodness and happiness. The human person's search for supreme fulfillment builds upon this lower ordering as a necessary first step. Our internal attraction to created bodily goods sets us on a trajectory toward that good which alone is uncreated and unsurpassed. Our passions and desires are like the steeds, to use Plato's legendary metaphor, which, needing to run and while unruly, are the "erotic" drive that propels us on toward the highest Beauty and the highest Good.[166]

To ensure that we remain on this trajectory toward the supreme good, upon which our mental well-being depends, we must maintain strict governance over our internal movements. This means subordinating the lower, affective ordering to the higher,

---

[166] Plato, *Phaedrus*, trans. Benjamin Jowett (New York: Random House, 1937), 246–256; cf. Plato, *Republic*, bk. 4. Completing the metaphor, Plato says reason is the charioteer by which the steeds are properly harnessed and ordered to the highest of the forms, the Good. This holds even if, as Plato admits, such harnessing "of necessity gives a great deal of trouble to [the charioteer]." Pope Benedict XVI's inaugural encyclical, *Deus caritas est*, which opens with an attempt at reconstructing a renewed and purified understanding of eros and agape, approximates the Platonic understanding of eros when he writes that eros is a form of love the Greeks see as "a kind of intoxication, the overpowering of reason by a 'divine madness' which tears man away from his finite existence and enables him, in the very process of being overwhelmed by divine power, to experience supreme happiness" (no. 4; Vatican translation). At the same time, Plato's position on the moral quality of the passions is ambivalent, due especially, no doubt, to his disdain for the body. For example, in *Phaedo*, 6484, Plato asserts that one must move beyond sensible pleasures in order to attain true spiritual joy.

rational one, which in turn requires a careful balancing of our emotional states. Should the lower, sensitive ordering usurp the higher, rational one, or should reason simply scorn outright our internal attraction to goods of the body, the door swings open to some psychological disorder. Morally and behaviorally speaking, an accomplished human life requires a proper "humanizing" of the passions. It requires the integration of the emotions into the pursuit of the good of reason.

What accounts for Aquinas's integralist view of the twofold appetitive ordering to the universal good and to goods of the body in the human individual is his conviction that fundamentally the human person is a unified being. He rejects the view that would sever the emotions from the higher rational powers. This is the view that isolates the passions in their own lower, animal sphere with little or no interaction with the life of the mind. The Cartesian tendency to internalize only the life of the mind, where the appetites and emotions serve as mere mechanized tools of the mind yields an inadequate disembodied anthropology.

Aquinas's anthropology is one we could term a "participated psychology." In his view the lower, animal-like dimension of the human person participates in the higher, mental or spiritual one. It affirms an intimate synergy and interpenetration between the emotions and reason and will, making the emotions not merely "animal-like" acts but genuine *human* acts. Human reason (our higher cognitive power) and will can incite movements of passion, just as movements of emotion can rouse the will and influence a judgment of reason. Our passions and desires often shape how we think, thereby influencing how we act. For Aquinas, this offers plain evidence of the fact that the lower appetitive ordering to goods of the body truly participates in the higher appetitive ordering to happiness and fulfillment, to goodness itself.

Such a participated psychology, such a view of the human being that is termed hylemorphic or psychosomatic, inasmuch as it defines the human person as a substantial composite of body and soul, affirms the indispensable role that limited goods, to which the lower, appetitive ordering inclines us, play in an integrated human life. In the human person, a spiritual soul is united to a material body in the way that, as Aquinas explains, form is united to matter.[167] And just as matter is for the sake of form, so the body exists for the sake of the soul. The organic human body exists for the sake of its animating principle, the spiritual and rational soul.

At the same time, however, the soul, as the form of a material body, is so essentially bound to the body that it cannot operate without the body. The life of the body must be sustained if the soul, even in the operation of its rational or spiritual powers, is to act, let alone flourish. That the emotions move us toward those goods which sustain the life of the body evinces just how much the properly human, that is, rational or intellectual, dimension of our lives stands in need of our emotions. We see this particularly in the case of the desire (an emotion) for pleasures associated with eating and drinking, which directly sustain the life of our bodies.

A Commonality of Outlook

In my judgment, many clinical therapists would find that the participated psychology outlined above aligns closely with their own professional experience. The majority of therapists no doubt work from the conviction that mental well-being hinges directly upon the attainment of limited goods. More specifically, they realize, however intuitively, that attaining bodily goods *in a balanced fashion* is requisite for mental health. Since the emotions represent the internal mechanism by which we target bodily goods, therapy often consists in helping the patient gain a balanced mastery of his emotions.

---

[167] For more on this point, see the earlier study in this book by Matthew Cuddeback.

To this end, therapy frequently takes the form of helping adjust the patient's behavior according to a healthy differentiation of good emotional states from bad ones. We see this in the case of cognitive therapy especially, where the patient is helped to gain an objective, rational (or cognitive) appraisal of his emotions. This in turn is meant, negatively, to keep the patient's emotions from taking control and, positively, to allow the patient to regulate his emotions more optimally. Similarly, Dialectical Behavior Therapy for borderline personality disorder teaches patients to gain a detached, objective appraisal of their emotional reactions in order to help curb their tendency to emotional overreaction.

So whether it means correcting a depressed patient's emotional deprivation (such as excessive feelings of worthlessness and emptiness), or helping a patient to recognize that having certain emotional reactions, such as anger, is not necessarily bad in itself, or helping the patient with aggressive behavior to cope with the onset of intense emotion (say, again, anger), the goal remains the same: to harness the emotions in a properly balanced way so that mental well-being can be attained.

An example here, pulled from the same anonymous case of the depressed patient mentioned above, may help. To help this particular patient overcome paralyzing fears of being abandoned by her husband, traceable ultimately to painful childhood experiences of feeling abandoned and unloved by her father, the therapist (a cognitive therapist) encouraged her to take moments in which she felt such fears to question whether these fears were objectively based or were merely used as a mechanism to support her dysfunctional patterns of behavior. To assist in this rational, cognitive appraisal, and thereby challenge such emotions and the maladaptive patterns associated with them (the task, ultimately, as we shall see, of moral virtue), the therapist pointed to objective data as evidence of her husband's attachment and commitment to her. The evidence included frequent expressions of love, or expressions of being happy to see and be around her, repeated compliments for her, and the fact that there was no evidence that her husband had ever considered leaving her. The goal for the therapist, among other things, was to help the patient harness her fears in a properly balanced way, to gain mastery over her deep-seated fears of being abandoned by her husband.

Additionally, one could point to the fact that often couples seeking therapy for marital distress will be asked by the therapist to bring to light the various emotions each may be feeling, such as anger and resentment, as well as the emotions associated with feeling unloved and unappreciated or insecure. The goal is to help the spouses develop empathy for each other, as well as to exercise regulated control over their feelings and channel them to serve the good, not the bad, of the marriage.

Given the commonality of outlook between the participated psychology sketched above and clinical therapy, it is my contention that, while Catholic thought can learn much from the insights of modern psychology, clinical psychology can stand to benefit greatly from the more philosophically and theologically grounded view of the way Catholic tradition, following the lead of Aquinas, sees the integration of the emotions into the human person's overall pursuit of moral and spiritual excellence.

What follows is a more detailed, if still cursory, overview of such a view. This study shall conclude with a brief consideration of some important implications this teaching has for clinical therapy.

A. A METAPHYSICAL ACCOUNT OF HUMAN EMOTION

Typically the method clinical psychology observes begins with human behavior itself, or with a patient's actual emotional state, and seeks to determine therefrom a diagnosis. The more philosophically grounded view of Aquinas takes the opposite approach. For him, the study of psychology is first and foremost a speculative discipline, not a practical one ordered to bettering people's lives.[168] Its proper object of inquiry is the truth of the human being or, more specifically, the nature of the human soul along with its powers or faculties (that is, its various capacities for determinate action) and operations.

This explains why Catholic thought, following Aquinas, typically begins with the metaphysical substructure of the human person before examining the actions that flow from this substructure, such as the emotions, and how such actions become integrated into the moral life. To arrive at a truly satisfactory understanding of human emotion, we must start with a deeper ontology, with a proper metaphysics of human nature, that is, with a fundamental grasp of the objective nature of the human being. As the famous maxim invoked in the era of Aquinas puts it, action follows being (*agere sequitur esse*), or such as a thing is, such is the way it acts.[169] Certainly, Aquinas would affirm that in the order of knowing we come to know of a thing first by its actions, and then proceed back to the being, the nature, of the thing: powers are known by their acts, and natures by their powers. Nevertheless, a proper grasp of human behavior is fully attained only when it rests firmly on a clear-sighted metaphysics of the human person.

Movements of the Lower Animal-Like Inclination to Bodily Goods

It is with the metaphysical substructure of the human person in mind that Aquinas defines the emotions as internal movements

---

[168] Christopher Thompson notes this in his essay in this book.

[169] Cf., for example, *ST* I, Q. 89, art. 1; I-II, Q. 55, art. 2, ad. 1; III, Q. 77, art. 3; and III, Q. 19, art. 2, *sed contra*, where Aquinas cites John Damascene's statement (*De fide orthodoxa*, bk. 2, ch. 23 [ed. Buytaert, 142–144]): "operation follows upon nature." Ultimately, this methodology observes the order of Aristotle's *De anima* and was followed throughout the Middle Ages.

of our lower, animal-like inclination (the sensitive appetite) to created bodily goods that are suitable to the sentient dimension of human life (such as pleasures associated with sex or food and drink).[170] Because they are movements that result from an agent being acted upon, specifically the sensitive appetite being acted upon internally by the cognitive sense perception of created bodily goods, the emotions are classified as "passive" phenomena (hence the term *passion, passio*). The sensitive appetite marks a certain capacity for action that is actualized by the cognitive perception of a suitable, or desirable, sense good.

From this we can see that passions or emotions do not arise as blind surges of affect or as wild hormonal responses.[171] The emotions mark our internal affective responses to sense objects cognitively grasped as suitable or undesirable. We undergo the emotion of fear, say, when sensing something terrifying, such as when a patient suffering from depression dreads the thought of getting out of bed in the morning to face the day's responsibilities. Or we experience anger when feeling slighted by another, such as when a wife in marital distress gets angry when she feels her husband is berating and negatively criticizing her—although, in his mind, he may merely be attempting to offer counsel.

That cognitive therapy, in particular, recognizes the causal role played by the perception of sense images in the onset of emotion is implied in a number of techniques this mode of therapy employs. Take, for instance, the technique known as the re-experiencing of the origins of dysfunctional patterns of behavior. This technique consists in the calling to mind, the imagining, of sense

---

170 Cf. ST I-II, Q. 22, art. 3, *sed contra* (citation of Damascene, *De fide orth.*, bk. 2, ch. 22 [ed. Buyt., 132]): *Passio est motus appetitivae virtutis sensibilis.* Cf. as well Aristotle, *De anima* III.10.433a17ff.

171 I am indebted to William Mattison for this insight (in personal conversation).

images associated with the initiation of dysfunctional patterns of behavior. The therapist is most interested in the emotions and feelings triggered by such sense images, as they reveal the origins of unhealthy comportment.

Further, it should be clear that in Aquinas's account of the human person, it is perfectly natural to be subject to emotion, to be affected by emotional responses and moods. Whether we like it or not, emotions play an essential role in our lives. To deny this would be tantamount to denying the fact that the bodily, animal-like side of human nature forms an integral part of the essential makeup of the human person: "Man is similar to other animals in his sensitive nature," Aquinas explains in a key passage. "Hence, reactions that follow upon the sensitive nature are present in man naturally, just as they are in other animals. And what is natural cannot be totally suppressed."[172]

This view is implied in many therapeutic settings, such as the clinical technique known as irreverent communication. In encouraging patients to express verbally their anger at themselves and at the therapist—since "it is okay to be angry sometimes"—this technique seeks to underscore that the proper management of emotion, especially anger, means acknowledging the presence of the emotion in the first place. Therapists find this technique helpful when treating patients suffering from borderline personality disorder who struggle with tendencies to harm themselves physically to feel important and cared for because of the attention harming themselves would invite. By using this technique to validate these patients' emotions, that is, to assure these patients that it is perfectly natural to feel unloved and uncared for, to cry, and to feel angry about not being cared for, the therapist ultimately hopes to get the patients to realize that harming themselves is an inappropriate, dysfunctional response to their emotions.

[172] *Expositio super Job*, 6:4.

Balanced Emotions

The Bodily Side of Human Emotion

An emotion always involves a change of disposition in the person who undergoes it, as emotions issue only after the lower, affective appetitive ordering has been acted upon. This change in disposition includes, in every case, some kind of change in the body, such as an increased heart rate, trembling of the hands, flushing of the face, hormonal and biochemical changes (the chemical oxytocin, for example, has been linked to emotional feelings of love). The bodily alteration involved in every emotion explains why biochemical and neurological phenomena are so intimately bound up with the emotions, and why psychopharmacology and neuropsychology can be of therapeutic benefit in many cases. Bodily change caused by an emotion also explains why biochemical predispositions can play a significant role in a person's emotional states. Evidence, for instance, suggests that persons who suffer from borderline personality disorder possess a biological predisposition toward strong and prolonged emotional reactions.

At the same time, we must be careful not to reduce the emotions solely to the biochemical or to the neurological, such as when we reduce love merely to the release of oxytocin, or happy feelings to the chemical serotonin. Aquinas explains how the bodily change, what he terms the *transmutatio corporalis*, is merely one essential component of an emotion. The internal movement of the lower, animal-like appetite is the other, more determining side. The two accompany each other in the way that matter (the bodily change) accompanies form (the internal motion of the lower, sensitive appetite).[173] This explains how the bodily change marks an essential element to every emotion and how we could not even undergo passion if we did not have bodies (and why God

---

[173] Cf., especially, *ST* I-II, Q. 44, art. 1, but also Q. 17, art. 7; Q. 22, art. 3; Q. 28, art. 5.

is not subject to emotion). It also exposes the error of Descartes, whose radical separation of body from soul leads him to place the emotions in the soul only, and not in the body.[174]

The Concupiscible and Irascible Emotions

The lower, sensitive appetite inclines us to created bodily goods in a dual fashion. Some of the sense goods that attract us are relatively easy to acquire (such as fine-tasting food placed before us), while others are arduous to attain (such as an athletic victory). For this reason Aquinas divides the one sensitive appetite into the concupiscible (the inclination of simple desire which targets the *bonum simpliciter*, the sense good that is easy to attain) and the irascible (the inclination of struggled desire that targets the *bonum arduum*, the sense good difficult to obtain).[175] Following Aquinas's lead, we can distinguish those passions or emotions of the concupiscible appetite (love or like, desire, joy, hatred or dislike, aversion, sorrow) from those of the irascible appetite (hope, despair, courage, fear, anger).[176] Whereas the first group responds to objects

---

[174] For an interesting study, cf. Antonio Damasio, *Descartes' Error: Emotion, Reason, and the Human Brain* (New York: Putnam, 1994). Here Damasio shows how practical reasoning and affective states are severely impaired by damage to areas of the brain that are responsible for affectivity.

[175] The principal text affirming this comes in *ST* I, Q. 81, art. 2. For more on this distinction, cf. Eberhard Schockenhoff, *Bonum hominis. Die anthropologischen und theologischen Grundlagen der Tugendethik des Thomas von Aquin* (Mainz: Matthias-Grünwald Verlag, 1987), 183–186; and Letterio Mauro, "Umanità" della passione in S. Tommaso (Florence: Felice Le Monnier, 1974), 60–86.

[176] Original to Aquinas, this list of eleven specific passions is offered throughout the entirety of his career: *Sent.*, bk. 3, d. 26, Q. 1, art. 3; *DV* Q. 26, art. 4; *ST* I-II, Q. 23, arts. 2, 4; and his commentary on the *Nicomachean Ethics* (*In Ethic.*), bk. 2, lect. 5. For a detailed discussion of these eleven passions, cf. Etienne Gilson, *The Christian Philosophy of St. Thomas*

we sense as relatively easy to acquire or avoid, the latter are by definition more complex and more psychologically involved, as it were, since they engage us in a struggle to attain or avoid the sense good in question. This helps explain why psychotherapists routinely face a stiffer challenge in helping their patients overcome those irascible emotions that often lie at the heart of the patient's psychopathology, such as fear or despair, or even anger.

B. The Ordering of the Emotions to the Moral Good of the Human Person

As already noted, to say the animal-like dimension of the human person finds its satisfaction in the acquisition of those created bodily goods targeted by the passions expresses only a half-truth. The enjoyment of limited bodily goods will be properly "human" only when our internal desires, our emotions, accord with our higher, rational ordering to ultimate goodness and happiness, to the universal good (*summum bonum*).

Emotion and the Human Quest for the Highest Good

While the passions incline us to the lowest kind of goods, to bodily goods, which cannot bring us, as rational beings, complete fulfillment ,these goods *do* participate in goodness itself—they are, after all, good. Such interim lower goods, then, even if subordinate to the *summum bonum*, remain ordered ultimately to the perfect and sufficient good, to the absolute perfection of God. By being inclined internally to limited bodily goods, we are already on the road, as it were, to the highest good. We are already being ordered to the *summum bonum*, even if only in its initial stages.

Since the soul is essentially bound to the body as form is bound to matter, we could never attain our ultimate end, the end of our

Aquinas, trans. L.K. Shook (New York: Random House, 1956), 271–286.

rational souls, if the needs of the body were not satisfied by the procurement of those goods targeted by the emotions. The life of spiritual and moral excellence is not bereft of the enjoyment of earthly and bodily pleasures. On the contrary, the pursuit of holiness and perfection burgeons forth from the enjoyment of earthly and bodily pleasures.

To ignore or outright dismiss the movements of affectivity, the passions, then, would imply, by extension, the renunciation of our very yearning for true flourishing and fulfillment. Our sensitive appetite, our animal-like inclination to lower goods, acts as a kind of germinating seed from which sprouts forth our desire to possess the universal good. In this good our entire appetitive longing, both intellectual and sensitive, both rational and animal, finds its complete rest. The whole of man is made to be moved from within, moved even by his lower sensitive appetite, to the acquisition of happiness, to the proper end of human life. Because the passions set us on a trajectory that finds its completion in the universal good, in the absolute perfection of God, we can appreciate the indispensable role the emotions play in the moral life—and, by consequence, in the life of mental health.

Because Aquinas understands that our rational ordering to ultimate goodness and happiness burgeons forth from our lower, affective ordering to limited bodily goods, he unambiguously distances himself from any kind of Stoic disdain for the emotions. Failing to distinguish emotion, that is, an internal movement of our lower, animal-like inclination to bodily goods, from the movements of our intellectual appetite, the will, and preoccupied with emotion's ability to cloud our judgment and to hamper our duty to live virtuously, the Stoics can manage no better than to revile the passions as "sicknesses of the soul."[177] Neo-Platonism

---

[177] For references to Stoic texts (principally from Cicero, Seneca, and Virgil) affirming this moral disdain for the passions, cf. my own *The Passions of Christ's Soul in the Theology of St.*

would carry on this disparaging attitude of emotion.[178] In doing so, the Stoics (and neo-Platonists) revile an essential element of human life. With vivid imagery, the moralist Servais Pinckaers notes the danger in this:

> Some think that [moral excellence] can only be achieved by suppressing our feelings and passions in a kind of self-mutilation. But would we want an animal trainer to use such methods? Wouldn't we mock him if he showed us tigers without fangs or claws? On the moral level such

---

Thomas Aquinas in "Beiträge zur Geschichte der Philosophie und Theologie des Mittelalters. Neue Folge, 61" [Münster: Aschendorff, 2002], 281, n. 44, and for numerous texts from Aquinas criticizing this view and which span his entire career, cf. *ibid.*, 282, no. 46 (for two examples, in *ST* I-II, Q. 59, art. 3, Thomas denounces the Stoic view as "unreasonable" [*hoc irrationabiliter dicitur*], and in *Super Evangelium S. Ioannis lectura*, ch. 11, lect. 5 [n° 1535], he calls the Stoic disdain for emotion "excessively inhuman" [*valde inhumanum*]). For an analysis of the influence of Stoicism on Thomas's thought, including the morality of the passions, cf. E. K. Rand, *Cicero in the Courtroom of St. Thomas Aquinas*, "The Aquinas Lecture, 1945" (Milwaukee: Marquette University Press, 1946); Gerard Verbeke, *The Presence of Stoicism in Medieval Thought* (Washington, DC: The Catholic University of America Press, 1983), 1–19; and Michel Spanneut, "Influences stoïciennes sur la pensée morale de S. Thomas d'Aquin," in *The Ethics of St. Thomas Aquinas: Proceedings of the Third Symposium on St. Thomas Aquinas' Philosophy*, eds. L. J. Elders and K. Hedwig, "Studi tomistici 25" (Vatican City: Libreria Editrice Vaticana, 1984), 50–79.

178 Cf. Pierre Hadot, *Philosophy as a Way of Life: Spiritual Exercises from Socrates to Foucault*, ed. Arnold I. Davidson, trans. Michael Chase (Oxford: Blackwell, 1995), 136, as cited by Michael Dauphinais, "Languages of Ascent: Gregory of Nyssa's and Augustine of Hippo's Exegeses of the Beatitudes," *Nova et Vetera* English edition 1 (2003): 141–163, at 147.

tactics would be more serious, not to say ridiculous, for movements of sensibility exist and act within us.[179]

Aquinas knows this well. He realizes that emotion, although participating in human rationality, arises from the animal-like dimension of the human person, not the rational. Since only rational actions possess moral worth *per se*, it follows that, considered in themselves, the emotions are morally neutral.[180] What appends moral worth to the emotions is the manner by which reason and will interact with them, in other words, the manner by which the emotions fall under our control.

It is to underscore their essential role in the moral life that Aquinas places his exhaustive study on the passions in the moral part—the second part (*Secunda Pars*)—of his crowning work, the *Summa Theologica*. More particularly, he tactically situates the treatise on the passions amid his analysis of the ultimate end of the human person and of human happiness.[181] This marks a

---

[179] Servais Pinckaers, O.P., *The Pursuit of Happiness—God's Way: Living the Beatitudes*, trans. M. T. Noble, O.P. (New York: Society of St. Paul, 1998), 62–63.

[180] Cf. *ST* I-II, Q. 24, arts. 1–2; Q. 59, art. 5, ad. 2; and *In Ethic.*, bk. 2, lect. 3. Thomas's view on the moral neutrality of the passions takes its inspiration primarily from Augustine, *De civitate Dei*, bk. 9, chs. 4–5 (CCSL 47, 251–254), and bk. 14, chs. 5–14 (CCSL 48, 421–438), and from Aristotle, *NE* 2.3–7, and Albert the Great, *In Ethic.*, bk. 3, lect. 1 (ed. Colon., 137). For more on this, cf. Mark Jordan, "Aquinas's Construction of a Moral Account of the Passions," in *Freiburger Zeitschrift für Philosophie und Theologie* 33 (1986): 71–97.

[181] The treatise on man's end and on happiness is found in *ST* I-II, Q. 1–5, and the treatise on the passions in Q. 22–48. There are 132 articles contained in these twenty-seven questions of the treatise on the passions, making it the largest treatise in the entire *Summa* (for a schematic overview of this treatise, cf. my *Passions of Christ's Soul*, 103–104).

surprising move, since at first sight one would expect Aquinas to have placed his study on the passions earlier in the *Prima Pars* of the *Summa*, specifically amid the treatise on the human soul (Q. 75–90), whose prologue proposes to study "the essence of the soul, its powers, and its operations" (Q. 75). As movements of the sensitive appetite (a power of the soul), the emotions are certainly to be included among the operations of the soul.

But Aquinas prefers the backdrop of the moral life, not the more metaphysical study of the human soul, against which to locate his study on the emotions. Such a move allows him to drive home the point that the emotions play a necessary first step in our striving for happiness, in our attaining the end of seeing God.

Placing the treatise on the passions in the moral part of the *Summa* marks a surprising move for an additional reason. Christian spiritual writers, betraying the enduring influence of Stoic thought with its disdain for human emotion, traditionally relegated the emotions, or human affectivity in general, to the margins of the spiritual life, usually as inimical obstacles to be shunned.[182] To break ranks with the Stoic-inspired school

---

[182] Certainly an exception to this general rule would be the great twelfth-century mystic Bernard of Clairvaux, who stressed heavily the affective side of the human love for God. One could list as just two examples of spiritual writers who lived shortly before Aquinas and who repeated the Stoic charge that the passions are "sicknesses" of the soul William of St. Thierry (d. 1148), *De natura corporis et animae* (PL 180, 714), and Richard of St. Victor (d. 1173), *De statu interioris hominis*, I, 9 and 34 (PL 196, 1122, and 1141). One could also list Gregory of Nyssa, who, as Michael Dauphinais ("Languages of Ascent," 151–152) tells us, sees passion as signifying unruly, disordered desire as such; cf. his Homily 5, nos. 131–133, in *Gregory of Nyssa: Homilies on the Beatitudes: An English Version with Commentary and Supporting Studies. Proceedings of the Eighth International Colloquium on Gregory of Nyssa* (Paderborn, September 14–18, 1998), ed. Hubertus

of thought, then, and to stress that we cannot secure a happy life—the goal of moral action—without the emotions, Aquinas takes the unprecedented step of situating the passions at the heart of his study on human morality.

Happiness: An Equivocal Term

At this point, it might be helpful to note a different, if still complementary, use of language between Aquinas the medieval Catholic thinker and contemporary clinical therapists. It centers on the term *happiness*. Aquinas affirms that the emotions are an essential component in the ordering of our psychological lives to the good, or to what he terms the *happy satisfying life*. The emotions initiate this very ordering. Clinical psychology, too, affirms the essential role the emotions play in the ordering of our psychological lives to mental health, to a happy satisfying life.[183]

R. Drobner and Albert Viciano (Boston: Brill, 2000). For a recent theological article arguing that the Christian life should be devoid of the emotion of anger, to single out this emotion, cf. Paul Lauritzen, "Emotions and Religious Ethics," *Journal of Religious Ethics* 16 (1988): 307–324; cf. as well his *Christian Belief and Emotional Transformation* (Lewisburg, Pennsylvania: Bucknell University Press, 1992). Also, Dietrich Bonhoeffer carries on the Stoic heritage when he writes (in *The Cost of Discipleship* [New York: Touchstone, 1995; originally 1959 by SCM Press], 127): "Jesus will not accept the common distinction between righteous indignation and unjustifiable anger. The disciple must be entirely innocent of anger, because anger is an offence against both God and his neighbour."

[183] In this book, Christopher Thompson notes how the January, 2000 special edition of the *American Psychologist*, the leading journal of the American Psychological Association, is dedicated to the special questions of happiness, excellence, and optimal human functioning, including Martin Seligman and Mihaly Csikszentmihalyi, "Positive Psychology: An Introduction."

Balanced Emotions

Yet the clinician typically takes *being happy* to mean the patient's attainment of optimum affective or emotional wellness, a kind of transient state of elation. A patient is happy when he accepts himself and feels good about himself, when his symptoms have been totally or at least significantly reduced, and when he finds he is a well-adjusted individual who makes important contributions to society.

At the same time, clinical therapy seems intuitively aware that mental well-being means something *more* than mere emotional wellness and adjustment. Otherwise, how else could therapists insist that mental health comes only when one gains balanced self-mastery *over* one's emotions? In speaking of what is requisite for the attainment of psychological health, clinical therapy implicitly appeals to something higher than emotion, namely, that which has the duty of regulating and integrating emotion. The positive psychologist and former president of the American Psychological Association Martin Seligman explicitly affirms as much and, in so doing, approximates an Aristotelian doctrine of moral virtue.[184]

That therapists in practice, even if implicitly, recognize that happiness is not necessarily to be equated with an emotional state

[184] For instance, in his *Authentic Happiness* (Boston: Nicholas Brealey, 2004), 262–263, Seligman writes: "Happiness, the goal of Positive Psychology, is not just about obtaining momentary subjective states. Happiness also includes the idea … of deriving gratification and positive emotion from the exercise of one's signature strengths.… [A] *full life* [then] consists in experiencing positive emotions about the past and future, savoring positive feelings from the pleasures, deriving gratification from your signature strengths, and using these strengths in the service of something larger to obtain meaning." Seligman identifies these signature strengths with the virtues and even appeals to Aristotle in doing so. See also the work edited by him and Christopher Peterson, *Character Strengths and Virtues: A Handbook and Classification* (Oxford: Oxford University Press, 2004).

is supported, I think, by simple clinical examples. Take the case of a patient seeking treatment for alcohol addiction who has observed, for instance, that his marital satisfaction decreases when he abstains from alcohol and that he becomes "unhappy" when he stops drinking. Any sound therapist will know that such "unhappiness" serves this patient's long-term mental well-being much better than the "happiness" gained through drinking alcohol. The therapist understands that this patient's genuine "happiness" is not to be identified with the affective happiness obtained through indulging in the pleasures of drinking alcohol.

Similarly, the Dialectical Behavior Therapy (DBT) for the treatment of borderline personality disorder encourages patients suffering from this disorder to accept some unhappiness for the sake of greater long-term happiness. In cases where patients frequently allow their excessive affective moods to determine their behavior, therapists using DBT will seek to help their patients realize that behavior leading to genuine happiness is not to be equated with behavior simply reflecting one's emotional moods.

This opens the door to the much fuller and richer meaning Aquinas ascribes to the term *happiness*. While not necessarily excluding emotional balance and wellness, the term *happiness* is employed by Aquinas, and Catholic thought in general after him, to signify the fulfillment of every human yearning, spiritual, moral, *and* emotional. For Aquinas, the pursuit of happiness matches the pursuit of moral and spiritual excellence. The reason abstinence better safeguards the recovering alcoholic's genuine happiness is that it serves his *true good*, not necessarily his immediate affective good (although it would serve his long-term affective good). Abstinence for recovering alcoholics marks the morally proper thing to do.

One could use as another example those cases of marital therapy where one spouse expresses insecurity over the degree of commitment to the marriage by the other—who happens to be divorced from a previous marriage. Quite possibly this insecurity marks a byproduct of the fact that the divorced spouse (or even both) does not believe marriage is a lifelong commitment. It should come as no surprise, in other words, that in a marriage where one or both of the spouses do not believe in the permanence of marriage there sits a deep-seated insecurity over the other spouse's commitment to the marital relationship. For Aquinas, as for Catholic thought in general, the marital commitment, because it is indissoluble by nature, requires adherence to its permanence. So long as this adherence is wanting, the very meaning of the marital union is undercut, and marital problems can be expected to ensue. The indissoluble nature of marriage upholds the *moral* good of the union, and thus the total good of the spouses, including their genuine affective good. Adherence to the permanence of marriage, in other words, safeguards the very happiness of the spouses, both as married persons and as human individuals. The affective needs of the spouses, if they are to find genuine completion, must serve a higher end, namely, that of lifelong commitment.

Without consigning emotion to a merely peripheral role, Aquinas does not hesitate to insist that happiness is only consequent upon *rightly ordered* or *properly balanced* and *integrated* emotion, that is, emotion ordered to our moral good.

A Clash of Competing Appetitive Pulls

That the emotions need to be integrated in a healthy, balanced fashion follows upon the ubiquitous existential fact that lower bodily goods of themselves, and the corresponding inclination to them, do not always align with authentic human goods. Clearly they can, but many times they direct us only to apparent goods, illustrated in the previously cited *Oresteia* by the apparent good of blood vengeance desired by the Furies, the pre-Olympian earth goddesses associated with lower, instinctive drives.

Aquinas recognizes that this inclination to apparent interim goods sets off a veritable strife in the human being, a clash between competing appetitive pulls, the one to bodily goods (the lower, sensitive pull) and the other to our highest good, the good of reason (the superior, intellectual pull). Certainly, the highest faculties of the human soul, reason and will, retain a natural "power to command" the lower, animal-like powers (the Latin term used by Aquinas to signify this power to command is *imperium*). This explains why we always remain responsible for our actions, even when we act under the impulse of passion (which might nonetheless lessen our degree of culpability).

Yet this power to command, the *imperium*, enjoyed by the higher powers is not absolute, as the sensitive appetite retains a kind of quasi-autonomy. In short, the power of reason and will to command does not remove or suppress the proper inclination of our internal affective ordering to created bodily goods. Otherwise, there could be no satisfactory way of explaining the state of competing appetitive pulls in the human person, where the lower, sensitive appetite remains ever ready to rebel against the *imperium* of reason and will or, conversely, to consent to it. We know, by contrast, that our bodily limbs own no such quasi-autonomy, as these never, on their own, resist the commands of reason (or our higher cognitive power) and will. The hand, the foot, the arm, and the neck will always observe what the mind commands of them.

There exists, then, a unique relationship between the lower, sensitive appetite and the higher, intellectual powers in the human being. Echoing Aristotle, Aquinas likens this relationship to a political one (the Latin phrase signifying this is *principatus politicus*).[185] More specifically, he likens the lower appetite to free

---

[185] The classic text from Aquinas is *ST* I, Q. 81, art. 3, ad. 2; and from Aristotle, *Politics*, I.5.1254b2–5.

subjects that participate in limited ways, namely, through their free consent, in the governance of a sovereign, the sovereign in this case being reason and will. Today we would say constitutional monarchy best corresponds to the type of political model Aquinas describes.

Rife with tension, this relationship of *principatus politicus* between our higher intellectual powers and our lower, animal-like powers, implies a kind of face-off between the appetitive inclinations of each. Theologically, we know this competing clash of internal appetitive pulls, which St. Paul poignantly describes in Romans 7:14–24 as a "war among his members" making him "not do the good he wants," represents one of the consequences of Original Sin. Catholic thought has traditionally employed the term *concupiscence* to signify this contest of appetitive pulls in the human person. In Aquinas the term *concupiscence* (not to be confused with *concupiscible appetite*) connotes a state of general disorder in the human condition, wherein the sensitive appetite remains inordinately inclined to lower, mutable goods.[186]

Persons suffering from mental imbalance often know from experience this clash of appetitive pulls all too well. A depressed patient, for instance, may find at times that his ability for objective rational self-possession is completely prevailed upon by his fears of abandonment, that is, the deep-seated (irrational) fear that persons close to him will leave him.

At this point, it should be pointed out, particularly for the therapist, that since no one escapes the consequences of Original Sin, not one person is immune to the emotional "imbalance" that

---

[186] Cf. *ST* I-II, Q. 82, art. 3 and art. 4, ad. 1; Q. 91, art. 6; *Compendium theologiae*, ch. 192; *DM* Q. 3–4; and *DV* Q. 25, arts. 6–7. For a detailed analysis of this point, cf. M.-M. Labourdette, "Aux origines du péché de l'homme d'après saint Thomas d'Aquin," in *Revue thomiste* 85 (1985), 357–398, at 371–385, and my *The Passions of Christ's Soul*, 294–300.

comes with concupiscence, that is, that comes with the disordered inclination of the lower sensitive appetite. Every person finds himself subject at times to the inordinate pull of emotions that, to varying degrees, oppose our better judgment. Emotional balance and health, in other words, cannot be secured by external conditions alone, such as family upbringing, no matter how "ideal," or no matter the degree of "unconditional positive acceptance" one receives, to use terminology popular among therapists. Servais Pinckaers, again using vivid metaphorical imagery, expresses well the interior disordering that pertains to the experience of every human individual:

> If we look within ourselves and study our conscience and reactions a bit, we can perceive the shadowy figures of all kinds of animals who live there and threaten us.... We find the proud, domineering lion, the bragging rooster, and the vain peacock, the flattering cat and the sly fox.... We discover the brutal rhinoceros and the sluggish elephant, the scared rabbit and the sensual pig, the fierce dog and the gnawing worm.... What power and firmness is needed, what clear-sightedness and skill, if we are going to control all these instincts, bring them to heal, and compel them to obey and serve charity! Complete self-mastery is a long and exacting work.[187]

The Humanizing Integration
of the Emotions through Moral Virtue

Aquinas singles out the cultivation of the virtues, specifically, the moral virtues, along with the assistance of divine grace, as the key to achieving emotional control and balance. The emotions are integrated into the human person's overall good by means of

---

[187] Pinckaers, *The Pursuit of Happiness*, 62.

the moral virtues. In short, moral virtue marks the concrete way by which reason (our higher, cognitive power) and will exercise their *imperium*, their power to regulate our internal affective ordering to created bodily goods. Moral virtue therefore owns the task of "humanizing" the emotions. Recall how in the *Oresteia* this is exemplified in the way Athena employs wisdom to regulate, and thereby "humanize," the Furies' desire for blood vengeance, inasmuch as she integrates this desire into a higher form of justice informed by reason, namely, trial by jury.

The reason Aquinas assigns the role of humanizing the emotions to the specific type of virtue he calls moral (as distinct from the intellectual virtues) is that, following Aristotle, he insists that our passions and desires constitute the proper "matter" of the moral virtues.[188] In other words, moral virtue is about nothing other than the regulating and disciplining of our emotions, about transforming the internal movements of the lower, animal-like sensitive appetite into actions that conform to and participate in the genuine human good.[189] Moral virtue marks the specific way we act so as to ensure that our inclination to interim bodily goods

---

[188] Cf. ST I-II, Q. 59, arts. 4–5; and Q. 60, art. 3; and Aristotle, NE 2.6.1106b15–16, where he asserts that "moral virtue ... is concerned with passions and actions." Cf. as well Nemesius of Emesa, *De natura hominis*, ch. 31 (ed. Verbeke-Moncho, 126); and Albert the Great, *De bono*, tr. 1, Q. 5, art. 1, ad. 4 (ed. Coloniensis, 74).

[189] In different yet complementary language, Pope John Paul II (Karol Wojtyla) stresses the distinctive self-orientation of the appetites and of the emotions that stands in need of integration through "the personalistic norm." The emotions need to be taken up into the fuller context of human perfection, i.e., into the fuller context of human persons who do not admit of being used or treated as objects and who are ordered to self-giving love. Cf. his *Love and Responsibility*, trans. H. T. Willetts (New York: Farrar, Straus, Giroux, 1981), 41; and *The Acting Person*, trans. A. Potocki (Boston: D. Reidel, 1979).

truly does set us on a trajectory toward, rather than divert us away from, goodness itself, toward the absolute perfection of God.

To grasp fully what Aquinas means when he says our passions and desires constitute the proper matter of the moral virtues, we need merely to consider a specific virtue or two. The virtue of temperance regulates the enjoyment of bodily pleasures. Without such pleasures, including the desires for them, there would be no virtue of temperance. Similarly, the virtue of fortitude cannot exist without the emotion of fear. Fortitude consists in the balanced regulation of this emotion, helping us neither to succumb to our fears nor to condemn our fears outright as something inherently bad.[190]

We can see this played out in any number of clinical examples. For instance, there came a moment during treatment (from a cognitive therapist) of a certain patient suffering from depression in which the patient recognized the need to overcome her fears that her husband would take active measures to prevent her from following simple, yet significant, steps toward self-improvement, such as learning how to drive a car. What began as a brute choice of the will to accomplish this over time became easy to do, to the point that the patient was no longer subject to such fears. Fortitude equipped her with this freedom from her fears. And although at the outset this patient's fears were excessive and misplaced, it was important for her therapist to take her fears seriously and not dismiss them as totally baseless.

In the case of another patient receiving therapy for severe depression, fortitude was needed to overcome the fears abetting her dysfunctional patterns of behavior. Concretely, this meant, for instance, expressing to her husband that she had a desire to have a child, a desire that had crippled her for fear it would induce her husband to leave her. Because this patient had used such fears

---

[190] For more on the importance of fortitude in the moral life and its pertinence to clinical psychology, see the study in this book by Daniel McInerny.

to reinforce schemas, or deep-seated maladaptive patterns of behavior, for the better part of a lifetime, here as well the therapist needed to tread gently and firmly to help the patient strike a more balanced way of living with her fears.

Specifically, our emotions are converted into virtuous acts through right reason (our higher cognitive power) reaching a judgment about the appropriateness (or inappropriateness) of a given movement of emotion, and the will freely (and habitually) choosing to carry out this judgment. Right reason arrives at this judgment in light of the truth of the human person and of how the sensible good in question is ordered to our highest good, the *summum bonum*. We can see as well how essential the virtue of prudence is to living appropriately with our emotions, as Craig Steven Titus points out in this book: prudence "involves not only doing something well but also expressing appropriate emotions 'at the right time, with reference to the right objects, towards the right people, with the right motive, and in the right ways' (*NE* 1106b20–22)."[191]

That therapists can use cognitive-based treatment to help children who suffer from aggressive behavior and conduct disorder offers clinical evidence of the necessary causal role cognitive judgment plays in the educing of good behavior. Such cognitive-based treatment, which has enjoyed a good deal of success, includes teaching these children either the skill of reflecting on what might happen as a direct result of acting in a particular way (called the Consequential Thinking skill), or the skill of conceiving different options that might solve problems in interpersonal situations (called the Alternative Solution Thinking skill).

---

[191] C. S. Titus, "Reasonable Acts." For an enlightening study on the role of "right reason" in the moral life, cf. Laurent Sentis, "La lumière dont nous faisons usage. La règle de la raison et la loi divine selon Thomas d'Aquin," in *Revue des sciences philosophiques et théologiques* 79 (1995): 49–69.

Another type of therapy, Parent Management Training, consists in helping the parents of such children acquire a more cognitive-based approach to instilling appropriate behavior both in themselves and in their aggressive children.

Still, since moral virtue plays the key role in the humanizing integration of our emotions and desires, emotional health or balance and, by consequence, mental well-being, cannot be achieved without cultivating the moral virtues. Clinical therapy, as important as it is—even essential in some instances—can never serve as a replacement for moral virtue. Certainly, it can, and in cases of mental illness should, serve as a supplement and aid to moral virtue. Although necessary for emotional health and mental well-being, moral virtue may not always be sufficient for such balance and well-being. At the same time, clinical therapy, at least in practice, can often focus merely on the reduction of symptoms, rather than on removing the ultimate cause of the psychological malady as such. Conversely, the cultivation of moral virtue targets the very underlying, ultimate cause of happiness (or unhappiness) itself.

But this does not suggest that, in principle, there exists an inherent tension between moral virtue and clinical therapy. To be sure, clinical therapy can be propaedeutic to the acquisition of moral virtue, if not a ready partner to it. For example, in nearly every case of therapy for alcohol abuse and addiction, the virtue of temperance (although rarely, if ever, by this name) is prescribed, usually in the form of total abstinence. In cases of borderline personality disorder, the clinician will usually try to help his patient overcome his susceptibility to letting his emotions get the better of him. In some instances of this disorder, therapists use the technique termed the dialectical strategy of devil's advocate to make their patients realize that their emotions frequently control their behavior and that deliverance from their disorder would require them to sever the necessary link between their affective moods and their comportment. Ideally, therapists will want to help their patients to *desire* to sever this link and achieve willful control of their actions.

Cognitive therapy, especially, recognizes the need to take a therapeutic approach that works closely with the affective elements of a patient's underlying schemas (or underlying maladaptive patterns of thought and behavior), an approach the Catholic moralist would see as roughly equivalent to the cultivation of moral virtue. Cognitive therapy uses rational, cognitive appraisal to manage one's emotions better. In one specific case of a female patient suffering from depression, there came a moment in treatment when the therapist sought to correct the patient's proneness to the subjugation schema, or her proclivity to act in excessively nonassertive and emotionally stunted ways. He did this by helping her realize that even nice people, which this patient saw herself as, can and should behave assertively at times, and that this might even warrant getting angry (such as when this patient got angry, which she regretted, after she had blocked her neighbor's car and the neighbor had called the police about it). Cognitive therapy, in other words, operates with the understanding that sometimes a measured expression of anger is healthy and can even serve as an indication of mental fitness.[192]

C. Consequences: The Emotions Become Rational by Participation

Among the notable consequences of Aquinas's teaching on the humanizing integration of the emotions through the cultivation of moral virtue, two especially, I think, stand out for our

---

[192] For more on the possible moral goodness of the emotion of anger in particular, cf. William Mattison, "Virtuous Anger? From Questions of *Vindicatio* to the Habituation of Emotion," in *Journal of the Society of Christian Ethics* 24 (2004): 159–179; and Giles Mihaven, *Good Anger* (Kansas City: Sheed and Ward, 1989).

consideration because of the importance they bear on the field of clinical therapy.

Emotion Should Not Be Shunned as Such

The first marks a fruit of Thomas's metaphysically grounded moral system, wherein the objective nature of the human person sits at the basis of all moral considerations. It concerns Aquinas's conviction that the emotions form part of the essential fabric of our human lives and, because accruing to the animal-like dimension of the human person, are in themselves morally neutral. This means, considered in themselves, our initial emotional reactions to things are neither necessarily good nor bad. In fact, they *could* mark the *proper* reaction (although only a judgment of right reason can determine this). We need not dismiss categorically out of hand an initial reaction simply because it happens to be of an emotional nature.

Still today, this view smacks against popular, if even unspoken, opinion. Many times, we are conditioned to think our initial emotional reactions to things, as such, should be viewed with suspicion. In the case of the same depressed patient seeking cognitive therapy mentioned immediately above, this patient felt misgivings about being angry for the simple reason that she *was* angry. Stoic (and Kantian, as we shall see) in spirit, this approach looks upon the emotions as inherently subversive of our moral well-being (in the depressed patient's case, of her being a "nice person"). The passions are bad and should always be mistrusted.

Yet, again, clinical psychology adopts an approach that is easily akin to Aquinas's. Therapists almost uniformly recognize that it is perfectly natural to feel emotion, even anger, and that emotion should not be shunned as such. The same depressed patient's therapist, for instance, needed to help the patient come to see that feeling angry was not wrong in itself. In a sense, emotions and desires stand on psychologically "neutral" terrain, to adapt

Aquinas's term. If anything, clinicians understand that following the Stoic ideal of dismissing emotion outright opens the door to mental imbalance and pathology. Therapists do agree that it is unhealthy to control one's emotions too much or too little and that therapy should consist in helping patients overcome extreme mood swings or the habitual onset of excessive emotion. But eradicating emotion and desire from patients' lives never marks the goal of sound therapy.

"Rational by Participation"

This leads to the second, and even more significant, contribution Aquinas makes to the understanding of how the passions become integrated in the pursuit of the human good, and of how his participated psychology can be of service to clinical psychology. According to Aquinas, the lower, animal-like powers of the human soul flow from and participate in the higher, intellectual ones and are ordered back, drawn, to them. At the same time, the animal-like inclination to bodily goods, the sensitive appetite, while inferior, retains the ability to obey (or disobey) reason's *imperium*. From this Aquinas concludes that this lower appetite can act as the *active principle* of virtuous behavior. The lower, sensitive appetite can, by way of participation, become so radically assimilated into the practice of virtue that it becomes a copartner, as it were, with reason (our cognitive power) and will in the shaping of our lives into works of moral excellence. Moral virtue succeeds in converting the very emotions themselves into rationally appropriate acts, into virtue-oriented movements. As a consequence, Aquinas, drawing upon Aristotle, does not hesitate to assert that the lower appetite, our animal-like inclination to bodily goods, has the capability of becoming, in its very act, "*rational by participation.*"[193]

---

[193] Aristotle affirms that the sensitive appetite "participates in reason to some extent" (*NE* 1.13.1102b13–14). This leads Aquinas, in his commentary on the passage (*In Ethic.*, no.

This teaching, while plotting, as we shall see, a middle course, is radical. It seems nonsensical to hold that emotion can *give rise to* virtuous acts, can partake in human rationality. After all, emotion flows from the animal-like side of the human person, and virtue in any case is defined as the will's execution of what is cognitively judged to be rationally appropriate behavior. Human rationality and free choice, not emotion, make an act virtuous as such.

Many prominent philosophers have proposed positions that disagree sharply with Aquinas's on this matter, usually falling to either extreme of his. Before examining in greater depth Aquinas's teaching on the emotions' being rational by participation, then, we shall briefly consider how the history of philosophical thought, particularly after Thomas, has stood at odds with him on this teaching. This will place in relief the unique achievement of Aquinas's doctrine, a doctrine that, again it seems to me, can provide an enormous benefit to the field of clinical psychology. It will place in relief as well the difficulty of affirming the cooperative, consensual role emotion plays in cultivating moral virtue.

---

242) to call the sensitive appetite "rational by participation." Thomas outlines this position in three principal places: *ST* I-II, Q. 56, art. 4; *Quaestiones disputatae De virtutibus in communi*, art. 4 ("Whether the irascible and concupiscible appetites can be the subject of virtue"), which was written just after the completion of the *Prima Secundae Pars* of the *Summa*; and *Sent.*, bk. 3, d. 33, Q. 2, art. 4, qla. 2. The classic study of this issue is found in M.-D. Chenu, "Les passions vertueuses. L'anthropologie de saint Thomas," *Revue philosophique de Louvain* 72 (1974): 11–18; and M.-D. Chenu, "Body and Body Politic in the Creation Spirituality of Thomas Aquinas" in *Listening* 13 (1974): 214–232. See also William Mattison, "Virtuous Anger?," 159–179, and Bonnie Kent, *The Virtues of the Will: The Transformation of Ethics in the Late Thirteenth Century* (Washington, DC: The Catholic University of America Press, 1995).

Balanced Emotions

A Survey of Philosophical Thought Opposed to Affirming the Cooperative Role of Emotion in the Moral Life

Aquinas's position drew fire in his own lifetime from Bonaventure, his Franciscan colleague at the University of Paris, and after his death from the late thirteenth-century Franciscan John Duns Scotus. Neither of these Franciscan thinkers would allow Aquinas to ascribe an active principle of virtuous conduct to our animal-like inclination to bodily goods, to our sensitive appetite. For them, virtue can arise only from an act of the will, not from the lower appetite as well, since, they hold, free choice alone appends moral worth to our actions.[194]

In short, Bonaventure and Scotus conceive of the relationship between the higher powers of the soul and the lower powers more in terms of imposed submission, that is, more in terms

---

[194] Scotus sums up his position when he writes in *Opus Oxoniense*, bk. 3, d. 33, Q. 1: "[T]he moral virtues should not be posited as present principally in the sensitive part of the soul.... [For] the will [alone is related to acting] rightly and not-rightly.... And the only necessity of positing virtues in powers is so that powers that of themselves are able to act rightly and not-rightly might be ruled by them." Bonaventure forges his position in *Sent.*, bk. 3, d. 33, art. 1, Q. 3 (ed. Quaracchi, 715–718). For studies on Scotus's teaching on the passions, cf. Alan R. Perreiah, "Scotus on Human Emotions" in *Franciscan Studies* 56 (1998): 325–345; and F. de J. Chauvet, "Las ideas filosóficas de J. Duns Escoto sobre las pasiones," in *Estudios Franciscanos* 48 (1936): 244–265. For a general presentation of Scotus's thought, cf. Allan B. Wolter, *Duns Scotus on the Will and Morality* (Washington, DC: The Catholic University of America Press, 1986); Tobias Hoffmann, "The Distinction between Nature and Will in Duns Scotus," in *Archives d'Histoire Doctrinale et Littéraire du Moyen Age* 66 (1999): 189–224; and, for the virtue of prudence in particular, Mary Elizabeth Ingham, "Practical Wisdom: Scotus's Presentation of Prudence," in *John Duns Scotus: Metaphysics and Ethics*, eds. L. Honnefelder et al. (Leiden: E.J. Brill, 1996), 551–571.

of reason and will simply imposing its judgment on the lower, sensitive appetite. Virtue does not transform the emotions into virtue-oriented movements. It only "tames" the passions through what Bonaventure, whose neo-Platonic strain no doubt accounts for his failure to ascribe full integrity to the passions, calls a forced *submission to reason* (*optemperat rationi*).[195] This submission to reason comes from the rational powers from on high and as from without.

One could also list Descartes, the seventeenth-century father of modern philosophy, who derides the writings of his predecessors on emotion, as a proponent of the view that would truncate any real synergy or communication between the lower, affective dimension of human life and reasoned judgment. Stirred by his dualist anthropology, Descartes confines the passions exclusively to the realm of the body. And since the body is only superficially joined to the soul, the passions bear no intrinsic relation to the true human good, the concern of the soul; they "no longer involve the whole human being, spirit and body together," Servais Pinckaers observes, and "thus they lose their moral and spiritual

---

[195] Bonaventure, *Sent.*, bk. 3, d. 33, art. 1, Q. 3, ad. 1 (ed. Quaracchi, 717). Scotus's position, as cited in the previous note, matches Bonaventure's closely: "[T]he only necessity of positing virtues in powers is so that powers that of themselves are able to act rightly and not-rightly might be ruled by them." *Opus Oxoniense*, bk. 3, d. 33, Q. 1. As for neo-Platonism, Michael Dauphinais ("Languages of Ascent," 144–145), citing the research of Pierre Hadot (*Philosophy as a Way of Life*, 83–100) notes: "'In the view of all philosophical schools, mankind's principal cause of suffering, disorder, and unconsciousness were the passions: that is, unregulated desires and exaggerated fears.' The passions debilitate human beings; the spiritual exercises of the philosophers cure the sickness.... [T]o be a neo-Platonist meant that one submitted to a set of progressive spiritual exercises moving one away from the disturbance of the passions toward union with the One."

repercussions."[196] His view approximates the position of Bonaventure and Scotus in that Descartes assigns virtue the task of "reining in" or "domesticating" the emotions almost against their will, or at least in spite of the lower, sensitive appetite's proper inclination. The inclination of this appetite must be forced into submission, as it follows upon the external, less-than-human side of ourselves.

Not far removed from the position of Bonaventure and Scotus, or of Stoicism for that matter, is that of the modern influential German philosopher Immanuel Kant. Kant builds his moral system on an antirealist rejection of the objective nature of the human being serving as a basis for moral theory. That is, his moral thought presupposes a denial of any objective knowledge of being. This leads Kant to cast aside our inclinations and sensible movements, including our emotions (part and parcel of an "objective human nature"), in the pursuit of moral excellence. He insists that only the will can be the subject of good moral action.

---

[196] Servais Pinckaers, "Reappropriating Aquinas's Account of the Passions," 281. Descartes himself writes: "It is to the body alone that we should attribute everything that can be observed in us to oppose our reason.... [I]t must be observed [then] that (the passions) are all ordained by nature to relate to the body, and to belong to the soul only in so far as it is joined to the body" (*The Passions of the Soul*, pt. 1, art. 47, and pt. 2, art. 137 [ed. R. Stoothoff, pp. 346, 376]). This leads Descartes to isolate the passions from the work of virtue in pt. 2, art. 148 (ibid., 382): "For if anyone live in such a way ... [of] what I here call 'pursuing virtue,' he will receive from this a satisfaction which has such power to make him happy that the most violent assaults of the passions will never have sufficient power to disturb the tranquillity of his soul." Also, in pt. 3, art. 212 (ibid., 404), he writes: "[T]he chief use of wisdom lies in its teaching us to be masters of our passions and to control them with such skill that the evils which they cause are quite bearable."

Philosophical Virtues and Psychological Strengths

The only intrinsically good thing, Kant asserts, is a good will.[197] Human reason, Kant famously writes in a way reminiscent of the Stoic view, must issue its commands "with disregard and contempt" for the "impetuous" natural inclinations (including the emotions). The natural inclinations represent nothing more than "the powerful counterweight to moral duty." Simply put, moral duty requires us to tear ourselves away from our emotions and desires.[198] Our passions and desires have, or at least *should* have,

[197] "[M]oral worth ... can lie nowhere else than in the principle of the will" (Immanuel Kant, *Groundwork of the Metaphysics of Morals*, ed. and trans. Mary Gregor [Cambridge: Cambridge University Press, 1998], sect. 1, p. 13; emphasis his). We should be struck by how similar this statement is to the one cited above from Scotus, *Opus Oxoniense*, bk. 3, d. 33, Q. 1: "[T]he moral virtues should not be posited as present principally in the sensitive part of the soul.... [For] the will [alone is related to acting] rightly and not-rightly." To be sure, in the same section from the *Groundwork*, Kant ascribes "genuine moral worth" only to a good deed done "not from inclination but from duty" (p. 12), since "an action from duty is to put aside entirely the influence of inclination" (where inclination would include the movements of sensibility, the emotions) (p. 13); he holds up as honorable only that kind of love which "lies in the will and not in the propensities of feeling (*empfindung*)" (p. 13); and he asserts that the grounding for duty stems from the fact that "there is left for the will nothing that could determine it except objectively the *law* and subjectively *pure respect* for this practical law [emphasis his], and so the maxim of complying with such a law even if it infringes upon all my inclinations" (pp. 13–14). For an insightful concise study of Kant's moral philosophy, cf. Robert Sokolowski, *Moral Action: A Phenomenological Study* (Bloomington, Indiana: Indiana University Press, 1985), Appendix D, "Kant," 215–220.

[198] Kant writes in *Groundwork of the Metaphysics of Morals* (ed. M. Gregor, 17): "The human being feels within himself a powerful counterweight to all the commands of duty ... the counterweight of his needs and satisfactions.... Now reason issues its precepts unremittingly, without thereby promising

little or nothing to do with our moral obligations. We should do what we ought *regardless* of our passions and desires.

At the other extreme would be the antirationalist Scottish philosopher David Hume, whose moral philosophy, like Stoicism, blurs any real distinction between acts of the will and the lower, animal-like movements of sensibility. However, whereas in Stoicism this blurring leads to a disparaging attitude toward emotion, an attitude shared by Kant, in Hume it reaches the opposite conclusion. For him, virtue is *identified* as such with movements of passion. To say pleasure *is* to say virtue and to say pain *is* to say vice.[199] The good life, the life of moral excellence, consists in the

anything to the inclinations, and so, as it were, with disregard and contempt for those claims [of the inclinations], which are so impetuous and besides so apparently equitable (and refuse to be neutralized by any command)." Commenting on this element of Kant's thought, R. Sokolowski (Moral Action, 215–216) observes: "The good inclination is contrasted to the moral goodness of the will.... Reason thus legislates for itself; it does not have its rules set for it by nature.... Kant's moral philosophy [therefore] assumes a conflict between practical reason or will, on the one hand, and need, inclination, desire, aversion, or sensibility, on the other." Richard Taylor (*Good and Evil: A New Direction* [New York: Macmillan, 1970], 103–115) describes Kant's moral system accurately, then, when he writes: "To be genuinely moral [for Kant], a man must tear himself away from his inclinations as a loving being, drown the sympathetic promptings of his heart, scorn any fruits of his efforts, think last of all of the feelings, needs, desires, and inclinations either of himself or of his fellows and, perhaps detesting what he has to do, do it anyway—solely from respect for the law."

[199] Hume writes: "The chief spring or actuating *principle of the human mind is pleasure or pain*.... The most immediate effects of pleasure and pain are the propense and adverse *motions of the mind*; which are diversified into *volition*, into desire and aversion, grief and joy, hope and fear, according as the pleasure or pain changes its situation" (*A Treatise of Human Nature*, bk.

pursuit of pleasure and in the avoidance of pain, a conclusion reminiscent of another ancient moral philosophy: Epicureanism.[200]

In short, moral judgments, in Hume's view, are nothing other than expressions of feeling. We should not be surprised, then, when we read Hume assert, rather provocatively: "Reason is, and ought only to be the slave of the passions, and can never pretend to any other office than to serve and obey them."[201]

Closely related to Hume's position is that of his British predecessor, the seventeenth-century philosopher Thomas Hobbes.

3, pt. 3, sect. 1 [Oxford: Clarendon Press, 1960], 574; emphasis mine). Hume then follows with the stark moral implications of this position: "[M]oral distinctions [therefore] depend entirely on certain peculiar sentiments of pain and pleasure, and that whatever mental quality in ourselves or others gives us a satisfaction [i.e., pleasure], is of course virtuous; as every thing of this nature, that gives us uneasiness [i.e., pain], is vicious" (ibid., 574–575). He repeats this a bit later: "Each of the passions and operations of the mind has a particular feeling, which must be either agreeable or disagreeable. The first is virtuous, the second vicious" (ibid., 590). See Donald MacNabb, "David Hume" in *Encyclopedia of Philosophy*, vol. 4, ed. Paul Edwards (New York: Macmillan, 1972), 85–88.

[200] The materialist Epicurus, the founder of Epicureanism who lived from 341–270 B.C., writes: "[P]leasure is the starting-point and goal of living blessedly" ("Letter to Menoeceus," in *Hellenistic Philosophy: Introductory Readings*, trans. and ed. Brad Inwood and L. P. Gerson [Indianapolis: Hacket, 1988], 24). As Servais Pinckaers notes, "The Epicureans place their beatitude at the level of the emotions" ("Reappropriating Aquinas's Account of the Passions," 275).

[201] David Hume, *A Treatise of Human Nature*, bk. 2, pt. 3, sect. 3, 415. Later Hume states: "Moral good and evil are certainly distinguish'd by our *sentiments*, not by *reason*" (bk. 3, pt. 3, sect. 1, 589; emphasis his). Judith Barad observes accordingly: "David Hume .. hold[s] that the choice of ultimate values is always made by the emotional side of our nature" ("Aquinas on the Role of Emotion in Moral Judgment and Activity" in *The Thomist* 55 [1991]: 371–413, at p. 371).

Hobbes defines our internal life entirely in mechanistic terms, that is, entirely in terms of matter in motion. The human person's internal states consist in nothing other than sense perceptions of material objects that give rise to pleasant or unpleasant sensations. These in turn end, respectively, in desires or aversions (or fears).[202]

As with Hume, then, Hobbes's moral system is based entirely on our passions, on our affective likes or dislikes. The "good life," the moral life, consists in nothing other than the satisfaction of our self-interested desires. Like animals, we are entirely self-serving, self-interested creatures, for whom "good" is meaningful only in relation to bodily objects. "Good" simply names objects of our desires or aversions, not some ultimate, common end shared by all human beings.[203] If, for Aquinas, our emotions mark only

---

[202] "Life it selfe is but Motion, and can never be without Desire, nor without Feare, no more than without Sense" (Thomas Hobbes, *Leviathan* [first published, 1651], ed. C. B. Macpherson [Middlesex-Baltimore: Penguin Books, 1968, repr., 1981], pt. 1, ch. 6, p. 130).

[203] Hobbes affirms: "For these words of Good, Evill, and Contemptible, are ever used in relation to the person that useth them: There being nothing and absolutely so; nor any common Rule of Good or Evill, to be taken from the nature of the objects themselves; but from the Person of the man.... *Pleasure*, therefore, (or *Delight*) is the appearance or sense of Good; and *Molestation* or *Displeasure*, the appearance, or sense of Evill. And consequently all Appetite, Desire, and Love, is accompanied with some Delight; and all Hatred, and Aversion, with more or lesse Displeasure and Offence" (*Leviathan*, pt. 1, ch. 6, pp. 120–122; emphasis his). Hobbes's identification of good with pleasure and evil with pain, or his blurring of emotion with virtue and vice, is seen in *Leviathan*, pt. 1, ch. 6, pp. 122–127; here Hobbes lists what he calls the various kinds of pleasures (or delights) and displeasures (or aversions): appetite, desire, love, aversion, hate, joy, grief, pain, hope, despair, fear, courage, anger, confidence, diffidence, indignation, benevolence, good

one *lower* dimension of the inner life of the human being, for Hobbes they are part and parcel of the *only* dimension of human life, since he defines man as nothing more than a machine—a definition one modern author claims marks "a great step forward in thought"![204]

An equivalent of the Hume-Hobbesian view would resurface later in the utilitarianism of Jeremy Bentham and John Stuart Mill. For these philosophers, moral duty lies in strict correspondence with sensible inclinations to pleasure. What one ought to do is that which accords the greatest and most lasting pleasure. This is because, for them, pleasure marks the only intrinsic good (and pain the only intrinsic evil): happiness, as Mill starkly puts it, consists in "pleasure and deliverance from pain."[205] Enjoyment of the greatest number of sense goods by the greatest number of people marks the goal of British utilitarianism.

A Reductionist Psychology?

Whereas this essay has stressed points of commonality between the approaches of Aquinas and clinical therapy on the issue of emotional balance and integration, here a caveat must be introduced. One can safely say, I think, that many clinical therapists today hold a reductionist or materialist anthropology in mind. This

---

nature, covetousness, ambition, pusillanimity, magnanimity, valor, liberality, miserableness, kindness, lust, luxury, jealousy, revengefulness, curiosity, religion, superstition, panic, terror, admiration, glory, vainglory, dejection, sudden glory, laughter, sudden dejection, weeping, shame, blushing, impudence, pity, cruelty, emulation, envy, deliberation.

[204] See R. S. Peters, "Thomas Hobbes," in *The Encyclopedia of Philosophy*, 39.

[205] John Stuart Mill, *Utilitarianism*, in *Collected Works of John Stuart Mill*, vol. 10 (Toronto: University of Toronto Press, 1963), ch. 2, p. 210. Cf. Jeremy Bentham, *Introduction to the Principles of Morals and Legislation* (London: Athlone Press, 1970), I, 1.

leads them to equate psychological well-being simply with good feeling or agreeable emotion. We noted this earlier when remarking how happiness, the goal of therapy, is often understood by the clinician as meaning nothing more than the patient's attainment of optimum affective or emotional wellness; when a patient feels good about himself, when his symptoms are significantly reduced and he feels he is a well-adjusted individual. When this happens, I fear, clinical therapy adopts an anthropology not far removed from that of Hume, Hobbes, and utilitarianism.

In the philosophical anthropology adopted in this essay, mental health means much more than emotional wellness, since the human person is more than a mere mechanized bundle of animal-like feelings and desires. The human person is not reducible to the purely emotional, to the purely biochemical or neurological.

Yet, as was noted earlier, clinical therapy seems intuitively aware of this, for therapists almost universally recognize that mental health comes only when one gains balanced self-mastery over one's emotions. In short, clinical therapy, in speaking of what is requisite for the attainment of psychological well-being, implicitly appeals to something higher than emotion, namely, that which has the duty of regulating and humanizing the emotions. There is the need, then, both for correction and for appreciation of commonality of outlook.

Aquinas Stands Apart

From the foregoing brief survey of philosophical thought, we can see that Aquinas's position on good moral action flowing from our emotions—indebted to Aristotle's remark at the end of the first book of the *Nicomachean Ethics* that the lower, sensitive or animal-like part of the human soul possesses the ability to participate in reason "to some extent"—stands very much apart in the annals of western learning. Writing in the fifteenth century, the Thomist John Capreolus does not hesitate to place Aquinas in a

class of his own on account of his insistence that our lower, an-
imal-like inclination to bodily goods, our sensitive appetite, can
act as the principle, the source, of a genuine *human* act, and, thus,
of a virtuous deed.[206] Not rational per se, the passions become ra-
tional by participation, that is, by active collaboration with those
faculties—reason (our cognitive power) and will—unique to the
human person.

Aquinas would agree with Bonaventure, Scotus, and Kant that
virtue consists first and foremost in an act of the will: "[T]he prin-
cipal act of moral virtue," Thomas affirms, "is choice [election],
and choice [election] is an act of the rational power."[207] He would
be quick to add, however, that it need not consist exclusively in
an act of the will. In no case will he agree with Kant that our pas-
sions and desires have, or at least should have, little or nothing to
do with our moral obligations, that we should do what we ought
regardless of our passions and desires. Aquinas insists that what we
ought to do should include our passions and desires. After all, our
emotions significantly impact the way we think and choose.

Good Moral Action Should Flow from Our Emotions

We turn, then, to a more in-depth consideration of Aquinas's
position that the emotions become rational by participation, that

---

[206] Cf. Aquinas, *Quaestiones disputatae De virtutibus in communi*,
art. 4; *ST* I-II, Q. 56, art. 4; and John Capreolus, *Defensiones
Theologiae Divi Thomae Aquinatis*, bk. 3, d. 33, art.1, end
of concl. 1 (the English translation of this is found in *John
Capreolus, On the Virtues*, trans. K. White and R. Cessario
[Washington, DC: The Catholic University of America Press,
2001], 246–260, at p. 250). Here Capreolus defends Thomas's
position on the sensitive appetite's being the subject of virtue
against the objections of Scotus and Peter of Auriol.

[207] *ST* I-II, Q. 56, art. 4, arg. 4; *Quaestiones disputatae De virtutibus
in communi*, art. 4, arg. 2. The first part of this phrase is a
citation of Aristotle, *NE* 2.6.1106a36 and VI.2.1139a22–23.

good moral action should flow from our internal desires and emotions. To begin, we need to recall that, unlike such actions as digestion or bodily growth, over which the human person enjoys no real self-mastery, the movements of our lower, animal-like appetite, because of their rebellious nature (as owing to the quasi-autonomy, as it were, of the sense appetite), demand that we gain mastery over them. And self-mastery makes an act properly human, since it involves the engagement of reason and will, or reflective judgment and execution.[208] Insofar, then, as an emotion leads us to gain mastery over it, it is brought up into, it becomes one with, the work of our higher intellectual faculties. It becomes a properly human act, a rational act.

Put another way, the lower, animal-like appetite in the human person gives rise to the emotions, which, unlike, say, digestion and growth, are interior movements that always remain able to resist the commands of reason. This means they stand in need of perfection. Since virtue perfects human acts, it follows that the sensitive appetite acts as a goad to virtue. That is, the sensitive appetite gives rise to acts of virtue as from a principle or source.[209] The human sense appetite, our animal-like ordering to created bodily goods, relates to virtuous conduct in the way that cause relates to effect.

208 "Man differs from irrational animals in this, that he is master of his actions. Wherefore those actions alone are properly called human of which man is the master. Now man is the master of his actions through his reason and will" (*ST* I-II, Q. 1, art. 1).

209 As Capreolus succinctly puts it: "Every power that is able to be a principle of a human act, and is not of its nature determined … to obeying reason, can be the subject of a virtue" (*Defensiones Theologiae Divi Thomae Aquinatis*). Aquinas does affirm in *ST* I-II, Q. 77, art. 6, ad. 2 that emotion can lessen the freedom of an action when it acts as a cause of virtue. But this is not the same as what is at issue here, which Capreolus well explains.

Philosophical Virtues and Psychological Strengths

Because Aquinas recognizes an active, synergistic participation of the animal-like powers of the soul in the rational ones, he concludes that any power of the soul that operates as a principle of a genuine human act must participate in human rationality.[210] In short, since the sense appetite can become rational by participation, and since it belongs to virtue to perfect human acts by aligning them with reason, "it follows," Aquinas concludes, "that there [be a kind of] human virtue ... [which] is placed in what is rational by participation, that is, in the appetitive part of the soul."[211]

We see here just how far a participated psychology can be pushed. The rational powers, through their ability to penetrate the lower, animal-like part of the soul, empower the lower sense appetite of the human being to accomplish what properly belongs to reason and will. Rather than simply being forced to submit to reason and will, as Bonaventure, Scotus, and Kant would have it, the animal-like sensitive appetite, because of its transformation, is treated as a kind of equal; it is conscripted into service in the acquisition of the moral virtues. As Aquinas affirms in a key passage:

> It is not the function of moral virtue to make the sensitive appetite altogether idle, since virtue does not deprive the powers subordinate to reason of their proper activities, but instead makes them execute [*exequantur*] the commands of reason *through the exercise of their proper acts*. Virtue therefore ... orders the sensitive appetite to its proper regulated movements.[212]

The Lower Sense Appetite as a Virtuous Habit

Virtuous conduct consists in habitual choice (*habitus* is the Latin term denoting this), whereby our repeated good acts incline

---

[210] *ST* I-II, Q. 56, art. 4.

[211] Aquinas, *In Ethic.*, bk. 1, lect. 13 (no. 243).

[212] *ST* I-II, Q. 59, art. 5; emphasis mine.

us to acting rightly, or endow us with a stable, character-shaping disposition or skill at acting well. As a result, Aquinas sees little problem in attributing the notion of *habitus*, habit, to our lower, animal-like inclination to bodily goods, to our sensitive appetite.[213]

Some moralists, pointing to a text by Aristotle for support, continue to debate whether virtuous habits, because they incline us to a certain type of comportment, actually lessen our freedom.[214] We must recall, however, that the faculty of choosing, the will, has as its object the universal good, the good of reason. Because virtuous habits incline us to the rational good, they order the will to its proper object. In so doing they ensure a proper functioning, and thus the proper fulfillment or flourishing, of the will. Aquinas does not look upon free will as a radically open-ended, undetermined power, indifferent to whatever stands before it, whether good or evil. Rather, freedom is determined and perfected by, because inscribed in, the human person's natural inclination to the good.[215] While it may hold, then, that vicious habits (the type of habit, in fact, mentioned by Aristotle) lessen our freedom, just the reverse is the case for virtuous habits.

To attribute the notion of habit to the sensitive appetite means that this lower appetite, our internal affective ordering to bodily goods, can be shaped into a power that is disposed to working side by side, as an active consensual partner, with reason (our cognitive power) and will in the practice of virtue. Through

---

213 *Sent.*, bk. 3, d. 33, Q. 2, art. 4 and Q. 1, art. 2; and *Quaestiones disputatae De virtutibus in communi*, art. 4.

214 The key passage from Aristotle comes in *Nicomachean Ethics*, where he asserts that those who have cultivated the vicious habit of intemperance or injustice lack the ability, the freedom, to be anything but intemperate or unjust (*NE* 3.5.1114a3–22).

215 "The will does not desire of necessity whatsoever it desires ... [since] the appetible good is the object of the will" (*ST* I, Q. 82, arts. 2 and 3; cf. Q. 83, art. 3).

growth in moral virtue, the lower, sense appetite advances from a power that contests, no matter how vigorously, reason and will's power to command to one that cooperates with it more and more, through its own impulses. In fact, the very proof that moral virtue, such as temperance, has been attained lies in the fact that one is no longer foiled by one's passions (in the case of temperance, one no longer struggles with disordered desires for bodily pleasures).

If this did not happen, our attempts to act virtuously would meet often with resistance from our animal-like inclination to sense goods. This would severely limit the extent to which virtuous behavior perfects our character, for our emotions would never take on a perfectly human character, would never be genuinely "humanized." To attain the state of perfect virtue, the very inclination of the sense appetite, likened to a subject that must give its free consent to the governance of a sovereign, must itself become virtuous. To attain the state of perfect virtue, we need to become good in our emotions and desires and in the choices of our will.

The Case of Continence:
Doing the Good without the Affective Desire for It

Aquinas's discussion on the virtue of continence and how it differs from the virtue of temperance, which draws deeply from the thought of Aristotle, may help clarify the element of his teaching we are here sketching.

The continent individual, as Aristotle first noted, is the person who acts virtuously but only after waging a struggle against disordered bodily desires (the continent differs from the incontinent in that the latter succumbs to his disordered bodily desires, and thus acts contrary to his principles, contrary to what he knows he ought to do).[216] Although seduced by his sensual desires, the

---

[216] Aristotle notes that in the continent individual, "reason rightly induces to what is best, but something besides reason seems to

continent person, unlike the incontinent, does not yield to such desires and persists in accomplishing the good of reason: "[T]he continent man is to be praised," Aquinas observes, "because he is overcome not by sensual desire [as in the incontinent person] but by reason."[217]

Nonetheless, the continent individual's problem centers on the fact that he fights against strong desires for bodily pleasures not in accord with his better judgment. This is why Aristotle says such a person "acts on decision [that is, on rational judgment], not on appetite [or on sensual desire]."[218] The continent person does the right thing, although not because he has the affective desire for it. Put another way, the continent individual does the virtuous deed through raw willpower alone, not through the help of his passions.

If the continent person is to achieve complete moral perfection, he must attain a proper regulation of his sensual desires or, more generally, of his internal affective ordering to created bodily goods. He must be good not only in his rational judgment but in all his internal desires as well.

Contrary to the view, say, of Immanuel Kant, who holds that we should observe our moral duty in spite of what we desire, the moral life is meant to be a life of joy, both affective and spiritual. This can happen only when we act on rational judgment *and* on sensual desire together, when our virtuous actions flow from our passions and desires: "[I]t belongs to man's moral good to be moved toward the good both by the will and by the sensitive appetite," Aquinas insists.[219]

---

be innate ... which conflicts with reason and resists reason" (*NE* 1.13.1102b17–19; see also VII.9–10.1151a30–1152a35).

217 Aquinas, *In Ethic.*, trans. C. I. Litzinger (Notre Dame, Indiana: Dumb Ox Books, 1993), bk. 7, lect. 9 (no. 1443).

218 *NE* 3.2.1111b15.

219 *ST* I-II, Q. 24, art. 3.

The Case of Temperance:
Doing the Good with the Affective Desire for It

Aquinas understands that one can affirm precisely this of the fully temperate individual: the person who has acquired the habit, the character, of being temperate experiences little or no inordinate pull from his concupiscible appetite. He *is* pulled by his concupiscible appetite, although toward the rational good, as his internal desires assist him in acting temperately. He performs the virtuous deed not through raw willpower alone but with the help of his passions. In this way even his desires are morally praiseworthy. Such a person acts with pleasure and promptness, and finds ease, not burdensome toil, in living virtuously.[220] This person has attained the goal of the moral life.

The regulation of pleasures associated with sex, which more specifically concerns the virtue of chastity (temperance oversees the balanced enjoyment of bodily pleasure in general), illustrates well how the temperate (or chaste) person differs from the continent one. While both the chaste individual and the continent do what reason commands as regards sexual pleasure, the continent person does so only through struggling with desires for illicit sexual pleasure. Conversely, the truly chaste individual experiences no such struggle. This person enjoys *good* affective desires, chaste desires, and these help him accomplish the good of reason. Aquinas would argue that, whereas both observe the chaste duty, there remains a clear moral difference between the two. One has acquired the character (*habitus*) of being chaste, which results in rightly ordered internal desires, whereas the continent simply does the chaste thing without having chaste desires. As Aquinas affirms in a key passage from his commentary on Aristotle's *Nicomachean Ethics*:

---

[220] Cf. ST I-II, Q. 24, art. 3, ad. 1.

[I]n these men [endowed with the habit of moral virtue] nearly everything—both external actions *and internal desires*—harmonize with reason ... [And so when we consider the difference between the virtues of temperance and continence, we see that] the temperate man does not have the evil desires of the continent *because his sensual desire is well ordered by his habit of temperance* ... Hence, by his habit of temperance the temperate man takes no delight in desires contrary to reason, while the continent man is disposed to take unreasonable pleasure though he is not seduced by his passion.[221]

This leads Aquinas to conclude, rather boldly, that the chaste individual enjoys a *virtuous* concupiscible appetite, that is, a rightly (or rationally) ordered concupiscible appetite, which offers its active assistance to living chastely. His concupiscible appetite is inclined, of itself, to being chaste; it possesses the habit, the character, of the virtue of chastity ("his sensual desire is well ordered by his habit of temperance").[222] Conversely, the continent is troubled by his concupiscible appetite. His desires speak a different voice from his reason. Herein lies the greater moral perfection.

For Aquinas, then, there can be no doubt that the disordering of the passions can be healed to the extent that the virtuous individual is not merely untroubled by his passions; he is actually *helped* by his passions in living virtuously. Through growth in moral virtue, the passions attain the ability to incline us to our highest good. In practical terms, this means the more virtuous

[221] Aquinas, *In Ethic.*, bk. 1, lect. 13 (no. 239), and bk. 7, lect. 9 (no. 1453–54); emphasis mine.

[222] Aristotle affirms that in the fully virtuous person, "every act [of the lower, sensitive appetite] harmonizes [*homophonia* ('is of one voice')] with reason" (*NE* 1.13.1102b29).

you become, the more you can trust your emotional reactions to persons and events around you, and the less you will struggle with your lower, animal-like impulses, for there is a greater likelihood that your emotions will incline you to what is morally good for you. Certainly, your emotions may steer you away from the rational good. But if you are virtuous and therefore safeguarded by prudence against faulty judgments during particular movements of emotion, there is a greater likelihood that your emotions will draw you to created goods that share authentically in the good of reason and that are directly in line with our ultimate good (summum bonum). There is a greater likelihood that your emotions will help you become happy and attain your proper human flourishing.

The Penetrating Influence
of Reason on the Human Body

In view of the intimate (substantial) union between the body and soul, we might even extend this line of reasoning to include the bodily dimension of the human person. Although Aristotle affirms that only the sensitive appetite, because it retains a quasi-autonomy, can properly be said to be rational by participation, there seems, at the same time, no reason not to hold that the rational powers exercise a penetrating influence even on the body itself.[223] After all, we know this can occur at the level of the biochemical when a bad choice of the will, a vicious act, is repeatedly executed. For example, the choice of the will, say, to overindulge in alcohol can eventually, in the case of alcoholism, result in a bodily condition of biochemical dependency on the substance of alcohol.

---

[223] Aristotle writes: "[T]here is another part of the soul [viz., the sensitive or animal part], irrational also [like the vegetative, or purely nutritive, part] but participating in reason to some extent" (NE 1.13.1102b13–14).

It seems reasonable to conclude the same occurs as a result of good choices of the will. In the case of the chaste individual, may we not safely suppose that the release, say, of oxytocin, the hormone related to feelings of emotional love, is not triggered as it otherwise is in the unchaste individual (at least inasmuch as oxytocin would be bound up with inordinate sexual feelings)? And we can only speculate what neuroscience might additionally reveal about how psychological states impact the body, or vice versa.

In its own way, then, the body, too, becomes "humanized" through the cultivation of virtue. The virtuous individual, as Aquinas himself intimates, becomes virtuous even in his body, in his eyes, in his muscles, in his biochemical makeup, as it were: "[I]t pertains to man's good that the whole of human nature should be subject to virtue, that is, that virtue should involve the intellectual part, the sensitive part, and the body."[224]

D. CONCLUSION: IMPLICATIONS FOR CLINICAL THERAPY

The consequences that this teaching—in particular, that the passions can be healed to the extent that a person's virtuous character is actually helped, and not merely untroubled, by his passions—bear on the field of clinical psychology are, it seems to me, enormous. Martin Seligman's positive psychology testifies to how fertile the ground of clinical psychology is to receiving the virtue theory outlined above. His psychology, despite pre-scinding from all ethical considerations, places the focus more on a patient's psychological strengths (such as resilience, hope, or any of the virtues) and on how these might be exploited to ensure the patient's psychological well-being. To assert that the more we grow in moral virtue, the more our passions incline us to what is morally good for us speaks volumes of the emotions' ability to share in the healing power of restored mental health and

[224] DM Q. 12, art. 1.

well-being. The beneficial side effects of mental well-being are so extensive that the emotions, much more than just being healed, actually assist in sustaining one's life of mental balance.

The Case of Intemperance:
Doing the Bad As If It Were the Good

Most clinical therapists know that achieving this level of healing demands considerable, if not intensive, toil. This is due in large measure, no doubt, to the moral condition that Aquinas terms *intemperance*. To understand what he means by *intemperance*, and how it concerns the therapist, we need to see how intemperance differs from incontinence (similar to the distinction, examined above, between temperance and continence). The incontinent person is the one who, through the impulse of passion, acts against his proper moral principles. He pursues inordinate bodily pleasures against his better judgment. Like the incontinent, the intemperate individual also pursues bodily pleasures inordinately. However, the difference rests on the fact that the intemperate person pursues these pleasures with the sanction, albeit a perverted one, of his reasoned judgment, as if this were the good and rationally appropriate thing to do, or at least not the morally deficient thing to do. The intemperate person rationalizes to himself that there is nothing wrong with such conduct. He convinces himself, as Aquinas observes, that such bodily pleasures mark his proper good, his ultimate good, the good of reason.[225]

225 "[T]he incontinent exceed the limits of right reason because of passion overcoming them to this extent that they do not act according to right reason, but still not to the extent of convincing them that they should pursue bodily pleasures as good in themselves without restriction [as in the case of the intemperate].... The intemperate man on the contrary is convinced that these pleasures are to be chosen as good in themselves, because of an inclination he has by habit"

Balanced Emotions

Intemperance and Psychopathology

How does this concern the therapist? The therapist's typical patient suffers from a deeply rooted pathological condition, that is, from a *habitual* condition, to use the moral categorization. The typical patient does not suffer from incontinence, since of its very nature, this vice, which consists in a momentary capitulation to an internal impulse of affective desire, is transitory or passing.[226] Granted, many patients may consider their problem to be one of incontinence (although generally not by that name), since they probably see themselves as failing to act in accordance with what they know is good. More than likely, however, their condition results not from a momentary ill turn of the will, committed under a passing affective impulse. It results from a successive series of

---

(Aquinas, *In Ethic.*, bk. 7, lect. 8 [nos. 1430, 1443]). "[T]he intemperate man thinks he should follow carnal delights by perverse judgment on his goal. Quite otherwise the incontinent man has no such idea because his judgment remains unimpaired" (Aquinas, *In Ethic.*, bk. 7, lect. 9 [no. 1454]). Clinicians make a distinction in the treatment of patients suffering from alcohol addiction that would seem to be equivalent to the intemperance/incontinence difference. For therapists tend to consider that patients who have learned to cope with relapses of drinking by minimizing the length and severity of those relapses have attained a successful stage of treatment.

226 The classic study on continence as a momentary vice is found in Bonnie Kent, "Transitory Vice: Thomas Aquinas on Incontinence," in *Journal of the History of Philosophy* 27 (1989): 199–223; in particular Kent notes (pp. 201, 214): "[Aquinas] stresses that intemperance is habitual, incontinence only temporary. Incontinence is like a transitory vice. The incontinent judges from passion, though not from habit, that bodily pleasures are good in themselves.... In this the incontinent differs from the intemperate, who has a perverted conception of the good, but who chooses and acts in accordance with it."

bad choices of the will, doubtless also under some kind of internal affective pull, which has brought about a pathological condition.

The example of alcoholism illustrates this well. The road to alcoholism more often than not begins with a bad, if momentary, choice of the will (an imprudent act) to overindulge in drinking (incontinence). (Clinical psychology affirms that most cases of alcohol addiction begin to develop in a social context.) It continues with the habitual choice of the will (habitual imprudence), driven by affective desire, to do the same, which at this point converts it from incontinence to intemperance. Eventually, this condition of intemperance produces the pathological condition of biochemical addiction or dependency. It is not unheard of for patients receiving treatment for alcoholism to impede treatment by insisting there is nothing wrong with their drinking patterns, a clear case of intemperance. In one case of an alcoholic in treatment, he thought at an early stage of treatment that the only negative consequence of consuming an average of ten to twelve drinks per day was a nagging wife!

The experience of the alcoholic is not unique. Many patients who seek psychotherapy, no matter the nature of their illnesses nor the vastly differing circumstances surrounding them, have plodded similar courses. Habituated behavior sits at the ground level of deep-seated psychopathological conditions. Such behavior might mean accommodating a tendency to a moral flaw, such as overindulging in alcohol. Or it could mean seeking to offset past psychological wounds, such as the hurt incurred from an abusive parent.

Even this latter case may be considered a type of intemperance, since often patients attempt to overcome past hurts because they think, albeit usually subconsciously, this is an appropriate thing to do. The person who avoids intimacy in relationships as a consequence of the psychological pain incurred from unloving parents, or from divorced parents, provides a good case in point.

This type of person, thinking such spurning of intimacy is good, has spent a lifetime making a successive series of bad choices of the will, even if, again, such choices arise from subconscious factors and are made with the assistance of his affective desires. Cognitive therapy in particular explicitly affirms that schema change, or the change of dysfunctional patterns of behavior, presents a stiff challenge to therapists since schemas are so deeply imbedded in their patients. Schemas are examples of intemperance.

Encountering the Irascible and Concupiscible Passions in Therapy

Because pathological conditions are often the fruit of impaired habituated behavior, most patients will view their illness as an evil that is difficult to overcome and, correlatively, the restoration of mental health as a good difficult to attain. This means that, more often than not—and as Daniel McInerny notes in his essay in this book—the typical emotions the therapist will encounter in his patients are those that target a perceived evil that is difficult to surmount (namely, the psychological malady) or a good that is perceived as difficult to attain (namely, psychological well-being, or at least a resolution of the patient's unhappiness). These are the irascible emotions, principally fear, the feeling of wanting to avoid or flee from a difficult evil (such as one's pathological condition), and despair, the feeling of wanting to give up on attaining the difficult good (such as mental health). The therapist, following the lead of positive psychology, should therefore encourage his patients to foster those irascible passions that counter these: courage, the affective urge that impels us to overcome the difficult evil, and hope, the feeling that emboldens us to attain the difficult good.

At the same time, every emotion, even those targeting the arduous good or evil (the irascible emotions), has its origin in the inclination toward the simple good (or aversion from the simple evil) and culminates in the acquisition of the simple good (or in the succumbing to the simple evil). The simple good or evil, of course, concerns the concupiscible emotions. The concupiscible emotions, then, mark the *terminus a quo* and *terminus ad quem* — the beginning point and the end point — of the irascible emotions. Aquinas sees the irascible passions as intermediate movements between the concupiscible passions: the simple good targeted by the concupiscible appetite, Aquinas explains, "has the aspect of end, which is first in the order of intention and last in the order of execution."[227]

In terms of psychotherapy, this means the therapist will need to identify and treat, in addition to the irascible emotions, the fundamental (concupiscible) likes and dislikes, desires and aversions, joys and sorrows that the more complex irascible emotions have as their root cause and end point. We see this in the case of hope, for one can hope only in something to which one first has an inclination through affective love or like, or fear something to which one has had an initial concupiscible aversion. As an example of the former, therapists routinely seek to enkindle hope in couples with marital problems by recalling how the spouses were initially attracted to each other and how they continue to find each other attractive (the concupiscible emotions of love and desire will be at the source of such attraction). Such enkindling of love and desire is intended to equip these patients with (irascible) hope and courage, that is, with the affective drive needed to submit oneself to the grueling task of treatment, to which, in fact, patients often feel an aversion.

Therapists treating certain patients for borderline personality disorder might endeavor to help them overcome their (irasible) sense of despair, which has expressed itself in attempts at suicide, by getting them to recognize that they possess a more

---

[227] *ST* I-II, Q. 25, art. 2.

fundamental affective (concupiscible) desire to live. In certain instances, therapists might employ the so-called devil's-advocate strategy to get their patients to admit that, all things being equal, they would rather live than die.

A Final Word

This essay has broached an issue that merits more reflection and examination. The integrated anthropology, or participated psychology, and the virtue theory espoused by Thomas Aquinas offer a gateway to gaining a penetrating understanding of the invaluable work that clinical therapists accomplish. Both Aquinas and the therapist agree that the fundamental good of enjoying bodily pleasures, and the emotions associated with them, play no small role in the health and well-being of our psyches. Psychological wellness and happiness ensue directly upon the way we live in relation to this fundamental good.

The person of practical wisdom (philosopher and therapist alike) finds that a large part of anxiety and depression can be overcome when a person faces fearful situations courageously, hopes in worthwhile but difficult projects, and patiently holds true to his goals in the midst of suffering.

Shaping positive emotional dispositions, which are the expression of related philosophical virtues and psychological strengths (such as courage, hope, patience, and perseverance), is not an intellectual exercise, though. Rather, it involves a progressive dialogue between reason and will expressed in concrete actions. Moreover, overcoming negative emotional states with positive ones is not done alone. As Daniel McInerny demonstrates, poised strengths are acquired and expressed in social practices that constitute the life of the family, friendship, and school, as well as other civic, economic, and therapeutic communities.

When human development has been upset or the person traumatized the support of psychological therapy and spiritual counsel gives an opportunity to develop virtues by establishing stable practices that promote human flourishing and the common good.

Chapter 9

Poised Strength

Daniel McInerny

A man cannot think himself out of mental evil; for it is actually the organ of thought that has become diseased, ungovernable, and, as it were, independent. He can only be saved by will or faith. The moment his mere reason moves, it moves in the old circular rut; he will go round and round his logical circle, just as a man in a third-class carriage on the Inner Circle will go round and round the Inner Circle unless he performs the voluntary, vigorous, and mystical act of getting out at Gower Street. Decision is the whole business here; a door must be shut forever.

G. K. Chesterton, *Orthodoxy*

Like a man in a carriage endlessly circling an urban roundabout, those suffering from anxiety and depression find themselves trapped in a circular rut of distorted logic. Reason, as Chesterton observes, has become the problem—although it is probably more accurate to say that the problem is the reasoning embedded in distorted passions. Because of this, one might say that the solution to the problems of anxiety and depression, at least for those patients amenable to some form of cognitive behavioral therapy, is to stop thinking. What the anxious or depressed person needs, in short, is to get off the psychological bus whose destination is nowhere, that is, to perform what Chesterton calls the "voluntary, vigorous, and mystical act" of getting out at Gower Street.

This "mystical act" of stepping out of the circular rut is not of course literally thoughtless, but it is not driven by the thoughts that usually captivate the anxious or depressed person. Indeed, to a person used to going round and round the Inner Circle, the thought of getting off at Gower Street may seem like jumping off the edge of the world. Switching his metaphor, Chesterton conjectures that "if you or I were dealing with a mind that was growing morbid, we should be chiefly concerned not so much to give it arguments as to give it air, to convince it that there was something cleaner and cooler outside the suffocation of a single argument." It is the task of the cognitive therapist to provide what Chesterton here calls "air," that wider, saner view in which the anxious or depressed patient sees a new landscape of possibility outside of the suffocating enclosure of his malady. Only when this wider, cooler landscape is acknowledged and believed in is it possible for the patient to feel emboldened enough to step out into it.

The goal then, one might say, for anxious or depressed persons as they enter cognitive therapy is to acquire at least the rudiments of virtue, principally the virtue of *courage*. The various techniques of the cognitive therapist thus serve as so many tools for the development of this crucial feature of a good moral character.

Another way of making this point is to note that psychological disorder and disability can be understood only in light of order and ability. The lack of something in a thing can be understood only in light of what properly belongs to that thing. Thus, if it is true to say that the fundamental problem with anxious or depressed persons—whatever the pathological dimension of their problem—is a lack of courage, then it is obvious that their malady can be fully understood only in light of the nature of courage itself.

To so connect anxiety and depression illuminates a more general truth, namely, that the situation of therapy for the anxious or depressed person exists on the same continuum of moral development on which virtually all human beings exist (the severely mentally handicapped alone being excepted). While the anxious or depressed person may exist at a remedial point along this continuum, nonetheless his goal is the same as anyone's: to flourish as a human being, a goal that the chapters of this volume claim to be a life of virtuous activity.

The foregoing confirms that a philosophical discussion of the nature and development of the virtues would greatly benefit the work of cognitive therapy. But this claim must be understood very carefully. To urge the benefit of a philosophical discussion for cognitive therapy is to not to assert that philosophy can replace the work of cognitive therapy, as if picking up Plato were the automatic solution to the problems of the anxious or the depressed. Nor is it to say that cognitive therapy, when all is said and done, is really a philosophical exercise. No. The speculations of the moral philosopher can never substitute for the techniques of the cognitive therapist. But even as we strictly observe the distinction between the disciplines, we should see them as united in a common enterprise: that of aiding human beings in reaching their full potential in the exercise of virtue. The psychological discipline must be seen as providing special, technical assistance to persons who have encountered psychological difficulties in progressing toward that flourishing existence of which moral philosophers give an account. Clearly, then, the work of the cognitive therapist can be enriched only by the work of moral philosophy and, when it comes to the treatment of anxiety and depression, by an account of the virtue of courage.

What follows, therefore, is a very brief introduction to a philosophical account of courage, what it is and how we acquire it, an account inspired by the thought of St. Thomas Aquinas. It claims only to sketch the outline of this virtue, but to do so in a way that clearly shows the benefit of the account to the cognitive therapist. This will be done by underscoring the ways in which the development of courage manifests itself in what in many ways is a successful therapeutic case involving a woman suffering from depression: a woman we shall call Irene.

Irene and the Irascible Appetite

The ancient Greek word for virtue is *arête*, meaning an excellence or perfection of some sort. The English word *virtue*, from the Latin *virtus*, most literally means "power." So a virtue is a perfection that is also a power. And a moral virtue is a power to perform certain actions in an excellent way.

A perfection or excellence is always a perfection of something else. Excellence at translating French irregular verbs is a perfection *of* an intellectual power. Hence in speaking about virtues we must speak about two kinds of power: the basic power that serves as the potential or seedbed of the virtue, and the power of the fully realized virtue itself. This second power, the virtue itself, is qualitatively different from the basic human power that it brings to perfection—just as the ability to teach French irregular verbs is distinct from the ability of the student to master them.

So in speaking about virtue we must distinguish power as potentiality from power as full actuality. When it comes to the virtue of courage, what is the power as potentiality? As with many of the moral virtues, the power to be perfected is found in the passions. For that is what the moral virtues perfect: not the intellect, principally, but the passions under the tutelage of the intellect. Courage, in fact, perfects two passions, passions that are gathered together with other passions under the umbrella term *the irascible appetite*.

The irascible appetite refers to the passions that come into play when we encounter difficulties in our pursuit of happiness. As such, the irascible appetite is distinguished from the passions that the concupiscible appetite comprises. This distinction is based upon the principle that passions are differentiated by their objects. The concupiscible passions are ordered to sensible good or evil simply considered, whereas the irascible passions are ordered to good or evil under the aspect of difficulty.[228] So imagine someone desiring food, a sensible good. Considered just this way, this desire is a passion of the concupiscible appetite. But if a serious obstacle appears, say a natural disaster, preventing the person from obtaining food, other passions are elicited, passions belonging to the irascible appetite.

Aquinas names joy, sadness, love, and hate as examples of passions associated with the concupiscible passions, and fear and daring, along with hope and despair, as passions associated with the irascible passions.

In light of these distinctions, consider now the case of Irene, a young married woman suffering from depression.[229] The depressive symptoms Irene catalogues for her therapist are low self-worth, hopelessness, difficulty coping with her children, a sense of being kept back by her husband, and a feeling of being stigmatized and socially isolated because her husband has just been released from a drug-abuse treatment center and is now unemployed. Most, if not all, of these thoughts and feelings are expressions of Irene's

---

228 *ST* I-II, Q. 23, art. 1. We should note here an interesting relationship between the concupiscible and irascible appetites. Imagine someone whose life revolves around the pursuit of sensible comforts and who therefore develops a remarkable "courage" in facing up to the difficulties encountered in pursuing his sybaritic dream. What the example reveals is the way in which the irascible appetite follows the movements of the concupiscible appetite. The formation of the irascible appetite is thus only as good as the formation of the concupiscible appetite.

229 Taken from David H. Barlow, ed., *Clinical Handbook of Psychological Disorders: A Step-by-Step Treatment Manual*, 2nd ed. (New York: The Guilford Press, 1993), ch. 6.

irascible appetite, elicited by difficulties Irene experiences in her pursuit of happiness.

What is the happiness that Irene desires? From her catalogue of depressive symptoms one may extrapolate that she wants, first of all, a more flourishing family life. She clearly would like to enjoy a better friendship with her husband and a better relationship with her children. Along with the goods of family life she desires a greater sense of self-worth, an understanding that she is valued by those in her family and in her wider society. And finally, she desires to be better connected with those outside of her family, not to be so socially isolated.

What are the difficulties that are keeping her from these goods? Her husband's drug problem, unemployment, and the consequent social stigmatization she experiences; the unruliness of her children; her feeling badly about herself. In her depressed state, these difficulties are bound up in what can be called *schemas*, ruts of distorted thinking and feeling that keep Irene from attaining her desires. Through their conversations, Irene's therapist identifies three schemas that dominate the way Irene sees the world: (1) a subjugation schema—a fear of being controlled by other people; (2) an emotional deprivation schema—a fear that other people do not care about her; and lastly, (3) an incompetence schema—a fear that she cannot do anything right. These schemas constitute the psychological dimension of the difficulties Irene faces in her pursuit of happiness.

Notice that all three schemas are constructed around some fear, or as we more often say, anxiety. Difficulty naturally produces fear, a retreat from the evil embodied in whatever obstacle is keeping us from the good. Irene is trapped by the fear that she is being controlled by other people, that other people do not care about her, and that she cannot do anything right. At its extreme, fear tends to despair, the feeling that the desired good is beyond attainment. Although not quite at the point of total despair, Irene's captivation by her depressive schemas generates in her something that is at least very close to despair.

Another irascible passion evinced by Irene in her catalogue of depressive symptoms is a desire to be valued, to be recognized favorably by others for the person she is and for the good she does. Among ancient and medieval philosophers, including Aquinas, this passion is described as a passion for honor. Such a passion often confuses the public registrations usually associated with honor—awards, ceremonies, gifts, offices—with the moral excellence that really deserves such registrations (whether one actually receives them or not). Sometimes we want to be the center of some circle of attention when we in fact do not deserve to be. But in itself the passion for honor is a legitimate one. The public registration of our worth, and most of all those more intimate registrations made by our families and friends, is a genuine human good.

Anger, too, another irascible passion, although not explicitly alluded to in Irene's catalogue of depressive symptoms, is no doubt also in play within her schemas, although perhaps not in such a way that it directly manifests itself. The difficulty that anger specifically wants to attack is the difficulty of an injustice, real or apparent, that has been done to a person. Irene's feeling of being kept back by her husband and of being socially stigmatized quite likely involve anger toward her husband for not acting more responsibly and generously, thus giving her more room for action and more opportunity for the approval of others.

Irene's depressive schemas keep her in retreat from the difficulties in her path to a more flourishing life. She does not easily manifest those other irascible passions that urge us toward the difficulties in an attempt to win the good by overcoming them. Yet at a crucial juncture Irene does clearly manifest what Aquinas calls the "attacking" irascible passions: hope and daring.

Any progress toward a flourishing existence must initially be inspired by the notion that such an existence is truly possible.

Philosophical Virtues and Psychological Strengths

The goal may be remote, it may lie at the end of a perilous journey, but if the goal is a real possibility, however difficult to attain, it has the power to summon us to it, to inspire actions of which we did not know we were capable. Hope is the passion that encourages us to keep pursuing such difficult goods no matter the enormity of the obstacles keeping us from them.

The presentation of new possibilities for action is not, of course, the sole propriety of cognitive therapy. Normally, human agents find sources of hope in their parents and other family members, in friends and teachers, and the leaders of the social institutions in which they play a part. A young person's parents and teachers, for example, are two of the chief sources of a young person's ideas of what is possible in his or her life. A revered mentor may open up unseen vistas of opportunity. But one of the difficulties that anxious and depressed persons must face is the feeling of constriction of such sources of hopeful opportunity. But as with patients like Irene, cognitive therapy can step in and offer the hope that a flourishing existence remains possible. On a local radio show Irene hears a piece about the successes of cognitive therapy, and this news gives her hope that she might find some solution to her problems, that her dreams for a happier existence might be realized. Hope is thus the opposite of despair. While despair gives up on ever obtaining the good, hope maintains the sense that obtaining the good is still possible, despite the difficulties.

Daring is a passion that springs from hope. It desires to attack the threatening obstacle on account of the good that is hoped for. This passion is very familiar to us from watching sports, when we speak of offensive players "attacking" defenses as they attempt to score a goal. In the language of sports, the passion of daring is often referred to as a player's "heart," his ability to look an opponent square in the eye and not back down. Irene's daring is on display when, after hearing the radio show, she calls up a cognitive therapist and makes an appointment in spite of her fears, which very probably included the fear of the social stigma often attached to those who undergo psychological therapy. Irene's situation makes clear that hope and daring do not rule out fear, although hope does rule out despair. One can hope for a difficult good and even face up to evil obstacles with some daring, and all the while feel fearful of the evil that one confronts.[230]

Learning How to See Again

In speaking of Irene's decision to enter cognitive behavioral therapy, we have already crossed over from a discussion of the passions strictly speaking, to a discussion of human action. Successful human action always involves some kind of passionate response to the world, but it also moves beyond the mere feeling of passion to the making of a reasonable choice. To borrow a metaphor from Aristotle, the passions stand to the reason as children do to a parent. The parent's job is not simply to suppress the child's unruly emotion, but to educate the child's passions through an artful combination of discipline and persuasion. Once the passions have become mature under the tutelage of reason, we say that a person has become morally virtuous.

Irene's decision to call a cognitive therapist and make an appointment is itself an act of virtue, specifically, the virtue of courage. This is Irene's first bold step into what must seem to her a perilous new world. However, at this juncture it cannot be said that Irene possesses the virtue of courage. There is a distinction between an isolated act characteristic of a given moral habit, and the possession of the moral habit itself. The first successful attempt to actualize a potency is not the same as the full actualization of that potency—although it is a necessary and laudable first step.

---

[230] These distinctions are taken from Aquinas's discussions throughout ST I-II, Q. 40–46.

Philosophical Virtues and Psychological Strengths

But for an action even to be an isolated act characteristic of a given moral virtue, it must be directed by reason. When reason itself becomes perfected in its work of disciplining and persuading the passions, moreover, we say that reason itself has acquired a virtue: the virtue of prudence.

As the discussion of prudence in this volume makes clear, prudence, while always connected to the moral virtues, is an intellectual virtue necessary for right action. The work of prudence is essentially one of bringing a person's global view of the good to bear upon a particular action. It begins with universal considerations—however vague and unarticulated—and ends with very specific considerations based upon the circumstances of a particular individual. Irene, for example, has a general notion that a greater sense of self-worth is a significant part of her flourishing. This is the difficult good that she hopes for. By the time she enters cognitive therapy, she has realized that one of the best ways, if not the only way, of achieving a greater sense of self-worth—in her particular circumstances—is to undergo cognitive therapy. This judgment is not one that applies universally to all human beings. While everyone desires a robust sense of self-worth as part of his flourishing, not all require cognitive therapy as a means to attain it. Prudence is always directed to the particular case, however much it gets its start from universal considerations about the human good.

Prudence is best described as that part of virtuous action which hooks us up to reality, with what truly is the case, as opposed to what we simply feel (which may be based upon appearance rather than reality). By entering cognitive therapy, Irene, with her therapist's help, endeavors to scrutinize in light of a more accurate view of reality the distorted reasoning that drives her passions. To amend a phrase from an essay by Josef Pieper, Irene's goal in cognitive therapy is to dismantle her depressive schemas and to learn how to see reality again.

Poised Strength

Precisely how this will be done is in the provenance of the therapist. It is up to the therapist to plumb the origins of Irene's depressive schemas and to discover the therapies that will best help her. In probing Irene's perspective on her marital problems, for example, her therapist makes a decision not to focus on the marriage as the first therapeutic target, reasoning that it would require too much time before providing symptom relief. The theoretical distinction between symptom and root cause and the judgment not to focus on Irene's marriage right away, so that Irene might more quickly experience symptom relief, are just the sort of discernments only the professional therapist can provide.

Yet it is interesting that in cognitive behavioral therapy as in moral philosophy, dialectic, or what Irene's case study calls *collaborative empiricism*, is of paramount importance in helping someone arrive at a clearer appreciation of reality, and thus in developing the virtue of prudence. This is not to say that the dialectic practiced by the therapist is the same as that practiced by Socrates. Rather, the claim is that the activity of questioning, of helping others test their assumptions against their own and others' experience, is one of the chief ways in which human beings gain insight into moral reality.

Of further interest is that such dialectic in the context of both therapy and moral inquiry often arises out of some conflict. Plato's dialogue *Euthyphro*, for example, arises out of the moral conflict between a son's pious duty to his father and the son's duty to ensure that murderers are brought to justice — even if a murderer happens to be one's father. Similarly, the dialectic that Irene undergoes in therapy is generated by her marital and other conflicts.

The aim of both sorts of dialectic, philosophical and therapeutic, is to resolve moral conflict by gaining insight into a truth that resolves the conflict. This insight is in no sense automatic or guaranteed. When it comes, as we see both in Plato's Socratic dialogues and in Irene's case study, it often comes only after much turmoil, through which a deeply cherished belief is reduced to absurdity.

Take a very simple example from Irene's case study. Early in their sessions Irene's therapist focused on Irene's inactivity and withdrawal, in particular, her tendency to stay in bed all day. As the case study makes clear, Irene's therapist did not directly debate or exhort Irene to get out of bed. Instead, through a form of dialectical questioning, he challenged her to test her own assumption that staying in bed all day was a solution to her problems. In reference to Irene's testing of this assumption, the case study even employs the Platonic language of examining a hypothesis.[231] By the second session, Irene admits the deficiencies of staying in bed:

> About staying in bed versus getting up, I thought about that the other day. I thought when I told you—like I said something about like keeping the bad things away from me. Like when I was under the covers or just staying in bed, they weren't really kept away from me. Like I always felt like I was always beating them down, I always had to ward them off. I don't know. I thought I told you it made me feel better to stay there, but I don't know if it really did. I don't think it did, now that I am thinking about it.[232]

As she reflected upon staying in bed all day, Irene discovered that staying in bed did not even provide the temporary relief from her depressive symptoms that she first told her therapist it did. Through a dialectical exercise, in which she puts herself to the question, Irene's view of what truly is the case about herself and her problems is adjusted. The hypothesis is swiftly reduced to absurdity—and discarded. Irene literally comes out of the

---

[231] As at *Republic*, 511a and following.
[232] Barlow, *Clinical Handbook*, 288.

suffocating enclosure underneath her covers into the clean, cool air of reality.

This very simple example makes clear the falsity of regarding cognitive therapy as a value-neutral exercise, as an activity that not only is distinct but also disconnected from the concerns of the moral philosopher. For in calling into question and ultimately discarding her practice of staying in bed all day, Irene is not merely redefining what works for her. She is rather, with her therapist's help, engaged in identifying the act of staying in bed all day (in *her* circumstances) as a moral evil to be overcome. True enough, Irene's report to her therapist emphasizes her feelings. Where before she felt that staying in bed all day made her feel better, on reflection she realized that it did not really do so. But Irene's change of feeling is caused by a closer examination of the reality of staying in bed all day. When she provides for herself a more thorough description of staying in bed all day, she remembers it as a constant struggle against the "bad things."

Reality, in short, causes a change in perception and a consequent change in feeling. And it is clear from the therapist's response to Irene's comments quoted above that this change in perception and feeling is positive yardage toward the goal of a more flourishing human existence: "It is funny that when you talked about it, your recollection was that [staying in bed all day] actually was comforting, but that sometimes happens with people. It happens to me too. I think that something is really good that's not so hot when I actually check it out."[233]

The therapist here is not merely massaging Irene's feelings, going with what works and leaving moral truth to the philosophers. He is acknowledging the objective good in getting out of bed and taking responsibility for one's life. To link this to another discussion in this volume, the therapist's and Irene's grasp of this

---

[233] Barlow, *Clinical Handbook*, 288–289.

objective good is ultimately grounded in their respective grasp of the first precepts of the natural law. All human beings perceive, in other words, that part of the reality of being a rational agent is that we should strive to be pro-active in our pursuit of a flourishing life. This does not mean seeking some caricature of independent self-expression. It means becoming a source of virtuous action—always in conjunction with others—in service to the common good, a service which entails, at very least, the act of getting out of bed in the morning.

Desiring Life Like Water, Yet Drinking Death Like Wine

We have noted that Irene's decision to undergo cognitive therapy is an act characteristic of the virtue of courage, a decision that embodies the beginnings of a transformation of the irascible passions by prudence. Let us now talk more about the structure of courage.

An act of courage evinces a double, apparently conflicting movement. Chesterton makes this point eloquently in *Orthodoxy*:

> Paganism declared that virtue was in a balance; Christianity declared it was in a conflict: the collision of two passions apparently opposite.... Courage is almost a contradiction in terms.... A soldier surrounded by enemies, if he is to cut his way out, needs to combine a strong desire for living with a strange carelessness about dying. He must not merely cling to life, for then he will be a coward, and will not escape. He must not merely wait for death, for then he will be a suicide, and will not escape. He must seek his life in a spirit of furious indifference to it; he must desire life like water and yet drink death like wine.[234]

[234] G. K. Chesterton, *Orthodoxy* (New York: Image Books, 1990), 93.

Poised Strength

What makes an act of courage a seemingly paradoxical reconciliation of irreconcilables is the opposing tendencies of fear and daring. Fear wants to get away from the evil obstacle; daring, for the sake of the good hoped for, wants to attack it. But to bring fear and daring into harmony in an act of courage that requires the direction of prudence. Prudence orders the good that one stands to lose in confronting an evil obstacle to the good that one stands to gain by confronting it, as when a solider subordinates his personal safety to the good of preserving his entire city. He does not cling to his personal safety at all costs — that would lead him to cowardice; nor does he disregard the good of his personal safety — that would lead him to recklessness. What the soldier does is live the hierarchy of goods in his passions and his choices, respecting the intrinsic value of each good while recognizing that one is still more important than the other. This is what leaves him free to "seek his life in a spirit of furious indifference to it"; to "desire life like water and yet drink death like wine." This is one way of talking about Aristotle's Golden Mean.

Aquinas provides further insightful analysis of the act of courage, distinguishing two features of the attacking movement of courage (the movement motivated by daring), and two features of the enduring movement of courage (the movement that checks fear).[235] The first of the features connected to attack is called *confidence*. This is that attitude of hopeful trust that one will be able to perform a great and honorable deed, such as aiding in the defense of one's city. The second feature of a courageous attack Aquinas calls *magnificence*. This feature pertains to the actual execution of the courageous deed; it is the quality of following through on the action determined by prudence. This following through includes both the planning and the performance of the courageous deed.

[235] *ST* II-II, Q. 128, unicus.

Philosophical Virtues and Psychological Strengths

The two features connected to the endurance of evil have familiar names: *patience* and *perseverance*. Patience is the ability not to be overcome by sadness when evils arise. It is that quality by which we are able to choose to stay put and endure difficult things for the sake of the good. Perseverance brings in the time element. When our troubles are prolonged, we need a quality by which we are able not just to stay put and endure, but to stay put even when no end to our suffering is in sight.

At the beginning of therapy, Irene remarks that for a long time she has wanted to join something. In particular, Irene yearns to be involved with others in a local tennis club. However, Irene's sense of self-worth and self-confidence are so diminished that she does not even know how she should go about doing it. But after her therapist walks her through the necessary steps, breaking the process of joining a team into manageable parts, Irene realizes she can do it. What is happening in this situation is that the therapist is helping Irene recognize that an act of courage will help her dismantle the depressive schemas that control her life and thus pave the way for future acts of virtue and greater fulfillment. Realizing that a strong sense of self-worth comes in part from a sense of accomplishment within the context of community, the therapist breaks down for Irene a simple act of virtue. In joining the tennis club, Irene once again manifests the harmonious action of courage: the double movement of hopeful daring and patient endurance by which she faces up to her fears.

This example is particularly important because it manifests an aspect of the irascible appetite that is of special import for those suffering from anxiety or depression. In cataloging the irascible passions, we noted the passion having to do with recognition, or honor, and how this passion is connected to a strong sense of self-worth, as recognition by others, especially by those we admire, is one of the most important ways in which we establish a strong sense of self-worth. Yet a focus on feelings of worthlessness is one of the preoccupations of the anxious and depressed, preoccupations that are distortions of what really is the case. What Irene needs, for instance, is not to feel worthless. Such feelings involve the wrong estimation of her value, first of all as a person and secondly as a person with particular talents. Instead Irene needs to feel that she is someone of inestimable worth, yet someone who, like everyone else in one form or another, needs the assistance of others to help her realize her capabilities.

Thus the virtue that is of great moment to the anxious and depressed is the virtue by which we rightly regard the difficult good of achieving recognition by others. Actually, we should say two virtues related to recognition, for as Aquinas points out, two virtues are needed in order to perfect the two opposing tendencies related to recognition: on the one hand, the tendency to focus on those gifts and achievements of ours that deserve the recognition of others, and on the other hand, the tendency to focus on our inability and weakness.[236]

For Irene, of course, her depressed schemas keep her focused on her inabilities and failures, to the point of causing her grossly to distort her weaknesses. In helping her join the tennis club, her therapist hopes to counteract these schemas by giving her a sense of accomplishment and pride in herself. As her courage matures, a harmony between the opposing tendencies related to recognition is established, a harmony established, once again, by a prudent grasp of reality. For it is prudence that rightly discerns that for Irene to participate in a tennis club is worthy of recognition, if by no one else than by her husband and her therapist. And it is also prudence that rightly discerns that Irene is still much in need of her therapist's assistance if she is going to grow in such virtuous self-sufficiency. The virtue that embodies the former discernment might be called *proper pride*. The virtue that embodies the latter

---

[236] *ST* II-II, Q. 129, art. 3, ad. 4.

discernment is called *humility*.[237] Because both virtues have to do with the difficult good of recognition, they are both virtues of the irascible appetite.

To round out this brief discussion of the virtues associated with the irascible passions, it would be appropriate to turn now to the virtue known as *meekness*, which perfects the passion of anger, with particular emphasis upon how depressed persons like Irene may need to practice letting their anger be shown to others in appropriate ways, rather than keeping it all in.[238] But another dimension of the virtues requires attention before we bring this discussion to a close, and that is the social context required for the exercise of virtue.

The Household of the Virtues

Irene's case study makes clear that her negative thoughts about herself, her feeling of being overwhelmed by her difficulties, and her sense of hopelessness about the future are all directly related to the dysfunction of her marriage and, more deeply, to the dysfunction within her own family while she was growing up. Maturation in the virtues of the irascible passions thus seems to require the proper functioning of the family. Indeed, all the virtues require a well-functioning social context if they are to flourish, the kind of social context that we find in practices.

---

[237] But humility, it should be needless to say, is not a virtue by which we judge ourselves, in whatever circumstances, incapable, small, of little or no worth. Humility is the ability to make a *true* estimate of our ability to attain a difficult good. Human nature being what it is, a true estimate must always involve an assessment of some weakness that we have. This estimate is a sober one, but it is not an exaggerated one. To exaggerate one's weaknesses—or even to invent some—in an effort to be humble is only to parody this virtue. See *ST* II-II, Q. 161.

[238] See *ST* II-II, Q. 157.

Poised Strength

Practices are social contexts in which the common goods central to human happiness are pursued according to established rules and standards, in such a way that encourages the human capacity to acquire virtue.[239] Practices, one might say, are the household of the virtues. Let us break down this definition of practices by staying with the example of the family.

It is generally the case that human beings are raised within the context of a family, whether natural or surrogate. Within the family human beings exhibit their natural desire for certain common goods, such as the moral goods of mutual affection and friendship, and the intellectual goods of play, learning, and conversation.

The pursuit of the common goods of family life, however, is not willy-nilly. Certain rules and standards of action establish the broad boundaries within which we participate in them. Within the family parents will no doubt lay down certain rules ("Three major acts of disobedience during the week means no television on the weekend"). Even prior to the house rules of particular parents, there are rules governing the pursuit of family goods. When a parent instructs a three-year-old not to hit his sibling when that sibling takes his toy, the parent ultimately relies upon a rule — "Do not harm those with whom you live" — that has an internal, essential relationship to the common good of sibling friendship. This kind of rule, as distinct from the no-television rule, is not

---

[239] This definition of *practices* is paraphrased from Alasdair MacIntyre, who defines a practice as "any coherent and complex form of socially-established cooperative human activity through which goods internal to that form of activity are realized in the course of trying to achieve those standards of excellence which are appropriate to, and partially definitive of, that form of activity, with the result that human powers to achieve excellence [i.e., virtue], and human conceptions of the ends and goods involved, are systematically extended" (*After Virtue*, 2nd ed. [Notre Dame, Indiana: University of Notre Dame Press, 1984], 187).

a mere matter of parental prudence. For without obedience to this kind of rule, the common good of sibling friendship, and the virtues required to sustain it, would not simply be difficult; they would be impossible.

This kind of rule is another example of what Aquinas calls a first precept of the natural law, a precept, discernible by human reason, that governs our natural desires for a range of human goods, including the common goods of family life. The first precepts of the natural law provide human reason with its original direction to the common goods genuinely fulfilling of human beings.

So when it comes to developing the virtue of courage, a child must first be confirmed by his parents in obedience to the natural precept proscribing harm to family members. He must learn that this rule is essential both for the protection of the family in its very existence and for the pursuit of the other common goods of family life. The good example of his parents and siblings, along with teachers and other social influences, will further help the child move beyond obedience to this simple rule and toward the fully mature habit by which he protects the goods of the family against evil influences of all sorts.

Within the context of family life, therefore, we can discern an interrelationship between our natural desire for common goods that perfect our nature as human beings, and the standards, natural and prudential, that guide our pursuit of these goods. At their best, practices like the family allow us to internalize and habituate ourselves to the proper pursuit of the common goods that make up the core of human happiness.[240]

---

[240] The common goods that we pursue within practices, however, are not the only goods that human beings pursue. Money, pleasure, and honor are goods that contribute to human fulfillment. They are also goods that can be achieved externally to practices and so can compete with the common goods and virtuous activities involved with practices. When external

Even against this sketch, it is clear that without a well-functioning family, it will be extremely difficult for Irene to grow in the virtues of the irascible passions—precisely because her family is the central practice in her life, the main source of moral nourishment for her growth in virtue. As the city is to the solider, so is the family to Irene. True, the situation of cognitive therapy provides a remedial sort of practice in which Irene, like a plant brought out of a dark closet, can begin to reorient herself toward the light of virtue. Moreover, her participation in the tennis club, as well as the job she eventually takes, provide other social contexts that might well function as practices. But nothing can replace the family as the most important practice in her life, and so the goal of her cognitive therapy must be the renewal of the practice of Irene's family life. For this reason, it is disappointing at the end of the case study to find Irene deciding to leave her husband. Had she been more attuned to the nature of the virtues and their necessary relationship to the proper functioning of practices, perhaps she would have recognized that her psychological well-being was intimately bound up with that of her husband and children and so would have wanted to do more to endure and overcome the difficulties in her marriage, such as seeking out marital counseling. This backing down from the difficult situation of her marriage only works against Irene's maturation in courage.[241]

Conclusion

In his book *Sources of the Self*, the philosopher Charles Taylor observes that it "has frequently been remarked by psychoanalysts

---

goods are pursued for any reason other than for the better pursuit of virtuous activity, practices begin to dysfunction.

[241] Of course, there is no guarantee that marital counseling would have helped save their marriage or that Irene's husband would even have agreed to participate in it. Success is not always the reward of virtue.

that the period in which hysterics and patients with phobias and fixations formed the bulk of their clientele, starting in their classical period with Freud, has recently given way to a time when the main complaints center around 'ego loss,' or a sense of emptiness, flatness, futility, lack of purpose, or loss of self-esteem."[242] It is fair to assume that such a view would be shared not only by contemporary psychoanalysts, but also by contemporary cognitive therapists. Throughout the world of psychological counseling, complaints of ego loss, loss of self-esteem, and a sense of emptiness are commonplace, just as we see in the case study of Irene's depression.

Taylor himself speculates that these complaints, whatever their pathological or non-pathological expression, are due in some way to what he calls a "loss of horizon."[243] By this he means a moral and spiritual framework that helped human beings make ultimate sense out of their lives. What the modern world has lost, according to Taylor, and which the premodern world seemed to possess, is a framework that stands unquestioned, "which helps define the demands by which [people] judge their lives and measure, as it were, their fullness or emptiness: the space of fame in the memory and song of the tribe, or the call of God as made clear in revelation, or, to take another example, the hierarchical order of being in the universe."[244]

No form of psychological therapy can hope, all by itself, to retrieve for the modern world an unquestioned moral and spiritual framework that will save depressed patients like Irene from the condition of being, in Walker Percy's phrase, "lost in the cosmos." But by holding fast to the tradition of the virtues, especially as that tradition is articulated by St. Thomas Aquinas, cognitive

[242] Charles Taylor, *Sources of the Self* (Cambridge, Massachusetts: Harvard University Press, 1989), 19.
[243] Ibid.
[244] Ibid., 16.

therapy can play a critical role in helping anxious or depressed patients find their place again within the world. When its own practice is in good order, cognitive therapy can inspire in patients a real sense of confidence that a wider, saner life devoted to the virtues within the context of healthy practices is still possible. And with that hope in their hearts, patients will be able to take that first, modest, yet decisive step into a more fulfilling life—a step as simple, yet as full of mystical purpose, as getting out at Gower Street.

Human love is neither animal impulse nor impersonal encounter nor commercial commodity. As David Franks affirms, love in one form or another underlies all human emotion, commitment, and action. However, since diverse loves, desires, pleasures, and joys so often conflict with each other, the better part of human life involves the ordering of love, that is, the personalizing of love at all levels and in all relationships according to one's commitments and according to the good of reason. Human love and true joy is won in the tempering of desire, in its testing, and in its purifying. Such tempering of desire differentiates the types of love and responsibility that are proper to the home, the community, and the workplace. Finally, it underlies the therapy and practices that contributes to the fullest expressions of the human person and society.

Chapter 10

Tempered Desire

J. David Franks

My three virtues are no different than men
and women in their homes.
Children are never the ones who work.
But no one ever works except for children.

Charles Péguy[245]

What is desire? What does it mean for a human person to desire? Is it a matter of brute animal impulse or of a fate that overcomes us? Or is it a matter of human freedom, of the integration of the human personality? The pursuit of this question is crucial for theology, philosophy, and psychology[246] and can serve as a fruitful point of contact for these disciplines, for here we get to the heart of what it means to live a fully human life.

Our most urgent and fundamental desires pertain to the maintenance of life, both in the individual human organism as well as in the species: the desires for food and for sex. This is as it is for

---

[245] Charles Péguy, *The Portal of the Mystery of Hope*, trans. David Louis Schindler, Jr. (Grand Rapids, Michigan: Eerdmans, 1996), 12.

[246] When I use the term *psychology* in this essay, I primarily intend it to mean psychotherapy in its theoretical self-appropriation.

all animals. But we are peculiar animals, ones who also seek truth and seek to love and be loved. We are animals who aspire to live in truth, goodness, and beauty, and we craft a peculiar ecosystem called culture in which to live out our intelligent animality. How our primordial desires for food and sex relate to the desires of our minds and hearts is a key question that theology, philosophy, and psychology must address. And it would be best if they addressed it in common.

In Christian tradition, it is the virtue of temperance that properly orders our natural, necessary attraction to objects that serve the requirements of biological life and orders this attraction according to our intelligent recognition of the full amplitude—the possibilities and responsibilities—of human personhood. Our intelligence integrates these impulsive passions into the wholeness of our personality through the virtue of temperance.

As can be confirmed by common experience, nature has joined the most immediately felt pleasures to the satisfaction of the requirements of biological life. It only makes sense that something so important as the preservation of the individual organism and the preservation of the species as a whole would have such an incentive. What can also be confirmed by reference to common experience, however, is the fact that given precisely the intensity and necessity of the pleasures involved, we can get lost in them, losing sight of the horizon of human community, the arena of human exertion and aspiration. The danger is that our desires for the great goods of food and sex, truly perfective of our animal nature, should become willfully wrenched out of their full human context, become atomized and depersonalized, broken into blind urges without reference to human wholeness—without reference to the true, the good, and the beautiful, without reference to the ones we love and for whom we are responsible.

This is a perpetual danger, for we can easily fall into a selfish fixation on maximizing pleasure. But this danger has been uniquely heightened in our age, with the ideological pressures of a consumerist culture bending us back upon ourselves, so that our desires for objects that should be for the sake of serving life, in the individual and in the species, serve instead a decaying self, a tyrannical desiring-machine.[247] Even so seemingly self-focused an activity as eating ought to belong to the great rhythms of human culture. When we eat, we do so at the table of human fellowship, so that we may be strong enough to provide for our families, to work for the common good, and to pursue truth.

And yet, we have an epidemic of obesity in a country like the United States and an epidemic of self-destructive sexual activity. Intrinsically related to these unhappy frustrations of human nature is a widespread selfish seeking after sensual gratification inflamed by a consumerist culture. Theology, philosophy, and psychology ought to march in the vanguard of the cause of advancing the human good, and so these disciplines must each be concerned with the particular historical conditions that have exacerbated a persistent tendency to depersonalize the natural desire for bodily goods. Thus, to varying degrees, each of these disciplines must

---

[247] The reduction of human persons to desiring-machines is to be found in the nightmare sexual-revolutionary vision of the philosopher Gilles Deleuze and the clinical psychoanalyst Félix Guattari in their *Anti-Oedipus: Capitalism and Schizophrenia*, trans. Robert Hurley, Mark Seem, and Helen Lane (Minneapolis: University of Minnesota Press, 1977). These authors claim the banner of "desire" and "life" against "capitalism." Such is the irony of ideology. Their failure to make intelligent distinctions concerning, say, the amplitude of human desire exposes the vulnerable, especially women and children, to the unchecked rapacity of a phallocentric sexual regime. This regime is controlled by a deformed masculine desire that exploits women, violates girls, makes war on female fertility, and aborts children—all to obtain pleasure without commitment. Deleuze and Guattari are pleased to call this liberation. This is the colonizing logic of the sexual revolution.

engage in a critique of ideology—in particular, a critique of the consumerist, bourgeois ideology that threatens the human person. And, to do so, theology, philosophy, and psychology must each have a clear sense of the nature of the human person, and of the importance of temperance for human flourishing.

This essay begins with a section that briefly traces the main lines of consumerist ideology. I propose that—given consumerism's profound negative impact on human desire—psychotherapy, as a healing art, might have an interest in demystifying this ideology in light of the true requirements of human happiness. The consumerist betrayal of human desire can be rectified only through the virtue of temperance, and so the second section concentrates on giving an account of that virtue. Section three fleshes out the relation of temperance and desire against the backdrop of the sexual revolution, leading in the fourth section to a focused treatment of the virtue of chastity—one of the component virtues of temperance. Sexual desire can be either intensely elevating or fundamentally disintegrating for the human personality. It tends toward the latter without the virtue of chastity, especially given the particular disposition of our consumerist culture and the hegemony of the misogynist regime of exploitative sexuality.[248] The

[248] This phallocentric socio-sexual regime depends on an ideology of loveless sex, which fractures human desire by separating sex from self-sacrificial love and procreation. Thus this ideology must wage war on female fertility, for the natural, dynamic rhythms of female fertility demystify the ideology of loveless sex: the female body as such reveals the untruth of separating sex from faithful, fruitful, and lifelong love. Women who embrace the natural rhythms of their fertility pose a mortal threat to the phallocratic regime.

For the French feminist Luce Irigaray, *phallocracy* refers to the rule of the phallus, where the phallus is understood in a generally Lacanian sense (see her *This Sex Which Is Not One*, trans. Catherine Porter and Carolyn Burke [Ithaca, New York: Cornell University Press, 1985]). In my usage of the term,

consequences of this disintegration are indicated in section five. The concluding section presents a literary image of healed desire to give a glimpse of human wholeness, beyond the fracturing of desire—an image of human desire in all its beauty, a desire that

phallus retains more of its physiological reference. For my purposes, I would emphasize that the phallocratic order has everything to do with a sexual order that serves a perverse (in the technical Augustinian sense) masculine *libido dominandi.* This sexual order is not merely a private one: it is the social-political reality. It is so much the social-political reality that we do not even see it. The utilitarian-consumerist culture, for instance, is fundamentally phallocratic. This reality, which comprises everything from the massive objectification of women in advertising (and the destruction of young girls' psyches that this entails, so that they internalize their slavery to the male sexual order) to hormonal contraception (which is the phallocratic colonization of the female body, rendering it completely disposable for the service of male desire) to, above all, abortion (which is the most brutal weapon wielded against women and girls to discipline their unruly fertility). The so-called "feminist" establishment embraces this violence against the female body as liberation: here the introjection of heteronomy is total. Only a new feminism, starting from an affirmation of the female body, can break the spell of such ideological sorcery.

For too long "feminism" has colluded with the ideology of deformed masculine (that is, bourgeois) desire, the ideology of loveless sex. As the sociologist Arlie Russell Hochschild has pointed out, commenting on the "abduction of feminism" as evidenced in advice books for women: "[These books] conserve the damage capitalism did to manhood instead of *critiquing* it .... In recycling male rules of love, modern advice books for women assert that it's a 'feminine' practice to subordinate the importance of love, to delay falling in love until after consolidating a career, to separate love from sex, and for married women to have occasional affairs" (*The Commercialization of Intimate Life: Notes from Home and Work* [Berkeley: University of California Press, 2003], 27).

expends itself for the sake of other persons, loosing into the world the graciousness of love.

I. Consumerist Depersonalization
and the Mission of Psychotherapy

At the end of the nineteenth century, this nation underwent what has been called the second industrial revolution: the shift from the factory system to the vertically integrated corporation (which encompassed everything from the extraction of natural resources to advertising and marketing). Thus a mass-production and mass-consumption economy emerged. This fundamental change in economic structure led to an explosion in urbanization, as well as to a massive increase in the number of women entering the workforce. With these changes came the bohemian mixture of intellectuals, socialists, trade-union activists, and the wealthy typified by New York's Greenwich Village. And with the elitism of this new pattern of urban life came a contempt for traditional views of sex and marriage. Thus, the second industrial revolution slowly brought about a significant restructuring of social life. Indeed, the sexual revolution, popularly thought to have emerged out of nowhere in the sixties, in fact began during this *fin-de-siècle* transformation. And this was the advent of the consumerist economy: there was now a corporate interest in redirecting desire away from the moderation of the Victorian family system into self-indulgence.[249]

---

[249] For more on the second industrial revolution, see David S. Landes, *The Unbound Prometheus: Technological Change and Industrial Development in Western Europe from 1750 to the Present*, 2nd ed. (Cambridge: Cambridge University Press, 2003), 520 and elsewhere. Eli Zaretsky links the emergence of psychoanalysis to this revolution in his *Secrets of the Soul: A Social and Cultural History of Psychoanalysis* (New York: Alfred A. Knopf, 2004). In a way particularly relevant to this essay, he notes the link between consumerism and sexual

Tempered Desire

Why this historical excursus in an essay on the virtue of temperance? The desires of the human person have to be treated in light of the ideological pressures exerted on them. The history of our desire must be investigated. If our concern as psychologists, philosophers, and theologians is to help advance the human good through a clear understanding of the desires of the human person, it is necessary to engage in ideology-critique to analyze the deformations of desire.

Significant elements of the current economic order seek maximization of profit through the inflaming of desires for sensual gratification—sex sells, as they say.[250] This necessarily involves a reorientation of human desire from its expansive natural habitat of ethical commitment and spiritual aspiration to a contracted focus on bodily desire now sundered from its personalizing context. Such advertising keeps consumers in a state of sensual excitation, vaguely uneasy until the next thing is acquired. This diverts emotional energy from the true ends of sensual gratification: to maintain the human organism for the sake of personal co-existence, for loving well and living in the truth. It is

---

revolution: "[Men and women] separated from traditional familial morality, gave up their obsession with self-control and thrift, and entered into the sexualized 'dreamworlds' of mass consumption on behalf of a new orientation to personal life" (p. 9). A more incisive analysis of the connection between sexual revolution and the massive socioeconomic changes of the late Progressive Era can be found in Angela Franks, *Margaret Sanger's Eugenic Legacy: The Control of Female Fertility* (Jefferson, North Carolina: McFarland & Co., 2005), 22–29, for example.

250 It should be noted that consumerism and capitalism cannot simply be equated. There is no logical or historical entailment such that an economic order that favors free entrepreneurial initiative over statist social engineering need depend on the inflaming of desires for sensual gratification. There are real human needs to be served by economic activity, after all.

no accident that our consumerist economy, which expanded so rapidly in the Internet globalization of the 1990s, has seen an explosion in pornography.

The consumerist contraction of the human spirit is clear from the anti-natalist (the anti-child) bias of the consumerist economy, which assumes that consumption need be in competition with reproduction. (If we attend to the fact that our two basic biological drives are those for food and for sex, we can see how inverted this opposition is.) Many corporate leaders calculate that population control, for example, is in their best interests, for childless individuals have much more disposable income to purchase consumerist superfluities than do large families, who must spend a much higher percentage of family income on the necessities of life. So we have this massive project of population control that seeks to colonize the desires of persons of color in the developing world by exporting a sexual and consumerist lifestyle that has no room for raising many children. This is high imperialism, but it flies the flag of feminism and humanitarianism.[251] Even though a childless couple in the developed world consumes far more resources than a large family in the developing world, the ideological claim is that it is "overpopulation" that threatens the world's environmental balance.

---

[251] Again, the book by Angela Franks, *Margaret Sanger's Eugenic Legacy*, is important for the discussion here; see, for example, chapter 7. Franks shows how a certain bourgeois project of sexual liberation, that of Sanger, a project generally considered to be feminist, in fact has led to the maiming and deaths of untold numbers of women and girls. Franks gives a genealogy of the population-control movement, tracing Sanger's crucial role in advancing negative eugenics by means of population control. Sanger managed to combine a eugenic distaste for the poor, the exportation of the contraceptive sexual lifestyle, and the demonization of female fertility in her immensely successful campaign for population control.

Tempered Desire

This consumerist manipulation of human desire leads to an addictive pattern in which we structure our lifestyles around the requirements of consumption. Decisions that bear primordially on our humanity, such as how well we will care for our elderly parents or how open we will be to raising children, become a function of the "standard of living" we want to attain or maintain. And what do we get in return for our contracted, increasingly atomized desires? Not happiness; not the simple pleasure of a good meal or of the face-to-face conjugal embrace. Instead we restlessly pursue a depersonalized sensual gratification. And it does not satisfy.

The role of psychotherapy in the face of this human unhappiness must be considered. Because dealing with the fate of desire in the human person is a special concern of psychology, it is pertinent at this point to ask the following question: Should psychotherapy seek more than adaptation to a bourgeois pattern of life — to consumerist routines of self-gratification, which tend towards a low-level and depersonalizing addiction, a rhythm of excitation and temporary relief based not on interpersonal relations but on consumerist satisfaction?[252] Psychotherapy that aims

---

[252] The term *bourgeois* is usually used as a piece of opprobrium hurled at suburbanites by intellectuals and other members of the doxic elite (the opinion makers, those who control the production and dissemination of ideological *doxa*, including the media, the culture industry, and the education establishment). That is not how the term is intended here. I want to reclaim the term for critical social analysis, which requires demystifying its ideological use as a way of demonizing the middle class.

To honor the general usage of the word, with its overtones of disapprobation, while making that usage more precise, I propose that it does not really denote an economic class per se. Rather, it denotes a form of desire, the vectors of which include libertarian self-gratification, pleasure maximization, avoidance of moral and intellectual exertion, evasion of familial responsibilities, utilitarian calculation, and religious

beyond bourgeois consolation requires attention to questions of our ultimate end: Who are we? What are we to desire? But once this line of thought is initiated, certain hesitations arise. Especially given that much psychotherapy is now brief therapy, can such a seemingly grandiose project as liberation from the consumerist contraction of desire be pursued? And is it not the case that a therapist's only concern is to target the maladaptive behaviors and dysfunctional cognitions that have led a client to have difficulty maintaining basic routines of life and to facilitate a change process that will restore the client to normal functioning? Would it not be beyond the competence of the psychotherapist to address the impact of consumerist ideology on a client's desire? In any case, should that not be left to religious counselors?

These are serious questions that must be seriously confronted by prudent psychotherapists. Nevertheless, if the goal is psychic healing and consumerist ideology deforms desire in such a way as to lead to unhappiness, it seems that psychotherapists must consider whether their healing art requires an engagement with the effects of consumerism on persons. The proper pursuit of this engagement would require an understanding of the full amplitude of the human person and of human desire, which consumerism would be compromising. Does psychotherapy have an emancipatory dynamism

---

indifferentism or reflexive anti-religiosity. Its foremost expressions are consumerist and phallocentric. Bourgeois desire, thus defined, obviously cannot be restricted to any one economic class. Indeed, the irony is that intellectuals tend to be even more radically bourgeois than the rest of the middle class. What saves the middle class is its closer experience of family life, piecemeal piercing the veil of ideology at random points along the libertarian continuum.

The most fundamental question for social analysis must be the Augustinian one: What or whom do you love? Is one's love self-sacrificial or purely self-serving? Bourgeois desire drives consumerism and depersonalized sexuality.

to realize, a mission to attempt to crack open the ideological total-ity and foster the search for ultimate meaning?

This is a propitious time for philosophy and theology to ask this question of psychotherapy, for psychotherapy has entered a period of heightened theoretical self-appropriation. Even though it is now more than a century old, "the field of psychotherapy is in its late adolescence at best."[253] And within the last couple of decades, a clear shift toward integration in psychotherapy has occurred. Indeed, we have reached a point that "research con-sistently demonstrates that integration/eclecticism is the most popular orientation of mental health professionals."[254]

Such a prodigious rise in integrative psychotherapies marks a watershed in the history of psychology, for going all the way back to Freud, school-dogmatism and school-rivalry have character-ized differing theoretical orientations in psychotherapy.[255] And this despite the fact that psychotherapy has always been open to other disciplines: "This stubborn isolationism in the field of psy-chotherapy stands in contrast to the fact that psychotherapists have always been interested in, and long have attempted to use,

[253] Linda Seligman, *Selecting Effective Treatments: A Compre-hensive, Systematic Guide to Treating Mental Disorders*, rev. ed. (San Francisco: Jossey-Bass, 1998), 424.

[254] James O. Prochaska and John C. Norcross, *Systems of Psycho-therapy: A Transtheoretical Analysis*, 5th ed. (Pacific Grove, California: Brooks/Cole, 2003), 3. Among clinical psycholo-gists, for instance, 27 percent claim integration/eclecticism as their primary theoretical orientation.

[255] Ibid., 481. "Integrative psychotherapies are the result of the synthesis of theoretical concepts and clinical techniques from two or more traditional schools of psychotherapy (such as psychoanalysis and behavior therapy) into one therapeutic approach" (Jerry Gold, "Integrative Approaches to Psycho-therapy," in *Encyclopedia of Psychotherapy*, eds. Michel Hersen and William Sledge, vol. 2 [San Diego: Elsevier Science, 2002], 26).

new developments in the natural and social sciences, philosophy, theology, the arts, and literature."[256] That is, it is only natural that psychotherapy would come seek to overcome school-dogmatism to fulfill better its nature as a healing art.

This general movement toward integration in psychology would seem to depend on a more expansive vision of the human person. For example, no longer do we have a one-sided emphasis on either personal character traits or on environmental determinants. Rather, there is a general recognition of the complex interaction of personal traits and environmental states — integrative theories that balance behaviorist and psychodynamic approaches have long been ascendant. Corresponding to this tendency is a willingness to engage in technical eclecticism, to take up effective techniques regardless of their provenance. But does not the very nimbleness of eclecticism require the orientation of a more inclusive vision of human well-being, one that would be theoretically appropriated? Perhaps; for example, psychologists could entertain an even broader notion of environment, one that includes ideological conditioning and that reaches up toward the ultimate spiritual significance of our existence. Indeed, integrative approaches are becoming more and more inclusive.[257]

---

[256] Gold, "Integrative Approaches," p. 26. It is this openness to insights from other fields, and especially the tendency toward an integrative self-appropriation, that makes so promising a conversation between philosophy and theology, on the one hand, and psychology, on the other, to which this book hopes to contribute.

[257] As just one example, there is the multimodal therapy of Arnold Lazarus: "There is far-reaching agreement that treatment needs to be holistic and must consider intraindividual, interpersonal and systemic factors at all levels of functioning — physical, psychological, social-environmental, and political. Some also argue for the inclusion of a separate transpersonal or spiritual dimension" (Arnold A. Lazarus, "Multimodal Strategies with Adults," in *Brief Therapy with Individuals and Couples*, ed. Jon

Tempered Desire

Such a synoptic view primes psychotherapy to be receptive to virtue theory and should make clear the importance for psychic health of the virtue of temperance in particular: attention to the civic and spiritual context of human personhood reminds us of the higher ends that measure our desires for bodily goods.[258] (By the same token, the ideological forces that seek to thwart the internalization of temperance can be recognized as psychotherapeutically relevant.) Already with, say, cognitive-behavioral therapy, there is a basis for training in virtue: cognitive therapy depends on the fact that the power of truth can bring about psychic healing, while behavior therapy indicates how, say, in the raising of a child, operant conditioning can be used to foster virtue.[259]

Carlson and Len Sperry [Phoenix: Zeig, Tucker & Theisen, 2000], 106–107).

[258] An explicit recognition of the need to make the strengthening of natural capacities (that is, virtue formation) a goal for psychology can be seen in positive psychology. Here we see a broadening of the horizons of psychology to include questions of what conduces to true human flourishing, both in the individual and in social life. As Martin Seligman puts it, "Psychology after World War II became a science largely devoted to healing. It concentrated on repairing damage using a disease model of human functioning. This almost exclusive attention to pathology neglected the idea of a fulfilled individual and a thriving community, and it neglected the possibility that building strength is the most potent weapon in the arsenal of therapy. The aim of positive psychology is to catalyze a change in psychology from a preoccupation only with repairing the worst things in life to also building the best qualities in life. To redress the previous imbalance, we must bring the building of strength to the forefront in the treatment and prevention of mental illness" ("Positive Psychology, Positive Prevention, and Positive Therapy," in *Handbook of Positive Psychology*, eds. C.R. Snyder and Shane J. Lopez [Oxford: Oxford University Press, 2002], 3).

[259] Multimodal therapy brings an even more sensitive appreciation of the powers of the human organism: "[Multimodal therapy] is

237

Philosophical Virtues and Psychological Strengths

But, again, serious reservations can be put forward concerning the propriety of a therapeutic intervention that seeks to achieve a result that exceeds the modest aim of restoring normal day-to-day functioning. Would not attempting anything more risk an un-ethical, proselytizing imposition of the therapist's spiritual values upon the client? It is a serious consideration, to be taken seriously. But the counterclaim will not easily yield: Can the client seeking help actually be helped without reference to what it means to live a flourishing human life?

Say Paolo and Francesca come in for therapy because they have found themselves becoming distant from each other. Having been married for ten years, they have not had sex in several months. Divorce has recently been discussed, but they both want to try to avoid that outcome for the sake of their four-year-old son. They each work more than full-time, partly because they have grown accustomed to a certain standard of living.

To deal with the presenting problem of atrophied intimacy, a therapist could reasonably suggest to the couple the goal of setting aside an hour each day, and a half day on the weekend, to be alone together. But, although this intervention strategy may indeed help reestablish some form of intimacy, have all the relevant human factors been taken into account? First of all, is their child being well-served by having to spend so much time in daycare because of his parents' work schedules? That is, are the couple meeting their basic parental responsibilities? Do they

---

predicated on the assumption that most psychological problems are multifaceted, multi-determined, and multilayered, and that comprehensive therapy calls for a careful assessment of seven parameters or 'modalities'—behavior, affect, sensation, imagery, cognition, interpersonal relationships, and biological processes" (Lazarus, "Multimodal Strategies with Adults," 107). Attention to imagery, for example, would be highly relevant for a therapy that would deal with the effects of consumerist ideology on the imagination.

seek fulfillment at work rather than at home? If so, can they really attain a durable and profound happiness without addressing this problem? Let's say that it turns out that Paolo works over fifty hours a week. When he is at home, he spends his time watching DVDs and researching and buying new electronic equipment: he is inattentive of his wife and child. Francesca, for her part, feels overtaxed by responsibilities at home and at work. Their son resents the dearth of parental attention and misbehaves when they are at home. Francesca is the one who usually has to deal with this, and it makes her look to work as a haven from the rigors of home, seeking more work hours.[260] Like her husband, when she is

---

[260] Hochschild speaks of the "time bind syndrome" (*Commercialization of Intimate Life*, 175–181). Her profound sociological analysis tracks how we have gone from being producers of care in our families to being consumers of care (as, for example, in daycare). This is the ultimate extension of consumerist logic, and it impacts the whole structure of our emotional lives. A socially hegemonic ideology that honors working-world productivity over caring will tend to obscure our basic human vocation, which is to love and be loved. If we are the kind of creatures that cannot be happy unless we live out self-giving love, then this consumerist ideology will lead to society-wide psychological difficulties. Hochschild presents a "sociology of emotion," which must at the same time be a critique of ideology immediately relevant for psychology.

As a healing art operating in a society with a particular configuration, psychology should find such considerations relevant, for they identify factors contributing to the unhappiness many psychologists treat: "But caring has become increasingly associated with 'getting stuck' outside the main show. When in the mid-nineteenth century, men were drawn into market life and women remained outside it, female homemakers formed a moral brake on capitalism. Now American women are its latest recruits, offered membership in the public side of market society on the same harsh terms as those offered to American men. The result makes for a harshness of life that seems so normal to us we don't see it. We really

at home, she detaches herself from the common life of the family, spending much of her time shopping on the Internet. The family rarely sits down to a meal together, and they have all taken to eating too much.

Would a therapist be serving these clients well by not having Paolo and Francesca think about what constitutes a flourishing human life? Would not a serious intervention plan have to address their compulsive shopping, as well as the root causes of that compulsion? Must the therapist not somehow communicate the desirability of redirecting personal energy into parenting and civic engagement and aesthetic appreciation? That is, the therapist may indeed be able to facilitate a renewed intimacy, at least in the short term, with the spend-more-time-together strategy, leaving the basic rhythms of the household intact. But can the therapist be said to have really helped this couple, having left their desires in fundamental disarray, with their vital forces fundamentally broken under the pressure of a consumerist lifestyle that has almost completely occluded the wide horizon of human community and aspiration?

II. Temperance

Temperance has nothing to do with driving to zero the vital impulses of the human organism, like some pale habit of constraint. Rather, temperance forges and tempers the impulsive powers of the human soul into an integrated and harmonious whole, generating a person capable of dynamic, effective, noble action. We can either enjoy the good things of this world in the self-possession of temperance or lose ourselves in those things in our consumerist fragmentation: obsessive, addictive, unfree, nervous.

---

need, I believe, a revolution in our society and in our thinking, one that rewards care as much as market success, one that strengthens a nonmarket public sphere—like the old village commons" (*Commercialization of Intimate Life*, 8).

Tempered Desire

Without the virtue of temperance, one eventually loses one's self-possession due to selfishness, in a frenetic, narcissistic seeking for sensual stimulation and gratification. It is not so with the temperate person, who seeks the natural goods of food and sex, and enjoys the accompanying pleasure, according to the ultimate human commitments: to family, country, humanity. Temperance does not run counter to our desire, for we are meant for greatness, meant to be athletes of the human spirit. We are meant for self-gift, meant to communicate ourselves in self-sacrificial love—and this requires self-possession, for to give oneself away one must be free in human wholeness to do so. There are times in our lives when we must be able to give up natural pleasures so that we may be true to love: fathers and mothers have to be able to give up sleep to care for their babies; husbands ought to attune their sexual desires to the natural dynamisms of their wives' bodies;[261] citizens may sometimes have to sacrifice in defense of their country.

Let us look at temperance a little more technically. Bodily appetite is naturally drawn toward the indispensable goods of food and sex, which are true goods because they are perfective of human nature (in the individual and in the species). That is, it is simply the case that without the right kinds of food, we die; without reproduction, cultures, and eventually the species, would die (the demographic suicide of Europe makes this startlingly clear[262]). If one recognizes that, no matter what, eating only sand will end in death, then one recognizes the objective reality of a human nature, according to which certain things lead to

---

[261] Indeed, a wife should be able to expect that her husband not be driven by selfish, and depersonalized, sexual need, so that if she were, say, to become disabled, even brain-damaged, she would not be somehow "replaced" by another woman.

[262] See, for example, Mark Steyn, *America Alone: The End of the World as We Know It* (Washington, DC: Regnery, 2006).

our flourishing and other things frustrate that flourishing. Some things in the world conduce to our happiness, and other things make happiness impossible. This is clear when it comes to what we ingest; it is no less true for our capacity to know and love. Our desires (ideological conditioning aside) help to indicate what we need, bodily and spiritually, if we are to realize our deepest yearning: to love and be loved.

A problem arises, however, if the passion for a good is inordinate. If we pursue desires without paying heed to the demands of true love or of human intelligence, we will desire even good things wrongly, addictively, exploitatively. Here is how the philosopher Josef Pieper puts it:

> The natural urge toward sensual enjoyment, manifested in delight in food and drink and sexual pleasure, is the echo and mirror of man's strongest natural forces of self-preservation. The basic forms of enjoyment correspond to these most primordial forces of being, which tend to preserve the individual man, as well as the whole race, in the existence for which he was created (Wisdom 1, 14). But for the very reason that these forces are closely allied to the deepest human urge toward being, they exceed all other powers of mankind in their destructive violence once they degenerate into selfishness.[263]

It is the virtue of temperance that moderates these passions according to the order of right reason, that is, according to a reason intelligent enough to recognize what is good for us and what is bad for us. Temperance makes our desires reasonable by elevating and integrating the bodily passions themselves, so that our very viscera impel us toward our true end. A temperate person

---

[263] Josef Pieper, "Temperance," in *The Four Cardinal Virtues*, trans. Daniel Coogan (Notre Dame: University of Notre Dame Press, 1966), 150.

does not continually have to battle urges to eat beyond the mean or have sex with someone other than his or her spouse. The urges themselves are attuned to the true good of the person, the perfection of human knowing and loving.

Therefore, temperance is not rigorist self-control, not mere continence, if we understand continence to be the sheer restraining of passions that are in themselves disordered—the lid on a pressure cooker. This is why St. Thomas Aquinas maintains that continence is not strictly speaking a virtue. [264] Virtue is not a precarious self-restraint; it is the attunement of our desires themselves to what is truly good for us.

Reason shapes the impulsive passions, our bodily desires, through the virtue of temperance, so that we are freed from the fragmentation of ideologically manipulated and addictive desires—free to love well, to live in solidarity, to participate in the pursuit of truth that alone can ground common life. Continence, on the other hand, resides not in those passions, but in the will. Continence is the Kantian ideal of morality: one wills to restrain the inordinance of one's passions. This is certainly a good place to start, but it is not sufficient.[265] To love well, we need the creative power of a soul liberated from the sterility and fragmentation of bourgeois desire. We need the power of a tempered soul.

III. What Is Desire?

We have not really begun to grapple with the profound psychic damage attending the practices widely disseminated by the sexual revolution. For example, our youth are increasingly subject

---

[264] *ST* II-II, Q. 155, art. 1.

[265] Here is how the *Catechism of the Catholic Church* puts it: "Moral perfection consists in man's being moved to the good not by his will alone, but also by his sensitive appetite, as in the words of the psalm: 'My heart and flesh sing for joy to the living God'" (no. 1770).

to dislocations in identity formation and severe diminishment of their ability to form attachments due to a rising tide of casual sexual activity. The misuse of the sexual faculty quickly suppresses all questions of ultimate end, so that our libidinal lives rush along while our faculties of knowing and loving plod haltingly behind a *cordon sanitaire* that keeps them from the libidinal wellsprings of organic life. The history of our desire becomes sundered from the activity of our intelligence. We think without desire, and we desire without thought. Many indeed experience the spiritual vertigo of living out patterns of life that allow no quarter for seriously asking and answering questions about the meaning of life — questions such as: Who am I? How am I to live? Unfortunately, theology and philosophy in the contemporary academy generally serve as handmaids of ideology, justifying the prevailing sociosexual routines, while much of psychotherapy involves strategies of achieving some kind of normal functioning while maintaining addictive, and destructive, sexual patterns (or at least addictive consumerist patterns, as in the example of Paolo and Francesca given above).

The cause of advancing the human good and human happiness requires that we demystify ideology and seek to understand the true relation between desire and our powers of knowing and loving. We must heal the Gnostic, Cartesian modern dualism that splinters these human powers. We must recognize how necessary temperance is for the perfection of human desire, how the unity of the human person requires that our bodily impulses be integrated and personalized. We cannot know and love well without doing so *through* and *from* the most basic impulses of the body. Romanus Cessario brings it to a point:

> In sum, moral realism rejects the view that the rational part of the soul forms the only significant characteristic of the moral person. Virtue shapes the whole body-soul

composite, the *per se unum* that is the human person, with the result that the practice of virtue need not always entail a conscious figuring out of what one ought to do; sometimes the *recta ratio agibilium*—the truth about what to do here and now—flows directly from well-ordered and fully developed sense passions.[266]

If there really is such a thing as the virtue of temperance, and this is not some more-or-less useful fiction, then the sense passions, our most basic bodily desires, cannot be treated as if they are autonomous drives that can be only haphazardly managed, having no intrinsic relation to human knowing and loving. This would destroy the integrity of the person. Indeed those who engage in casual sex may find themselves feeling alienated from their bodies, as if "who they really are" is not really implicated in their sexual practices. It would seem that psychic survival would require such a breakdown in the integrity of the personality in an individual who goes from one impersonal sexual encounter to another, from one relationship to the next. And this effect would only be magnified in the young.[267]

---

[266] Romanus Cessario, O.P., *The Virtues, or the Examined Life* (New York: Continuum, 2002), 164.

[267] Indeed, an analysis of data to be found in the National Longitudinal Survey of Adolescent Health shows that 25.3 percent of sexually active girls aged 14 to 17 said they were depressed a lot, most or all of the time (compared with 7.7 percent of girls who are not sexually active) (Robert E. Rector, Kirk A. Johnson, and Lauren R. Noyes, "Sexually Active Teenagers Are More Likely to Be Depressed and to Attempt Suicide," a report of the Heritage Center for Data Analysis [June 2, 2003]). There are other indicators that the separation of sex from faithful, fruitful, and lifelong love frustrates human nature and its fundamental dynamism toward self-giving love, especially the epidemic of sexually transmitted diseases among our youth. At least one-quarter of America's sexually active teens

Where does the path to healing lie? Happily, our natures are oriented toward recovery. Just to engage our intelligence, to pursue the spontaneously arising questions concerning what it means to live a human life—Who am I? What am I doing here? How does my longing for intimacy actually get satisfied? Or even, why does that rose bush put out flowers? —just to pursue these questions with some seriousness will be to set out on a path that liberates desire from determined mindlessness. The liberation of one's libidinal life from the narrowness of a thoughtless sexual voracity will open up the richness of an affective life that involves friendships and family, in which one recognizes where sexual intimacy does and does not belong.

As Cessario explains, there is a distinction to be made between sensitive love (*amor sensitivus*) and rational love. The former is the resting of the passions in that which has moved them: enjoying that tasty doughnut, for example. Rational love, on the other hand, has to do with the movement of the rational appetite, the will, our capacity to love in a fully human way—in which our bodily or sense appetite should find its indispensable context.

Sense appetite is aroused by values sensibly perceived or imagined, whereas intellectual affectivity, or will, is the power to enjoy things that come within the focus of understanding. Rational love differs from sensitive love in that its object is the good as known by the intellect.[268]

The forces of free-sex and consumerist ideology resist the personalization of desire precisely by training persons to confront objects merely as perceived or imagined, and not as understood. One hears a lot these days about "desire," but this rhetoric usually involves the occlusion of the distinction between sensitive and rational desire. This serves the ends of ideology. If one speaks

have been infected (Meg Meeker, Epidemic: *How Teen Sex Is Killing our Kids* [Washington, DC: Regnery, 2002], 12.)

268 Cessario, *The Virtues*, 158.

flatly of "desire," he is invariably speaking of what his gut or loins feel like doing right now, which is certainly not a measure of the true good when one has fallen victim to an addictive desire or to ideological conditioning. What gets covered up is recognition of the existence of *rational* appetite, that is, human freedom. To pretend that the sense appetites are not intrinsically oriented to intelligence (as if they were absolute in themselves) is to refuse human wholeness.

To treat our bodily, especially sexual, desires as blind urges is to atomize and mechanize the movements of bodily desire, separating those passions from their inherent ordination to the higher faculties of the soul. This is to carry through the fetishization of, in Michel Foucault's famous phrase, "bodies and pleasures," which is a nominalist refusal of personalist realism.[269] Only an intelligent sexual appetite can desire a person: anything less must necessarily depersonalize.[270] And, of course, this "less" is not even simply animal innocence: for humans, untutored passion is always a function of ideology, and in effect involves the subjection of

---

[269] Michel Foucault, *History of Sexuality. Vol. I: An Introduction*, trans. Robert Hurley (New York: Random House, 1978), 157.

[270] Roger Scruton nicely encapsulates "the peculiar intentionality of human sexual emotion": "Sexual desire is not a desire for sensations. It is a desire for a person: and I mean a *person*, not his or her body, conceived as an object in the physical world, but the person conceived as an incarnate subject, in whom the light of self-consciousness shines and who confronts me eye to eye, and I to I. True desire is also a kind of petition: it demands reciprocity, mutuality, and a shared surrender. It is therefore compromising, and also threatening. No pursuit of a mere sensation could be compromising or threatening in this way" ("Sacrilege and Sacrament," in *The Meaning of Marriage: Family, State, Market, and Morals*, eds. Robert P. George and Jean Bethke Elshtain [Dallas: Spence Publishing, 2006], 15). Scruton lays out his full argument for this claim in *Sexual Desire: A Philosophical Investigation* (London: Phoenix Press, 1986).

reason to "desire." We bend our intelligence toward gratifying our desires, which in turn are not somehow authentic expressions of a deep-down personal core, but are instead usually the remainder of a program of manipulation by, for example, what critical theorist Theodor Adorno called the culture industry.

IV. Chastity

Temperance regards both the pleasures of food and drink and of sex. Vices surrounding food and intoxicating substances are certainly not uncommon in our culture, but even more profoundly destructive of the integrity of personality, and of the integrity of social life, is the abuse of sexual pleasure. So, sex is a special concern here, and therefore so is that part of temperance that is the virtue of chastity.

Aquinas provides a clear analysis of temperance and the particular virtues that fall under that encompassing virtue. He distinguishes between the principle of actions relating to the use of food, which preserves the nature of the individual, and that of actions relating to sexual pleasure, by which the nature of the species is preserved.[271] That is, the proper matter of chastity is the use of the organs intended for procreation. The truth of human sexuality is that it is ordered to the preservation of the species, and it flourishes only in the sharing of a whole life (that is, in marriage).

Sexual desire is not private. It is not an individual matter, but one pertaining to the preservation of the species. Our age of bourgeois individualism and privatization radically separates the household from the public square. We no longer think in terms of family or children (or the common good). And here Freud bears much responsibility: one of the great mistakes that dominates "modern" consciousness is pansexualism, a mistake entailed by

---

[271] *ST* II-II, Q. 151, art. 3.

the Freudian assumption that interpersonal attachment is always a function of libidinal energy understood as the id's brute seeking of "sexual" satisfaction. This mistake destroys awareness of the analogous levels of human attachment: contracting our understanding of the amplitude of human friendship, distorting family life, and suppressing the desire for the gift of divine friendship. The only way we could have come to this reduction of human attachment to sexual desire is to ignore familial attachment (or, as in Freud, to sexualize such attachment).

Sexual desire as an absolute: a good father or mother knows how unreal such a view is. Freud's focus on sexual attachment has hampered research into the true scope of libidinal life, the irreducibly complex articulation of human relationality in terms of friendships and family. And so theology and philosophy, no less than psychology, have not thought deeply enough about the healing of desire, and certainly have not thought enough about desire in terms of the dynamics of human relations or the relations of parents and children.

To recognize again the complexity of desire will, for example, restore a crucial component of civic-mindedness, against the prevailing individualism. There is an immense, and largely unknown, fruitfulness to addressing the political question "What is the good life?", beginning with the recognition that true friendships and a sound family life heal desire and build up the common good.

Of course, much is at stake in having theology, philosophy, and psychology maintain a political horizon for the pursuit of their particular questions. It would be important for all three disciplines, for instance, to consider the social impact of sexual vice. Pieper notes, "Only the combination of the intemperateness of lustfulness with the lazy inertia incapable of generating anger is the sign of complete and virtually hopeless degeneration. It appears whenever a caste, a people, or a whole civilization is ripe for its decline and fall."[272] Which is to say that fatherhood is dying. (The fact that motherhood too is dying has other symptoms.) This is a crisis that psychology, philosophy, and theology must each address.

Chastity, and temperance in general, clothes a person with graciousness and steels a person for the responsibilities of communal life. It gathers one's forces up into an intensity such that one can truly offer oneself to another. Chastity is what makes sexual difference truly fruitful, for the most intense physical realization of self-gift is the face-to-face sexual embrace of a man and woman who share a whole life together, without reservation. (So, without chastity, society is not possible.)

Now, the sexual faculty is often employed outside of this completeness of self-gift, and it is then that the wonderful gift of sexual pleasure becomes darkened by self-seeking. This surpassing good, with all of its wonderful intensity, so fundamentally expressive of the drive for intimacy and love that animates the human person, when taken out of its context of total self-giving becomes frustrated. Consumerist ideology tells us that pleasure can be had atomistically, in a depersonalized context, but this goes against our experience of what actually satisfies our deepest hunger: we eat and drink and have sex, and take great pleasure in performing those activities so basic to human life, as persons in community, as persons who seek intimacy, who want to carry out the responsibilities of love for the sake of our family, friends, and fellow citizens. That is simply what it is to be human: to want to love and be loved, to be a blessing to those we love. And this basic fact recommends itself as relevant to psychotherapeutic practice. How exactly is a different matter, one that professional psychologists have to work out. But this is simply a plea that psychotherapeutic practice be set within a wider horizon.

[272] Pieper, *Four Cardinal Virtues*, 197.

V. Unchastity and Anti-Realism

"Among the vices of intemperance, venereal sins are most de-
serving of reproach, . . . because by these sins especially, the reason
is absorbed."[273] Because of the power of sexual passion, when it
is misused, it leads to the destruction of the capacity to contem-
plate. This is a phenomenon with which many a teacher is famil-
iar, seeing how sexual vice destroys the minds of students. The
taste for spiritual things withers; their very existence becomes
incredible. And the question of God and of one's ultimate end
does not arise at all, questions that had been asked in various ways
since childhood.

What is at stake again is social: this suppression of the taste
for higher things such as beauty strikes at the very basis of cultural
creativity and appreciation, at the nobility of man. Something
like appreciation of the beauty of Mozart or Bernini or Cather
requires that one's eyes not be set on satisfying disordered carnal
desire, which contaminates every look with self-interest. And not
just beauty: metaphysical and moral antirealism easily flow from
unchastity.

Pieper explains this connection:

Unchaste abandon and the self-surrender of the soul to the
world of sensuality paralyzes the primordial powers of the
moral person: the ability to perceive, in silence, the call
of reality, and to make, in the retreat of this silence, the
decision appropriate to the concrete situation of concrete
action. [Why? T]he destructiveness lies in the fact that un-
chastity constricts man and thus renders him incapable of
seeing objective reality. An unchaste man wants above all
something for himself; he is distracted by an unobjective
'interest'; his constantly strained will-to-pleasure prevents

273 *ST* II-II, Q.151, art. 4, ad. 3.

251

him from confronting reality with that selfless detachment
which alone makes genuine knowledge possible."[274]

274 *Four Cardinal Virtues*, 160–161. E. Michael Jones puts the
situation starkly: it is either masturbation or prayer (*Libido
Dominandi: Sexual Liberation and Political Control* [South
Bend, Indiana: St. Augustine's Press, 2000], 262). He takes
his cue from the renegade Freudian Wilhelm Reich, making
clear Reich's crucial importance for the sexual revolution.
For example, the widespread and quite destructive delusion
that autoerotic behavior is somehow intrinsic to healthy
psychosexual development stems from Reich. He explicitly
framed his project in terms of a struggle with the Catholic
Church: "Church = sexual-political organization of the pa-
triarchy" ("Bottom Line," trans. Derek and Inge Jordan, in
German Essays on Psychology, eds. Wolfgang Schirmacher and
Sven Nebelung [New York: Continuum, 2001], 160). The
hoary chestnut about Christianity's opposition to healthy
human sexuality is given paradigmatic expression by Reich:
"It was not until relatively late, with the establishment of an
authoritarian patriarchy and the beginning of the division of
the classes, that suppression of sexuality begins to make its
appearance. It is at this stage that sexual interests in general
begin to enter the service of a minority's interest in material
profit; in the patriarchal marriage and family this state of af-
fairs assumes a solid organizational form. With the restriction
and suppression of sexuality, the nature of human feeling
changes; a sex-negating religion comes into being and gradu-
ally develops its own sex-political organization, the church
with all its predecessors, the aim of which is nothing other
than the eradication of man's sexual desires and consequently
of what little happiness there is on earth" ("The Social Func-
tion of Sexual Repression," trans. Mary Boyd Higgins, in *Ger-
man Essays*, 156). More radical than statist totalitarians, the
Freudo-Marxist Reich wanted a total revolution, one that
inverted the very soul of each person. And so sex ed and por-
nography are to serve the ends of overthrowing the authority
of God and Church and, in fact, of neutralizing the attraction
of any spiritual value such as beauty or truth.

The sexual revolution must necessarily strike at the family,
the heart of ordered communal life, especially by destroying

Tempered Desire

What is desire? It certainly has something to do with sex, but not without the embracing and personalizing realities of intelligence, creativity, friendship, family, and country. The integration of a human life requires this richness. Only thus can we begin to understand how to love well and to live free, moving in this world with that surprising creativity and power of personality that marks the one whose deepest physical drives are spiritually saturated.

The care of our youth is at stake above all: how do we lead them on the way toward a fully human life, a life of freedom, of true love, of intelligent activity and creativity? We have thoroughly analyzed the depersonalizing and disintegrating effects of contemporary consumerist desire, showing its especially destructive manifestation in unchastity. We have seen that education in temperance is indispensable. We have also seen that psychology, philosophy, and theology have much to think together concerning the unity of the human person and what that has to do with

---

the authority of the father. Reich initiated that persistent pop-psychoanalytic claim that conservatism stems from sexual repression: "The moral inhibition of the child's natural sexuality, the last stage of which is the severe impairment of the child's *genital* sexuality, makes the child afraid, shy, fearful of authority, obedient, 'good,' and 'docile' in the authoritarian sense of the words. It has a crippling effect on man's rebellious forces because every vital life-impulse is now burdened with severe fear; and since sex is a forbidden subject, thought in general and man's critical faculty also become inhibited.... Man's authoritarian structure—this must be clearly established—is basically produced by the embedding of sexual inhibitions and fear in the living substance of sexual impulses.... The result is conservatism, fear of freedom, in a word, reactionary thinking" (Ibid., 156–158).

The flight from reality is complete here, driven by an all-consuming sexual vice. Too many, especially our young, are threatened by this life-denying madness that destroys thought, friendship, love.

our common life. Finally, we have raised the question concerning how all three might aid in a therapy of desire, a healing and liberation of desire that frees human persons to enrich this world through glorious self-expenditure.

VI. For Children

We saw at the beginning of this essay that the consumerist contraction of desire concretely necessitates the relinquishing of fertility in favor of a higher standard of living and the pursuit of sexual self-satisfaction. This is the ultimate depersonalization of desire, and its remedy must involve (as I have argued) a renewed recognition of the intrinsic connection between sexual desire and the begetting and raising of children. In that spirit, here is a meditation on fatherhood that reveals what is at stake in human sexuality, an antidote to radicalized Freudianism and consumerist desire, from the French poet Charles Péguy. We have seen, in the case of Paolo and Francesca, an all-too-typical example of intemperate desire; let us attend now to Péguy's description of healed, selfless, personalized desire, as found in a fully tempered human person. Philosophers, theologians, and psychotherapists must have before them an image of human wholeness to break open the ideological totality of bourgeois desire, of consumerism and loveless sex.

Mothers live out this self-sacrificial love all the time, along with many fathers. But many more men than women have forgotten their vocation to human love in its full amplitude, in this culture of deformed masculine desire. For the sake of human happiness, for the sake of women and children, as well as of men themselves, we must meditate on both motherhood and fatherhood, but especially on what it takes to be a father.

My three virtues, says God.
Master of the Three Virtues.

Tempered Desire

My three virtues are no different than men and
    women in their homes.
Children are never the ones who work.
But no one ever works except for children.
It's never the child who goes to the field, who tills
    and who sows, and who reaps and who harvests
    the grapes and who trims the vine and who fells
    the trees and who cuts the wood
For winter.
To warm the house in winter.
But would the father have the heart to work if he
    didn't have his children.
If it weren't for the sake of his children.
And in winter when he works hard.
In the forest.
When he works the hardest.
With his billhook and with his saw and with his
    felling axe and with his hand axe.
In the icy forest.

. . .

He thinks tenderly of the time when he will no
    longer be needed.
And when things will go on all the same.
Because there will be others.
Who will bear the same responsibilities.
And who will perhaps, and who will undoubtedly,
    bear them better.

. . .

His children will do better than he, of course.
And the world will go better.
Later.

He's not jealous of it.

On the contrary.

Nor for having come to the world, as he did, in an ungrateful time.

And to have no doubt prepared for his sons a time that is perhaps less ungrateful.

What madman would be jealous of his sons and of the sons of his sons.

Doesn't he work solely for his children.[275]

---

[275] Charles Péguy, *The Portal of the Mystery of Hope*, 12, 17, 18.

Part III

Connections

Chapter 11

Modern Philosophical Anthropology

Roger Scruton

The expression *philosophical anthropology* may have been first used by Baumgarten, Kant's mentor. Kant himself delivered lectures on "anthropology" throughout his life, and they were published after his death, although Kant does not clearly distinguish in those lectures between the philosophical and the empirical parts of his study. More recently Etienne Gilson has written of the "Christian anthropology" of St. Thomas, and the term has since come to have a fairly settled meaning in the writings of those influenced by the personalism of Max Scheler (such as the late Pope John Paul II). A philosophical anthropology, as exemplified in the studies in this book, is a conceptual account of our conduct in this world and our destiny in the next. It is not an empirical science; rather, it explores deep-rooted features of the human condition (freedom, individuality, personality, and so on) with a view to understanding our social nature and moral and spiritual life. But it has an important empirical application, since it aims to tell us how we differ from the rest of creation, and how we are both corrupted and fulfilled. Much that is said and believed about the human condition, and has been built into medical practice, exhibits some account of human nature, and philosophical ideas concerning freedom, the emotions, and the relation between persons and their bodies have had far-reaching consequences in the practice of psychotherapy. The topic of philosophical anthropology is therefore as relevant for us, in a world of secular values, as it was for St. Thomas, in the great days of Christian belief. Our societies are suffering from the adverse effects of theories and practices built upon wishful thinking and ideology rather than upon sound philosophical argument; and one purpose of this book, as I see it, is to point to another, more fruitful foundation for the psychological sciences and their application.

Philosophical anthropology has roots in Greek philosophy. Plato's theory of the dual nature of the human being, as rational soul embodied in a passionate animal, had a revolutionary effect on all subsequent thought in the ancient world and inspired the first attempts to give cogency and substance to the Christian doctrine of the afterlife. Plato situated the soul of man in the eternal realm, the realm of ideas. He was well aware of the problem that this created: the problem of the relationship between time and eternity, between the empirical world in which we live and the divine realm to which we are destined. This problem resurged again and again in early Christian theology and was given a new life by Boethius in his *Consolation of Philosophy*, a book whose influence can be seen in countless works of medieval and Renaissance literature, from the *Divine Comedy* to the *Fairie Quean*.

Plato's doctrine of the soul seemed to make sense of many puzzling features of the human condition: for example, the intense focus of all our interpersonal attitudes on the inward and conscious aspect of the other; the constant tension that all people feel, between soul and body—between the pursuit of virtue and the appetites of the flesh; the relation between rationality and rational choice, on the one hand, and appetite and desire on the other. And, of course, it vindicated the great promise of religion. The Platonic theory of the soul therefore held sway among the Fathers of the Church, was built into his system of Christian theology by St Augustine, and was refashioned for Islamic purposes by al-Farabi.

However, it was difficult to be fully satisfied with the theory, since it presented such intricate metaphysical difficulties concerning the relationship between soul and body and between the temporal and eternal realms. It seemed to grant only accidental existence to the body and to downgrade much that we believe to be essential to human beings and their fulfillment. Moreover, as Aristotle recognized, it presented an insuperable problem of individuation. How can we individuate the human being, if what he essentially is lies hidden from us and revealed only to the inner eye of introspection? And how are souls to be individuated in that timeless and changeless realm to which they are destined? Only if we give a full and proper place to the body, in our concept of the human being, can we solve the problem of individuation. Moreover, it is our existence as individuals that underlies all our projects and hopes and determines our interpersonal attitudes and interests. Hence individuation is always going to be at the heart of philosophical anthropology and provides the test for any theory of the soul.

Aristotle solved the problem through his distinction between matter and form. Every individual object, he argued, is composed of matter organized by its form, just as a statue is composed of bronze cast in a certain shape. The relation of soul to body is that of matter to form; the human individual is composed of his body and shaped by his soul or *psuche*. All living things have souls on Aristotle's view; what distinguishes the human being is the part of the soul that is given to reason or *nous*, which concerns itself with everlasting things and which is itself everlasting.

The form/matter distinction implies that the soul is a kind of organization of the body and its behavior. This implication aligns Aristotle's theory with modern functionalist theories of the mind, which see the mind as software and the body as the hardware in which the soul is, so to speak, installed. But the theory also implies that the individuality of the human being persists only so long as body and soul are united. Avicenna attempted to synthesize the Platonic and Aristotelian positions, arguing that the soul is *both* the form that organizes the body *and* an individual object capable of persisting in its own right. But this seems to involve assigning the soul to two quite heterogenous categories—as though the shape of a statue could endure even when the material has been dissolved.

Those controversies were inherited by Aquinas, together with another and quite distinct idea, which came to him *via* Boethius: the idea of the person. The word *persona*, taken by the Romans from the Etruscan theater, denoted first a mask, then a theatrical character, then the legal bearer of rights and duties, and finally the human being in his moral aspect. Defined by Boethius as "an individual substance of a rational nature," the person was identified by Aquinas as the human essence, that in which individuality, intellect, and the moral life are all united and incarnate. This idea became the core component of Thomist anthropology, and it is what unites that anthropology with the later developments that I shall be principally considering in this foreword.

Aquinas argued that the crucial aspect of the soul, which governs our destiny and happiness, and in which personhood resides, is the rational part, the intellect. All those aspects of the mental life that we share with the lower animals—such as sensation, perception, and appetite—are, for Aquinas, subsumed into the intellect, which elevates us to a higher order of being than that occupied by dogs, horses, and bears. It is in virtue of his rational intellect that a human being is an autonomous source of activity, spontaneously initiating events for which he is also accountable. This is what we mean, or ought to mean, by *personality*, and Aquinas goes on to develop a theory of the person as the highest kind of creation, in which freedom, reason, accountability, and self-knowledge are given the prominent position that they were later to regain, from a completely different metaphysical perspective, in Kant.

Between Aquinas and Kant, however, lies the great shadow cast by Descartes, whose "method of doubt" caused him to reject out of hand the speculative account of human nature given by the scholastics and to found his philosophy on the indubitable, because self-verifying, propositions "I exist" and "I think." Descartes argued from these indubitable premises in the following way: since I cannot conceive of myself except as thinking, it is of my essence to think. (*Think*—*cogitare*—was a word of wide application for Descartes, and covered all conscious manifestations of the mental life.) Now, however hard I try, I can find no other property besides thought that belongs to my essence. For example, although it seems to me that I have a body that I can move at will, I can readily conceive of myself as existing without this body. Hence it is not an essential property of me that I have a body. I could conceivably exist after the body's demise. And in so existing I will continue to exist as a thinking thing—a *res cogitans*.

Descartes begins from the question "How can I know, be certain of, the things that I know?" Immediately his thought turns inward, to the contents of his own mind and the certainties attached to them. Although the peculiarity of the "*cogito*" lies in its self-verifying nature (it can be doubted only if it is true), there lurks behind it a host of other certainties: I am able to know what I think, feel, experience with an authority that is quite distinct from any authority that attaches to my knowledge of another person or thing. In the case of my own mentality, what is, seems, and what seems, is. The phenomenon of first-person privilege leads directly to the Cartesian view of the mind. My immediate certainty of my own mental states is contrasted with my uncertainty about all corporeal things, in such a way as to lend support to the contention that what I am is an immaterial, substantial being, accidentally and temporarily connected with the body by means of which I act. I am a substance, but not a corporeal substance, and my privileged awareness of the contents of my own consciousness is supposed somehow to be explained by that.

It is fair to say that philosophical anthropology suffered an enormous setback with Descartes. The person, his individuality, his body, his form of life, and his virtues have all dropped from the picture, to be replaced by the "I," the disembodied thinker. The Cartesian "I" is supposedly substantial, but in another sense quite insubstantial precisely because viewed only from within and therefore without reference to action in a shared and observable world. All constructive anthropology takes second place to meditation on the "first-person case."

It was not until Kant that the enterprise of a philosophical anthropology was resurrected, and the concept of the person placed once again at the heart of it.

The Kantian Tradition

As I remarked at the outset, the term *philosophical anthropology* was probably coined by Baumgarten[276] and used only later of Kant, who distinguished moral anthropology from the "pragmatic" science that he broached in his *Anthropologie in pragmatischer Hinsicht*[277] and who describes both moral and pragmatic anthropology as applied or empirical sciences.[278] In his lectures on logic, however, Kant made the striking claim that the studies

---

[276] *Metaphysica*, 3rd ed., 1749, Section 747: *Anthropologia philosophica*. See Friedrich Delekat, *Immanuel Kant; Historisch-Kritische Interpretation der Hauptschriften* (Heidelberg, 1963), 171.

[277] First published in 1798, but deriving from lecture notes begun thirty years before.

[278] That the critical philosophy should be seen as a complex philosophical anthropology in the current sense, is argued in Frederick P. Van de Pitte, *Kant as Philosophical Anthropologist* (The Hague: Martinus Nijhoff, 1971).

of metaphysics, morals, and religion are all contained within an-thropology.[279] In the three *Critiques*, the third in particular, Kant approached this a priori theory through an account of the many "faculties" of the human being, by way of availing himself of a concept that seemed to lie in some undecidable region between empirical psychology and philosophical logic. I think that Kant was right to emphasize the possibility of an a priori theory of hu-man nature and to look to it, as he did, for the grounds of moral and aesthetic judgment. I also believe that Kant's philosophical anthropology was his greatest legacy, which survives, altered and embellished, but never entirely rejected, through all the often wild metaphysical theories of his immediate followers.

The following, I believe, are among the crucial components of the Kantian anthropology:

1) Human beings are both subject and object of their own awareness.

2) Human beings are characterized by self-conscious-ness—the "transcendental unity of apperception"—which endows them with a peculiar perspective on the empirical world, as though from the very edge of things.

3) From this transcendental perspective I, as the human subject, see myself as free, in the sense of being the origina-tor of my own actions. From the empirical perspective, by contrast, I see myself from outside, as one object among oth-ers, a part of nature, bound by the law of cause and effect.

4) Self-consciousness and freedom imply and are implied by rationality—which includes the ability to act from rea-son alone, so that reason provides a motive to action.

---

[279] *Kant's Introduction to Logic*, trans. T.K. Abbott, (London: Longmans, Green, 1885), 15.

5) From the transcendental perspective, therefore, I find myself constrained by a priori laws, which are binding on me and all rational beings. These are the laws of morality.

6) In particular I am constrained to see myself and others as ends, not to be used as instruments only, but to be respected as free, sovereign beings. A need for, and predisposition toward, justice is contained within the exercise of freedom.

These six propositions can be summarized neatly (if a trifle tendentiously) in the proposition that the human being is both a free subject obedient to reason and a determined object under nature's laws. My primary obligation is to respect subjects (myself included) as subjects and not to treat them as objects. And from the premise of subjectivity all anthropology begins, as Kant himself makes clear in the first sentence of the *Anthropology*: "That man is able to have among his conceptions the notion 'I,' lifts him infinitely over all other beings on earth." At first sight, this emphasis on the "I" approximates Kant to Descartes—suggesting that Kant is founding his vision of the human condition on a study of the first-person case. That is the opposite of the truth. Kant is describing the "I" from the third-person perspective, and the critical philosophy (as I read it) describes the place of the subject in an objective world.

Kant's immediate successors—Fichte, Schelling, Schiller, and Hegel—gave a peculiar twist to Kantian anthropology, and in doing so endowed it with a cultural and a political meaning that it has never lost. The theme is that of the self-determination (*Selbtsbestimmung*) of the subject. The root idea can be expressed in the following way. Self-consciousness and freedom exist *in potentia* in the human being. But they become actual only when realized as objects of their own awareness. This process of self-realization is also a self-limiting, since we can know the self only if we can distinguish self from not-self. The process of self-limitation is made possible by the objective forms of social life — law and institutions, culture, morality, and interaction with our kind. The free subject, therefore, requires a cultural context. And the highest form of political order is the one that maximally encourages self-realization and therefore self-limitation. Such a political order is an *Entäusserung*—a making objective—of the inner life. It is an objective order among subjects, who are subjects only because of the objective order that preserves and enhances their freedom.

One influential offshoot of this idea was the argument that occurs in Hegel's *Phenomenology of Spirit*, concerning the master and slave, which purports to show that relations of pure power involve a loss of freedom both for the victim and for the victor, and that freedom is realized for both of them only when their "struggle" is transcended into the comparative serenity of mutual respect. Another influential offshoot is the theory of alienation, as this occurs in Marx, which argues that under capitalism people treat one another as objects and so become alienated from their essence, which is that of the free and self-determining subject.

Kant's vision of the human person centers on autonomy. A person is free to act and free to will the maxim of his action as a law. Actions motivated by reason must obey the a priori demand of reason to be free from "empirical conditions," in other words, to be free from all reference to individual interests and desires. Hence reason commands me to will the maxim of my action not as an interest of mine, but as a universal law, binding on all rational beings, by virtue of their rationality alone. This command is the categorical imperative.

In developing that idea Kant brings to the fore two fundamental conceptions: the person and the self. Kant's self is conceived not as Descartes conceived it, as a retreat from the objective world, but as a point of view from which objects are observed, known, and acted upon. The metaphysic of the first-person case has little or no appeal for Kant; in the "Paralogisms of Pure Reason" in the first *Critique* he dismisses the traditional arguments for the individuality, substantiality, and immortality of the soul and replaces the soul with the merely grammatical idea of self-reference, which he summarizes as the "transcendental unity of apperception," which is a merely "formal" (i.e., grammatical) unity and not the substantial unity proposed by Descartes. Nevertheless, Kant suggests, we should not think that persons are merely objects, like the other particulars we encounter in the empirical world. We can indeed *see* them as objects, as things to be used, as means to our ends. But that is precisely to violate the categorical imperative, which tells us to respect reason in all its manifestations and therefore to treat persons not as means only but always as ends in themselves. To treat a person as an end is to acknowledge his autonomy, his freedom, his selfhood. It is to treat him not as an object but as a subject, one who addresses me I to I.

In this way Kant tries to reconstruct the concept of the person through ideas of self-reference, self-consciousness and autonomous choice. There is not some mysterious soul-substance that turns an organism into a person. There is a pattern of self-reference and individual choice, which creates a "first-person perspective" on the behavior of that organism and so converts passion to action and behavior to choice. And one task of philosophy is to describe this first-person perspective from the third-person point of view.

On one simple reading, Kant's radical reworking of morality, in terms of autonomous choice, ought to leave no room for philosophical anthropology. Reason represents a different order of motivation from the passions: its commands are clear and irrevocable, and the feature of the human condition that they presuppose — metaphysical freedom — is one about which, on Kant's view of the matter, nothing can be said. The Kantian theory therefore seems to detach the rational agent entirely from his passions, which are merely part of his "pathology," and to endow him with an abstract and formal motivation in which emotion, virtue, and happiness play no part.

In fact, however, Kant was well aware that the moral motive forms only a small part of our practical nature, that it stands always in need of supplementation from other sources, and that it entirely alters the emotional life and social aspect of the human being. Hence there is considerable scope for philosophy in examining the distinctive nature of interpersonal attitudes—attitudes directed toward other subjects and which involve treating them as subjects. In his lectures on ethics, and in the *Critique of Practical Reason*, Kant unfolds many fascinating arguments, concerning the emotional life of the rational agent, whose states of mind are informed by his practical reason. We constantly veer between the attitude that sees others as desiring animals and the attitude that sees them as autonomous agents like ourselves. Thus Kant builds an elaborate theory of respect for persons and its role in our social emotions and in the institutions of a free society. Although Kant was not so acute an observer as his contemporary, Adam Smith, who was perhaps the greatest philosophical anthropologist in the empiricist tradition (not only in *The Wealth of Nations* but also, preeminently, in *The Theory of the Moral Sentiments*), he covers much of the same ground as Smith, and recognizes, like Smith, that the rational demand for impartiality, which tells us to look on others as we look on ourselves, entirely transforms our emotional lives and governs the possibility of earthly happiness.

Kant bequeathed to German idealism conceptions that have proved influential and even dominant to this day. From the point of view of anthropology no Kantian idea was more important than that of the self—the screen on which the world is printed—with which Kant replaced the rationalist conceptions of the soul. As I have indicated, there is a tendency in Kant to see the self in purely grammatical terms, as a kind of projection of the logic of self-reference. The fundamental feature is not the first person, but the first-person case. Thus in many parts of the *Critique of Pure Reason* Kant refers to the "purely formal unity" of apperception and opposes this to the material or substantial unity of the soul, as the rationalists had presented it. And Kant's argument recalls the Aristotelian idea of the soul as the "form" of the living individual. As he turns from the abstract arguments of metaphysics to the questions of the moral life, however, Kant deploys a richer notion of the self. The self becomes an "idea of reason," a concept to which we cannot give empirical content, but which haunts our practical reasoning with the idea of a transcendental subject, lying behind experience, observing and acting on the world from the unique perspective that is I. It is in this self that freedom, autonomy, and personhood are all mysteriously but also transparently contained.

This is the aspect of Kant that was taken up by Fichte, in the *Wissenschaftslehre*, a work whose obscurity did nothing to prevent its enthusiastic reception in Germany as a new and radical exploration of the human condition and the true starting point for philosophy. The point from which all thinking must begin, according to Fichte, is that mysterious identity, I = I, which contains the whole secret of self-consciousness and whose seeming emptiness conceals vast depths of implication, as we unfold the preconditions under which such a simple-seeming truth could be known. The "I" that knows is the knowing subject; but the "I" that is known is the object of knowledge; so that the word *I* does not occur with equal force or significance in those two occurrences in the original equation. It denotes both the subject and the object, and it is only by realizing itself as an object among other objects that the self can be known. Self-knowledge involves the making objective, the *Entäusserung* of the subject, in the forms and structures of a shared and public world.

Modern Philosophical Anthropology

Fichte's hyperflated argument involves technicalities and jargon of a kind that no longer have much intellectual appeal. His importance lies in the idea that he bequeathed to his immediate successors, Schelling and Hegel, which was to form the basis of an entirely new kind of anthropology: the idea of the self as an entity to be *realized*, through its own "alienation" in a shared and objective world. Fichte uses the term *Selbstbestimmung*, which suggests both "making certain of" and "setting limits to" the self. His root idea is that I achieve self-knowledge, and therefore true freedom, only by adopting forms, customs, and laws that guide and limit my conduct. Self knows itself only in a world of others, in which self and others enjoy the benefits and the burdens of a shared moral life.

The argument has never been more fruitfully expressed than by Hegel, in *The Phenomenology of Spirit* and *The Philosophy of Right*, two works that take forward Kant's conception of the self so as to give a kind of archeology of human freedom. For Hegel we are indeed autonomous and self-conscious beings: but this is a condition that we achieve through our successive "objectifications" of the purely subjective perspective from which our life departs. In a series of extraordinary arguments—half parables, half logical dissections—Hegel shows the unfolding of self-consciousness and its achievement of self-knowledge through the encounter with the Other. The self comes to know itself as other, by giving objective flesh to its subjective inwardness. This knowledge is achieved through a "life and death struggle," through lordship and bondage, through the various stages of the unhappy consciousness and alienation, winning through to enlightenment and freedom only with the recognition of a universal moral law of the kind proposed by Kant. But this law too is only the starting point for the higher forms of freedom that depend upon our social membership and on the institutions of politics. Hegel attempts to give an a priori argument for the laws, customs, and institutions of civil society

271

and to show the human being as intrinsically directed toward a political order founded in law, property, and free association and enjoying a private life as an equal member of a public order.

Hegel began his intellectual journey in the study of theology, and there is always in the back of his mind the desire to provide a vindication of the Christian vision of human destiny. But it is also true that he was infected by the romantic skepticism of his contemporaries and intended his account of the human individual and human society to show what human beings essentially are, whatever their faith.

When Hegel was developing his Fichtean version of Kant's theory of practical reason, another theologically minded philosopher, Friedrich Daniel Ernst Schleiermacher, was developing Kant's ideas in another directon. The Kantian vision of the human subject seems to imply that my actions are to be understood not by explaining them as a scientist would, but by attributing them to my rational self and searching for the reasoning behind them. Reasons are discovered through dialogue. I come to understand your reasons by asking the question *why* and seeking out the maxim governing your action, the end pursued through it, and the means chosen to achieve that end. There is, in all such rational dialogue, a search for meaning: how you construe the world shapes what you intend, and there is no way in which I can understand the reasoning behind your action if I do not also understand the meaning of your words and gestures and the way in which you divide and classify the world.

Schleiermacher argued that there is a general problem of hermeneutics, manifest in the particular case of biblical texts with which he was especially concerned. Such texts are to be understood as actions, not as objects; and their meaning is revealed in the reasons for their creation. But those reasons can be understood only through the meanings contained in them. Hence we must first assign a meaning to the text if we are to understand the reasoning behind it; yet if we have not deciphered that reasoning, we will not be able to assign a meaning.

This "hermeneutical circle" was not described as such by Schleiermacher, nor is it clear that he would have seen it as an insuperable obstacle to biblical exegesis. (It was Heidegger who was to stress this difficulty, for purposes of his own.) What becomes apparent in Schleiermacher's writings is the contrast that he makes between explaining actions and understanding them and his view of meaning as what is *understood* in another's words and behavior, rather than what explains their origins. This idea was given a pivotal role in philosophical anthropology by Wilhelm Dilthey, who called himself a Kantian and who followed Schleiermacher in making a sharp distinction between explaining a person and understanding him. The distinction corresponds to the Kantian distinction between seeing a person as an object, part of nature, governed by natural laws, and seeing him as a subject, a citizen of the kingdom of ends, obedient to the law of reason.

There are not, Dilthey suggested, two parts of a human being, but rather two ways of approaching him, either with the objective eye of science, or with the interpersonal attitude he called *understanding*, or *Verstehen*. This interpersonal *Verstehen* looks for reasons rather than what an Aristotelian would call "efficient" causes, meanings rather than biological needs, and searches out the subjective perspective from which the other looks out on the world.

Science and *Verstehen* are, metaphysically speaking, approaches to the same phenomena. But these phenomena are conceptualized in contrasting and incommensurable ways. An analogy illustrates what Dilthey had in mind. Pigments spread on a canvas are conceptualized in one way by the scientist who reduces them to digital coordinates and in another way by the critic who describes the image that we see in them. The two descriptions are incommensurable, even though there is nothing described in the one that is not described (using other concepts and categories) in the other.

That idea of Dilthey suggested not merely two contrasting visions of people in everyday life, but also two contrasting forms of study, that of the natural sciences on the one hand and that of the humanities or *Geisteswissenschaften* on the other. From our point of view, however, the significance of Dilthey's approach is that it carves out a territory for philosophical anthropology that is both morally significant and protected from invasion by the biological sciences. We encounter everywhere today the belief that we can understand the nature and significance of human action and emotion by studying them as expressions of our biological nature and our species needs, explaining them, for example, as the bequests of evolution and reducing them to variants of behavior and emotion to be observed in animals. Thus, when biologists write of "altruism," they tend to assume that this term denotes one and the same phenomenon, whether it is applied to the bee that "lays down its life" for the hive or the man who lays down his life for his friend (although the bee does not lay down its life, of course, since it has no conception of life, no conception of sacrifice, and no ability to form the complex intention summarized as "laying down"). This "biologism," actively pursued by Richard Dawkins and his followers, is fast becoming the public doctrine concerning the nature and destiny of mankind. Against that doctrine I would claim that biology neither contains nor could contain the concepts through which human action is understood—any more than the digital representation of a picture could contain the concepts in terms of which it is seen. To understand people, we need to proceed in the way that Dilthey recommended, by conceptualizing the world as they do and not by explaining their behavior from the perspective of empirical science. Moreover, the intentionality of human emotions and the structure of human motives are both predicated on meanings that lie beyond the repertoire of nonrational animals. I have tried to give an example of this in my book *Sexual Desire*, in which I argue that sexual desire is a purely human phenomenon and is only genealogically related to the reproductive urges of other animals.

One of the philosophers who most influenced me in the writing of that book, and one of the few who has had anything interesting to say about its subject matter, was Max Scheler, and it is fitting to make a few remarks about this neglected thinker, in whom the Kantian tradition is combined with a deep respect both for the Thomist and the Augustinian legacies, and whose particular variety of "personalism" had such a profound influence on the late Pope John Paul II.

Scheler recognized that there was no understanding to be gained of human emotions and motives if we did not first see them as the mental states of rational beings, who conceptualize the world in terms of its meaning, whose concepts and categories are shaped by the needs of rational action, and who see other members of their kind not as human animals, but as persons, subjects of consciousness, and autonomous agents. Toward such beings we have sympathies (and also resentments) of a special kind. We feel shame and pride in their presence, as we do not in the presence of an animal. And all our relations with them are informed by the attitude of judgment, knowing that they too judge. It was from this premise that Scheler developed his remarkable studies of sympathy, *ressentiment*, and sexual shame, as interpersonal responses through which we shape the human world.[280] Scheler's approach has given hope to those philosophers, and I am one of them, who believe that there really is a conceptual study of

---

[280] Max Scheler, "Über Scham und Schamgefühl," in *Schriften aus dem Nachlass*, ed. Maria Scheler (Bern: Franck, Verlag, 1957); Max Scheler, *Ressentiment*, trans. L. B. Coser and W. W. Holdheim (Milwaukee: Marquette University Press, 1998).

human nature and that this study will show us not only what we are but also how we flourish and decline.

Therapeutic Implications

The ancient wisdom that made rationality part of the human essence was endorsed both by the medievals and the Kantians. Aristotle was also interested in the abnormalities of practical reason, in particular with the condition that he called *akrasia*, or weakness of will. But any concern for the mental health of the human agent was absorbed, by Aristotle, into the theory of virtue and vice. Since practical reason is expressed in action, and since actions can frustrate or fulfill our nature, the rational agent should acquire the dispositions that tend to our fulfillment. These dispositions are the virtues, and the four cardinal virtues — courage, temperance, prudence, and justice — must be instilled in each child as the only assurance, prior to living it, that his life will be lived for his good.

This emphasis on virtue recurs in Aquinas and can be seen as forestalling much of the current concern of psychotherapy. The virtuous person is one who is at peace with himself, freed from shame and self-reproach, and unhappy, if at all, only on account of external forces with which he has to contend and from which no therapy can release him. With the advent of the Kantian picture, however, the emphasis shifts from the concern with character to that beguiling and elusive thing, the self. Although Hegel shared Aristotle's view, that fulfillment comes through right relations with others, his way of arriving at this conclusion made room for the self-obsession that is observable in many forms of psychotherapy. The theory of self-realization officially assigns no identity to the self and no reality to freedom, save in the context of an active life in society. The theory is turned outward, toward the third-person view. It ought therefore to follow Aristotle and Aquinas, in regarding the well-being of the human individual as residing in a virtuous character and settled relations with others and with God.

At the same time, however, the idealist theory generates, like a shadow, the opposite idea, of the self as somehow fully real, free and pure, prior to its outward adventure in the world of others. In this view unhappiness resides in a dissonance between self and other. Hegel would argue that this dissonance can certainly occur, but that it is a sign of immaturity, like the "unhappy consciousness" to which he devotes some of his most poetic pages. It is a stage that the self must *pass through* if it is to be fully itself, the cure for which is a more disciplined and determined venture toward the other. For many schools of psychotherapy, however, this dissonance between self and other lies at the root of mental illness. Some practitioners, such as Laing and the existentialists, even blame others in general, and the family in particular, for the patient's sense of being sundered from the world of others by an existential divide.

Behind all such theories lies the adoption of that pernicious word *Ich*, not as a reflexive pronoun, but as a substantive noun. The error here reflects Freud's theory of the unconscious. Freud divides the mind into three parts, *Das Ich*, *Das Es*, and *Das Über-Ich*. This reification of the "I" (obscured by Strachey's translation into *ego*, *id*, and *super-ego*) comes from Fichte and Hegel and is a long-term consequence of Kant's own hesitation between the true view of the first *Critique*, which sees self-consciousness in terms of the grammar of the reflexive pronoun, and the false view often glimpsed in the second *Critique*, which represents self-consciousness as the acquaintance with a transcendental object: the reified "Ich." Although, properly understood, the idealist emphasis on the self can be reconciled with a sound anthropology; it is open to this tempting misinterpretation, which makes the self into a refuge from the world of others, rather than an aspiring part of it. And the reification of the self amplifies the quite dangerous tendency in much modern therapeutic practice to treat the patient as enjoying a prelapsarian innocence. In the view of Laing and Esterson, for example, the self is essentially pure, unsullied, longing for the freedom and spontaneity that society denies. If it is suffering, it is from "repression," and to remedy such a malady, the other, not the self, must change.

If, however, we reject the reification of the "I," we will find, in the Kantian tradition, a kind of philosophical anthropology that upholds much of the old morality of virtue. This is the lesson of Dilthey and Scheler, both of whom avoid the excesses of Hegelian metaphysics and rest content with emphasizing the categories through which we shape our goals and our reasons for pursuing them. These categories spread before us what Husserl called the *Lebenswelt*, the world of life. And although there is nothing contained in this world that is hidden from the scientist, there is no science that describes what it contains.

One task for philosophical anthropology today, therefore, is to adapt the insights of the Kantian tradition to the modern philosophy of mind. Ever since Wittgenstein's *Philosophical Investigations*, published in 1952, it has been apparent that the first-person approach to the mind, on which so much hope had been pinned by Husserl in his early years, and by Sartre in *Being and Nothingness*, will yield at best only engaging metaphors. Wittgenstein's decisive demolition of the first-person perspective opens the way to a new and more fruitful philosophical anthropology, in which the social nature of the individual is given due prominence. Although Wittgenstein rejected phenomenology, as based on a philosophical confusion, he agreed with Dilthey and Scheler that we perceive and understand human behavior in a manner different from the way in which we perceive and understand the natural world. We explain human behavior by giving reasons, not causes. We address ourselves to our future by making decisions, not predictions. We understand the past and present of mankind through our aims, emotions and activity, and not through predictive theories. All these things reinforce the Husserlian idea of a *Lebenswelt* distinct from the world of science.

Much of Wittgenstein's later philosophy is devoted to describing and analyzing the characteristics of human understanding and demolishing what he thought to be the vulgar illusion that science could generate a description of all those things with which our humanity is mingled. He argues not only that our knowledge of our own minds presupposes the knowledge of the minds of others (for how else could language, and the self-knowledge that depends on language, be taught?) but also that, as Scheler put it, "our conviction of the existence of other minds is earlier and deeper than our belief in the existence of nature." Wittgenstein shares with phenomenologists the sense that there is a mystery in human things that will not yield to scientific investigation. This mystery is dispelled not by explanation but by careful philosophical description of the "given." For Wittgenstein, however, what is "given" is not the immediate contents of first-person awareness, but the publicly observable "forms of life" that make that awareness possible. A Wittgensteinian anthropology would devote itself to examining those forms of life, to exploring the way in which self-consciousness is displayed in social behavior, and to showing how disorders might be rectified by adjusting the individual to his social context, so that the third-person perspective, the view from outside, can exert its controlling and mediating influence over the view from within.

In my own work I have attempted a synthesis between the "hetero-phenomenology" of Wittgenstein and the Kantian theory of the subject, in an attempt to make sense of key human experiences and to understand the place of freedom, rationality, and virtue in securing our fulfillment. The result is in one way very distant from the chapters presented in this volume, since it derives from a philosophical tradition that has been largely uninfluenced by Thomism and has only belatedly acknowledged Aristotle as its founder. But my conclusions are close to those presented here, and depend on the same fundamental perception, that the human being stands both in the natural world and out of it.

Chapter 12

Mental Health and Human Well-Being

Benedict M. Ashley

At a time when the question "What is the relation of the human mind to the human body?" is still hotly debated by scientists, it is not surprising that the goal of psychotherapy is also in question. As a step in a long-time program of research, the essays found in this volume seek to advance our understanding of these questions by especially considering the thought of St. Thomas Aquinas. Because it seeks to serve therapists within the large Christian tradition, this book wishes to take advantage of the Catholic Church's long-standing recommendation of Aquinas for his balanced summing up of the results of the Church's long experience in trying to understand human behavior. Our study looks forward to well-planned empirical research using current research techniques to correct bias and prejudice to test this Thomistic model.

What are the main points that have emerged from our study?

Mental health cannot be defined except in relation to human physical health, and human physical health must be itself defined in relation to the good of the total human person. Since human persons are essentially social beings, further consideration needs to be given to this social aspect of health. Matthew Cuddeback establishes this point and shows that it is a grave mistake to think of persons reductively: they must be considered in terms of their existential totality.

To understand the totality of the human person we must face the fact that we are inevitably moral or immoral persons or a particular mixture of both, that is, we are persons who have freedom and responsibility for our own lives and our relations to others. Human freedom, however, is not necessarily to do what we "want" to do, but requires us to respect human nature as a given fact, since doing what we desire can often destroy our freedom. One great source of mental illness is self-destructive behavior. The proper goal of psychotherapy, therefore, is to break this vicious circle so as to enable a client to be free to make realistic decisions. Realistic decisions are ones that face up to the natural moral law, as John Cuddeback shows, and then apply it prudently, as Craig Titus shows. The very concept of human freedom, however, runs into the tendency of scientists to insist that human behavior is explainable by psychological laws, that is, is deterministic. They, of course, have come to admit a certain type of indeterminism and thus are ready to deal with determinism and chance, but not with true freedom. Tobias Hoffman carefully clears up this confusion.

Modern rationalism since Kant, as well as ancient Stoicism, emphasized that freedom is made possible only by reason, but they exaggerated this to maintain that human emotion, as such, is essentially the enemy of reason. Aquinas, as Paul Gondreau shows, strongly opposes this rationalism and gives to human affectivity a necessary and positive role in human freedom and moral decision. Thus psychotherapy should seek to free the patient from defective emotion and promote, not degrade, virtuous affectivity, just as medicine should promote good physiological functioning.

Since Freud, no one would question that sexual affectivity is a principal factor with which the psychotherapist must deal, but sometimes less attention is given to what Aquinas insists is the other principal bodily drive or affection, namely, aggression.

Without courage to overcome the obstacles to life we will perish. Freud perversely called aggression "the death wish" when in fact it is, like the sexual and food drives, directed to life, not destruction as such. Daniel McInerny shows the rich thought of Aquinas on this human factor.

David Franks, in dealing with the sexual drive, enters more than any of our other authors into the sociological aspect of human behavior, which, as I have mentioned, requires further exploration. He well shows how today the lack of social support has left many persons sexually dysfunctional. The remedy, however, is not suppression of affective drives, including the sex drive, but their development through the skills we call *virtues*, in this case the virtue of temperance or moderation in our dependence on pleasure to support realistic living.

Mental health, therefore, is not as such a virtue, but is a state of affairs in which the person has become free to make realistic, prudent decisions and thus to begin to acquire the virtues which will enable them to work consistently to attain the goal of human happiness. Medicine has as its goal optimal physiological functioning of the person, yet this needs to be understood in the context of the person's whole life. Similarly psychotherapy, as such, can go no further than to help persons become free to make realistic decisions about their lives and must leave medical, ethical, and spiritual problems to other counselors of appropriate expertise; it must nevertheless view its task in the context of the total person, as all our essayists insist.

As I read these essays with admiration certain other questions for further research have occurred to me. The first concerns terminology, which may seem trivial, but it has done a good deal of harm in confusing our thinking about these so important issues. Obviously Aquinas's terminology, such terms as *form, soul, virtue*, and *happiness* raise problems for those trained in modern psychology. What is often not realized, however, is that modern philosophical terminology and even that used by Catholic writers, is often deeply colored with dangerous, especially dualistic, idealistic, and reductionist connotations that can have deleterious practical consequences. For example, what is "psychology" and what is "metaphysics? And what is "ontological"? Today we are faced with the "information explosion" and the resultant very difficult problem of interdisciplinarity: "How do we interrelate different types of knowledge without destroying their proper autonomy?" Aquinas addressed this problem in his synthesizing science, "metaphysics," which many today confuse with some kind of idealistic, a priori foundationalism or even with fortune-telling or else despise as nonsense. St. Thomas's intention, however, was to correct the Neo-Platonism that colored Christian thought (and still does) by carefully distinguishing and relating different types of knowledge.

In this "division of the sciences" the treatment of living things is the culmination of natural science and establishes that human intelligence, as well as some uncaused causes of our changing universe, must exist, yet the positive study of their transcendent natures exceeds the methods of natural science. Therefore, the study of the human person, as regards the body and the conscious life that we share with animals, including our sexual and aggressive drives, properly pertains to natural science, but human intelligence, reflective self-consciousness, and freedom exceed the methods of natural science and pertain to metaphysics. Metaphysics is a synthesizing discipline that introduces no new information, but argues by analogy from effect to cause, that is, from the empirically observable effects concerning which it is informed by the other special disciplines; that is, it is interdisciplinary.

This means first that, to be valid, metaphysics must rest on the proof of the existence of immaterial first causes in natural science. Furthermore, it presents difficulties to the learners that require mature experience. Hence, although it is "first philosophy" in the sense of the most eminent, it is last in the order of learning. Furthermore this arduous study would not be worth the effort if the ethical sciences, also based on what we have learned about human nature in natural science, did not show that human happiness is not complete without the unified understanding of our world and God, which only reasoned metaphysics and revealed theology provide.

Thus for Aquinas there are three great theoretical disciplines: natural science, metaphysics, and mathematics. Mathematics and the art of logic that it so well exemplifies are not of great importance for their content. Logic helps us order and check the consistency of our knowledge in other sciences and communicate it in proper language. Mathematics abstracts from the quantities of things studied in natural science and is a useful instrument for its researches.

The practical sciences are the technologies and fine arts that produce useful instruments of life and include medicine that aims at human physical health and furthermore the ethical sciences that govern our free decisions of means in our search for the goal of happiness. These sciences demonstrate why our happiness ultimately consists in the contemplation of God. The ethical sciences are three: those governing personal decisions, family decisions, and political or social decisions.

Where then does psychology fit in? The ancient Greek saying "Know thyself" shows that humans have always been interested in themselves and others. Yet *psychology* is a word that first occurs in 1590 in the writings of a rather pedantic German Protestant philosopher, Rudolph Göeckel (Goclenius). It did not become popular before 1719, when another, even more pedantic German Protestant philosopher, Baron Christian von Wolff (1679-1754), professor at the Universities of Marburg and Halle in Prussia, began publishing his immense textbook *Rational Ideas on the Power of Human Understanding*. It was so popular not only in German

Universities but throughout Europe that it became, as it were, the bible of the Enlightenment. The Enlightenment's greatest thinker was Immanuel Kant (1724–1804), who was educated in Wolff's philosophy and, although he came to criticize its dogmatism, never escaped from its idealistic rationalism.

Two volumes of Wolff's textbook were titled *Psychologia Empirica* (1732) and *Psychologia Rationalis* (1734).[281] Wolff had been a disciple of the great mathematician, scientist, and philosopher Gottfried Wilhelm Leibniz (1646–1716), who was a follower of René Descartes (1596–1650). Descartes had revived the ancient Platonic notion that the certitude of knowledge rests not on empirical evidence but on innate ideas. Like Descartes and Leibniz, Wolff was a thorough rationalist and assumed that metaphysics, because it deals with innate first principles, is what is first known to us. Although he gave more value to sense knowledge than Descartes and Leibniz had done, he accepted Leibniz's view that general metaphysics, or ontology (another term invented by Glocenius), is concerned not merely with what is actual but first of all with what is "possible." Hence he considered "rational psychology" a branch of "special" metaphysics, that applies "ontology," or general metaphysics, to particular fields of knowledge. Thus he distinguished it from "empirical psychology," based on sense observation.

This Wolffian distinction between metaphysical "philosophy" and empirical "science" was taken up by neo-scholastics and

---

281 Some sources attribute it to Luther's reformer Phillip Melancthon (1497–1560), who Protestantized the German universities, but it is not found in his published works. Others attribute the term to Otto Casmann (1562–1607), but he used it in print four years after Goclenius; see Marko Marulic (pseudonym for K. Krstic), "The Author of the Term 'Psychology,'" *Acta Instituti Psychologici Universitatis Zagrabiensis*, no. 36 (1964): 7–13; available from http://psychclassics. yorku.ca/Krstic/marulic.htm.

Mental Health and Human Well-Being

became common among Thomists even after Leo XIII's revival of Thomism, although in fact it is quite contrary to the views of St. Thomas Aquinas. The danger of this terminology, which Wolff did not foresee, is that in our modern universities "philosophy" has become a marginalized department grouped with the "soft-headed" humanities over against the dominant "hard-headed" empirical sciences. We ought, therefore, to avoid the term *philosophy* unless we mean *metaphysics* and should drop such terms as *philosophy of science* and *philosophy of this and that* as hopelessly confusing.

What then, again, is psychology? I believe that Wolff was right in thinking it is really two sciences but utterly wrong in thinking that there is a "rational" and an "empirical" psychology. All valid knowledge other than sacred theology, Aquinas insists, is derived from the senses and is thus empirical, and of course it is also rational. Properly, therefore, the term *psychology* should be taken for what St. Thomas called *De Anima* and should refer to the study of the sense knowledge and affectivity of animals, including the human animal, and should be considered the culminating part of biology and biology as the culminating part of natural science. This in fact is what current psychology is. Unlike current psychology, however, when it treats of the Mind-Body Problem, psychology should demonstrate that human behavior cannot be explained without admitting the unique existence in human persons of an immaterial intelligence and hence of a soul that is more than material. This discovery then refers the discussion of these topics to metaphysics and, for Christians, ultimately to sacred theology. Thus, instead of rational and empirical psychology, it would be better to speak of *comparative psychology*, relating this discipline to physical, animal aspects of human thought and feeling, and *personal psychology*, relating it to the specifically human aspects of intelligence and freedom. Psychotherapy, therefore, operates at the borderline of these two disciplines.

Philosophical Virtues and Psychological Strengths

Psychotherapy thus becomes the practical application of psychology to the achievement of mental health at the animal level, just as medicine is the practical application of biology to the achievement of physical health at that same level. It also means, however, that psychotherapy is unusual in that it operates at the borderline of natural science and touches not only on medical technologies but also on philosophy, that is, on metaphysics. Psychotherapy's goal is to enable persons who suffer from unhealthy behavioral patterns that limit their realistic view of themselves, the world in which they live, and the God who is their ultimate goal and joy, but it cannot as such provide ethical or metaphysical guidance. This limitation of scope does not, however, render psychotherapy unimportant; rather it shows its immense importance and the immense importance of educating psychotherapists in the basic results of the other disciplines.

The final topic I would like to outline from the results of this study is, as I have mentioned, further research that makes use of the current techniques, instruments, and mathematical methods in the study of psychology as the culminating part of natural science. This was what Wilhelm Wundt (1832–1920), commonly called the Father of Psychology, intended when in 1879 he set up the first laboratory of experimental psychology at the University of Leipzig. Wundt wrote in his *Principles of Physiological Psychology* (1902):

> Psychological inquiries have, up to the most recent times, been undertaken solely in the interest of philosophy; physiology was enabled, by the character of its problems, to advance more quickly toward the application of exact experimental methods. Since, however, the experimental modification of the processes of life, as practiced by physiology, oftentimes effects a concomitant change, direct or indirect, in the processes of consciousness—which, as we

have seen, form part of vital processes at large—it is clear that physiology is, in the very nature of the case, qualified to assist psychology on the side of method; thus rendering the same help to psychology that it, itself received from physics. In so far as physiological psychology receives assistance from physiology in the elaboration of experimental methods, it may be termed experimental psychology.

While more detailed classification is possible, one author offers this basic breakdown of the schools of psychotherapy. George Boeree[282] groups current theories into three "forces:"

- The *psychoanalytic*, which seeks explanation of human behavior in the unconscious.

- The *behavioristic*, which seeks explanations in external behavior in relation to the environment.

- The *humanistic*, which seeks explanations in conscious experience.

Psychoanalysis, once so dominant, has lost much favor both from a theoretical and a practical perspective. The humanistic approach has the disadvantage that it confuses the borderline I have described between natural science and philosophy, that is, metaphysics. Thus the best candidate and the closest to Aquinas's view is the behavioristic (with its cognitive emotive modifications) for two reasons: (a) it fits his axiom, "a thing is as it acts," and thus we can really know human beings only by their actions, although what they say is part of their behavior; (b) it tends to confine itself to being a part of natural science and does not move into metaphysics. Strict behaviorism, however, has its dangers. Watson and Skinner, who proposed a radical behaviorism,

---

[282] George Boeree, *Personality Theories*, http://webspace.ship.edu/cgboer/perscontents.html (last modified 2006).

neglected introspective evidence and communication, as well as the problem of consciousness, and this radicalism proved hopelessly inadequate. Modified forms of behaviorism, however, which would include cognitive theory, offer notable prospects for development.

What is needed is adequate research on problems that lie at the borderline where a scientific understanding of human behavior touches on human intelligence and freedom and thus on ethics and metaphysics. Let me give a simple example. A marriage counselor refers a married woman to a psychotherapist because her marital problems seem compounded by depression that results from her unrealistic view of her own sexual attractiveness. She and her husband have always had trouble communicating with each other because he is busy making a fortune and shows little interest in her and their three children. The counselor is trying to get the couple to sit down and discuss this issue, but the woman is so depressed that when they attempt to do so she does nothing but burst into tears. This makes the husband eager to escape counseling sessions. They no longer share even their one former common interest in vacation travel.

The cognitive therapist, of course, aims at getting the depressed wife to discuss her fantasies and feelings about herself and her family in relation to the real facts of her married life. To do this, however, the therapist must have in mind some model in behavioral terms of what good married life is like. Yet in forming this model and critically examining its adequacy, the therapist, if honest, will soon discover that his own worldview (which is at the metaphysical level) and value system (at the ethical level and related to the metaphysical) inevitably enter into that model to a degree.

For Catholics this presents the following problem. We fortunately have a very well-developed metaphysics and moral theology based on the Church's long pastoral and confessional experience. Nevertheless, for the most part we have neglected modern-type research on whether its conclusions can be verified in modern experience. We need to subject our view of the happy marriage and its possible defects to modern research techniques that yield mathematical measurements. Only then will we be able to meet the modern sense of realism and to answer those who say that our moral standards are not only hopelessly contrary to modern conditions, but are actually harmful to mental health.

Finally, I want to urge research on the role of the interior senses in free decision, not only the memory and imagination or fantasy so much emphasized in psychoanalysis, but on what Aquinas called the *vis aestimativa*, or instinct in animals, and its equivalent *vis cogitativa*, or evaluative sense in human persons. According to St. Thomas it is this interior sense that mediates between our intelligence and free will as well as between these spiritual acts and our affectivity. We can imagine something without recognizing it as either pleasant or unpleasant, that is, as attractive or unattractive because of our human needs. Animals, however, have instincts that tell them which stimuli are to be sought and which avoided, and these instincts can be further determined by experience. We also have such instincts, but in order to leave us free for more complicated learning than animals ever acquire, our instincts are relatively unspecified. Through experience and education, however, we acquire all sorts of likes and dislikes, attitudes and inclinations, and ultimately virtues or vices. I believe mental illnesses are probably in the main defects of the evaluative sense. Moreover, the transcendence of free intelligence over animal consciousness in which mental health consists directly involves the evaluative sense.

Chapter 13

Postscript

Paul C. Vitz

At the end of this collection of rich and relevant chapters, let us consider its title, *Philosophical Virtues and Psychological Strengths: Building the Bridge*, and ask the question: Have the two disciplines been truly bridged, that is, widely and strongly linked? The answer, I believe, is no, but much progress has been made. In view of the importance of connecting the philosophy and psychology of the virtues, the fact that significant progress has been made here is a real contribution.

A bridge commonly involves a foundation column on or near each of the two banks or sides that are being connected. The essays in this book (and probably some existing elsewhere) constitute a foundation column near the side of philosophy, which is no mean accomplishment. All of the preceding chapters contribute to this task. Already such a foundation has been built on the psychology side by such theorists as Martin Seligman and the established and still growing field of "positive psychology." Academic and research psychology have in the last ten to fifteen years spelled out a good psychological introduction to most but not all the virtues. One very important psychological understanding that remains weak, however, is the application of the virtues in psychotherapy, the kind of psychology of most relevance to this book. That is, a general theoretical and research-based psychological foundation of the virtues is available, but it is in the application to mental pathology and specific requests for help that psychological understanding is inadequate. This remaining weakness probably accounts for why I said the bridge has not been completely constructed—why the distance between the two disciplines has not been fully spanned.

It remains for concrete clinical intervention based on the virtues and applied to different pathologies and mental problems to be developed and verified before a truly useful bridge is possible. Let me briefly describe the work of two students at the Institute for the Psychological Sciences that illustrate what needs to be done.

Leslie Trautman addressed, in her dissertation, Narcissistic Personality Disorder (NPD), a notoriously difficult psychological condition to treat effectively. She proposed that by using techniques of Cognitive and Behavioral Theory (CBT) and the virtues of humility and altruism, she could intervene to help patients with NPD. She described cognitive understanding and specific behavioral practices whereby the patient learned about and practiced these two virtues. Each virtue had a simple, intermediate, and more advanced level of practice and understanding. The basic psychological rationale for each virtue was that it would help patients get outside of their ego or narcissistic preoccupations, thus alleviating their disorder (NPD). In the case of altruism patients are to practice helping and doing good to others that would require thinking about what others needed and were feeling and then responding to them in a positive way. Humility was not described using this word but as gaining true self-knowledge developed primarily through discussion with the therapist. As such the dissertation was a theoretical one and the all-important stage of testing whether the approach would work remains to be seen.

Eric Gudan, also in his theoretical dissertation, has proposed that practicing the virtue of gratitude should be an effective healing response for people suffering from ruminative depression. There is a good deal of psychological research with nonclinical subjects that supports the claim that practicing gratitude has positive effects on emotions and attitudes. But, again, whether this would be an effective CBT approach for people with depression of the ruminative type remains to be demonstrated. Many other such possible approaches remain to be spelled out and tested. For example, could training in courage help those suffering from intense anxiety and fearfulness? Can justice be effectively used with antisocial pathologies, perhaps in combination with altruism? How might training in the virtues be used with couples or in family therapy? When such theoretical approaches have been developed for the application of virtues to therapy, the difficult and time-consuming verification process still remains to be done.

Of course, the virtues are not just about recovering from mental pathologies and problems. Perhaps even more important is to test the claim that happiness and flourishing are the result of learning and living the life of the virtues. The research clearly demonstrating this traditional understanding of the virtue-based life also remains without convincing empirical support.

When and if the above types of research are published, an even more sophisticated philosophical/psychological interpretation of the virtues will be possible.

For example, can all or only some of the virtues be learned, and at what ages and with what procedures? I assume philosophers eagerly await such findings and the methods that reliably demonstrate them. For philosophers to evaluate these future contributions they will obviously have to keep in close intellectual contact with the therapists and psychologists applying specific virtues in their work.

There remains an even broader and deeper psychological topic that involves the virtues. In many ways the virtues have been understood as the positive flourishing of a person's natural good capacities. Although each person may be born with a greater potential for some virtues compared with others, the good life is what helps one's virtues to flourish. This theory implies that the virtues represent a kind of innate, latent structure for everyone. We already know that all humans are born with an innate linguistic structure expressed somewhat differently in each language. By analogy, then, humans can be thought of as being born with a latent virtue structure. Presumably this structure interacts with our experiences, both positive and harmful, so as to create a particular underlying virtue structure for each person. This actual virtue structure can be considered as each individual's personality. Such an approach to understanding personality has yet to be fully conceptualized and its measurement developed.

One last topic dealing with the virtues as understood in philosophy and especially theology should be noted. Reasonably enough, the preceding chapters have dealt with the natural virtues. But the nature and relevance of the theological virtues calls for some discussion. These virtues, faith, hope, and charity (love) may be theological and primarily the result of grace and the practice of religious activities such as prayer and almsgiving, but the effects of such virtues are nevertheless often observable in a person's attitudes and behavior. If the effects were not observable, there would be no way to judge people as being holy and saintly. But such people are identified with some reliability. Indeed, the official process of canonization in the Roman Catholic Church relies to a significant degree on reliable reports of the candidate's behavior and mental life. Therefore there is no reason why at least some of the effects of the theological virtues could not be part of psychological science and integrated with their philosophical and theological understanding.

Acknowledgments

This volume is the fruit of an initiative of the Scholarly Research Center of the Institute for the Psychological Sciences in Arlington, Virginia. We acknowledge with special gratitude the munificence of Mrs. Barbara Koch from Minnesota, whose devotion to the work of the institute prompted her to make up a majority of the benefaction. The faculty of the institute and others associated with its work take a special interest in multidisciplinary studies, especially the relationship between psychology, philosophy, and religious studies. The essays contained in this volume are the fruit of regular meetings held over a period of three years, in several cities along the East Coast of the United States. In addition to the contributing scholars, who represent mainly the disciplines of theology and philosophy, the research group held dialogue sessions with leading practitioners of psychology, especially Robert Coles and William Beardsley, MD, of Harvard University. Dr. Abbyann Lynch of University of Toronto participated in the common discussions for a certain period. These discussions allowed the authors who contributed essays to this volume to develop a unified presentation of the elements of a philosophical psychology. The editors gratefully acknowledge the support given by the officers of the Institute for the Psychological Sciences as well as the assistants of the institute, especially Mrs. Nancy Flynn, whose assistance proved indispensable to bringing the research project to fruition. The authors and editors express gratitude to the president of Sophia Institute Press, Dr. William Fahey, for the attentive way in which he and Dr. Christopher Blum have made the results of our important and innovative research available to students of religious studies, philosophy, and psychology.

Contributors

Benedict M. Ashley, O.P., is emeritus professor of moral theology at Aquinas Institute of Theology, St. Louis. He has been involved in interdisciplinary dialogue between science and faith for half a century, including at the Institute for the Psychological Sciences. Among his many publications are *Health Care Ethics* (with Jean de Blois and Kevin O'Rourke), *Justice in the Church*, *Living the Truth in Love*, *Theologies of the Body*, and most recently *The Way toward Wisdom: An Interdisciplinary and Intercultural Introduction to Metaphysics* and *The Ashley Reader*.

Romanus Cessario, O.P., completed doctoral studies at the University of Fribourg and continues to carry on research in psychology and moral theology. He is author of more than a hundred articles in theology and related fields and has published eighteen books mostly on the virtues and Christian ethics, including *The Moral Virtues and Theological Ethics*, *Christian Faith and the Theological Life*, and *Introduction to Moral Theology*. Father Cessario teaches at St. John's Seminary in Brighton, Massachusetts, and is a Fellow of the Pontifical Academy of Saint Thomas Aquinas.

John A. Cuddeback received a Ph.D. in philosophy from The Catholic University of America. He is a professor of philosophy at Christendom College in Front Royal, Virginia. He teaches, writes, and lectures in ethics, especially concerning friendship and law. His recent book is *True Friendship: Where Virtue Becomes Happiness*. He is married with six children.

Matthew Cuddeback received his Ph.D. in philosophy from The Catholic University of America and is assistant professor of philosophy at Providence College in Providence, Rhode Island. His research and published articles focus on philosophical anthropology in view of the metaphysical teaching of Thomas Aquinas.

J. David Franks received his Ph.D. in theology from Boston College. He is assistant professor of theology (systematic and moral theology) at St. John's Seminary, Brighton, Massachusetts. He serves as vice president for mission of the Theological Institute for the New Evangelization of Saint John's Seminary.

Paul Gondreau, S.T.D./Ph.D., did his graduate work in theology at the University of Fribourg, Switzerland, from which time he has been engaged in dialogue between psychology and moral philosophy and theology. He has authored several articles and has published a book on the role of the emotions in the life of Christ: *The Passions of Christ's Soul in the Theology of St. Thomas Aquinas*. Professor Gondreau teaches at Providence College, Rhode Island, and is married with five children. He is faculty resident director of the CEA/Providence College Center for Theology and Religious Studies.

Tobias Hoffmann (Ph.D., Fribourg) is an associate professor in the School of Philosophy at The Catholic University of America, Washington, DC. His numerous articles, edited volumes, books, and translations have concentrated on medieval metaphysics and ethics, and especially free choice and the problem of weakness of will; his edited volumes include: *The Problem of Weakness of Will in Medieval Philosophy*; *Weakness of Will from Plato to the Present*, *Thomas Aquinas and the Nicomachean Ethics*.

Contributors

Daniel McInerny earned his doctorate in philosophy from The Catholic University of America and has held positions at the University of St. Thomas (Houston), the Notre Dame Center for Ethics and Culture, and Baylor University. He is the author of *The Difficult Good: A Thomistic Account of Moral Conflict and Human Happiness* and of fiction for children and adults. He is the CEO of Trojan Tub Entertainment, a children's entertainment company.

Kenneth L. Schmitz is professor of philosophy at the John Paul II Institute for Studies on Marriage and Family in Washington, DC, and professor emeritus of philosophy at Trinity College, University of Toronto. He is the author of *The Gift: Creation; At the Center of the Human Drama: The Philosophical Anthropology of Karol Wojtyla/Pope John Paul II; The Recovery of Wonder: The New Freedom and the Asceticism of Power; The Texture of Being: Essays in First Philosophy;* and *Person and Psyche.*

Roger Scruton is resident fellow at the American Enterprise Institute, Washington, DC, and senior research fellow at Blackfriars Hall, Oxford. He is an academic philosopher, writer, editor, and publisher who has served as professor of aesthetics at Birkbeck College, London, and as professor of philosophy and university professor at Boston University. In addition to philosophical publications, he also writes fiction and political and cultural commentary. His most recent books are *The West and the Rest; Death-Devoted Heart: Sex and the Sacred in Wagner's Tristan and Isold; Culture Counts: Faith and Feeling in a World Besieged; Beauty;* and *The Face of God: The Gifford Lectures.*

Christopher J. Thompson is professor of theology at St. Thomas University in St. Paul, Minnesota, and academic dean at St. Paul's Seminary School of Divinity. He has published numerous articles and a book (*Christian Doctrine, Christian Identity: Augustine and the*

Narratives of Character) that contribute to the debate about the human capacity to develop character and the influence that faith can offer.

Craig Steven Titus (S.T.D./Ph.D., Fribourg) is associate professor and director of integrative studies at the Institute for the Psychological Sciences, Arlington, Virginia. His book *Resilience and the Virtue of Fortitude: Aquinas in Dialogue with the Psychosocial Sciences* engages in a dialogue between virtue theory and psychosocial research on resilience and overcoming difficulty. He is editor of eight volumes, including *The Pinckaers Reader*; *Renouveller toutes choses en Christ*; *The Psychology of Character and Virtue*; and *Philosophical Psychology*.

Paul Vitz is professor and senior scholar at the Institute for the Psychological Sciences, Arlington, Virginia. He was professor of psychology at New York University for thirty-nine years. His works are focused on the integration of Christian theology and psychology, breaking from the secular humanism, and post-modern relativism prevalent today. Dr. Vitz's books include *Psychology as Religion: The Cult of Self-Worship*; *Sigmund Freud's Christian Unconscious*; *Modern Art and Modern Science: The Parallel Analysis of Vision*; *Faith of the Fatherless: The Psychology of Atheism*; and *The Self: Beyond the Post-Modern Crisis*.

Abbreviations

DM   *Quaestiones disputatae de malo*, St. Thomas Aquinas

DV   *Quaestiones disputatae de veritate*, St. Thomas Aquinas

In Ethic.   *In decem libros Ethicorum Aristotelis ad Nic. expositio*, St. Thomas Aquinas

NE   *Nicomachean Ethics*, Aristotle

PL   *Patrologia Latina*

SCG   *Summa contra Gentiles*, St. Thomas Aquinas

Sent.   *Scriptum super liberos Sententiarum*, St. Thomas Aquinas

ST   *Summa Theologica*, St. Thomas Aquinas

Suggested Reading

Classic

Aquinas, Thomas. *Commentary on Aristotle's Nicomachean Ethics* (*Sententia libri Ethicorum*).

_____. *Disputed Questions on the Soul* (*Quaestiones disputatae de Anima*).

_____. *On the Virtues in General* (*Quaestiones disputatae de virtutibus*).

_____. *On the Truth of the Catholic Faith* (*Summa contra gentiles*).

_____. *On Evil* (*Quaestiones disputatae de malo*).

_____. *Summa Theologica*.

Aristotle, *Nicomachean Ethics*.

Augustine. *The City of God*.

Boethius. *Consolation of Philosophy*.

Plato, *Republic*.

Contemporary

Ashley, Benedict M. *The Way Toward Wisdom: An Interdisciplinary and Intercultural Introduction to Metaphysics*. Notre Dame: University of Notre Dame Press, 2005.

_____. *Theologies of the Body: Humanist and Christian*. Braintree, Massachusetts: Pope John XIII Medical-Moral Research and Education Center, 1995.

_____. *The Ashley Reader*. Naples, Florida: Sapientia Press, 2006.

Benedict XVI. Encyclical Letter *Deus caritas est* (2005).

Brennan, Robert. *General Psychology: A Study of Man Based on St. Thomas*. New York: MacMillan Company, 1952.

Capreolus, John. *On the Virtues*. Translated by K. White and R. Cessario. Washington, DC: The Catholic University of America Press, 2001.

Cessario, Romanus. *A Short History of Thomism*. Washington, DC: The Catholic University of America Press, 2005.

_____. *An Introduction to Catholic Moral Theology: Catholic Moral Thought*. Washington, DC: The Catholic University of America Press, 2001.

_____. *The Moral Virtues and Theological Ethics*. Notre Dame: University of Notre Dame Press, 2009.

_____. *The Virtues, or the Examined Life*. New York: Continuum, 2002.

Chesterton, G. K. *Orthodoxy*. New York: Image Books, 1990.

Cuddeback, John A. *True Friendship: Where Virtue Becomes Happiness*. Denver: Epic, 2010.

Damasio, Antonio. *Descartes' Error: Emotion, Reason, and the Human Brain*. New York: Putnam, 1994.

Dewan, Lawrence. "The Importance of Substance." In *Form and Being: Studies in Thomistic Metaphysics*, vol. 45 of the series *Studies in Philosophy and the History of Philosophy*. Washington, DC: The Catholic University of America Press, 2006.

Suggested Reading

George, Robert P., and Jean Bethke Elshtain, eds. *The Meaning of Marriage: Family, State, Market, and Morals*. Dallas: Spence Publishing, 2006.

Gilson, Etienne. *The Christian Philosophy of St. Thomas Aquinas*. Trans. L. K. Shook. New York: Random House, 1956.

Gondreau, Paul. *The Passions of Christ's Soul in the Theology of St. Thomas Aquinas* in "Beiträge zur Geschichte der Philosophie und Theologie des Mittelalters." Neue Folge 61. Münster: Aschendorff, 2002.

Griffiths, Paul J., and Reinhard Hütter. "Duplex Ordo Cognitionis." In *Reason and the Reasons of Faith*. New York: T&T Clark, 2005.

Hittinger, Russell. *The First Grace: Rediscovering the Natural Law in a Post-Christian World*. Wilmington, Delaware: ISI, 2003.

Hoffmann, Tobias. *Thomas Aquinas and the Nicomachean Ethics*. Cambridge: Cambridge University Press (forthcoming).

Hoffmann, T. J. Müller, and M. Perkams, eds. The Problem of Weakness of Will in Medieval Philosophy. Leuven: Peeters Publishers, 2006.

Hütter, Reinhard, and M. Levering, eds. *Ressourcement Thomism: Sacred Doctrine, the Sacraments, and the Moral Life*. Washington, DC: The Catholic University of America Press, 2010.

John Paul II. Encyclical Letter *Fides et ratio* (1998).

_____. Encyclical Letter *Veritatis Splendor* (1993).

Kass, Leon R. *The Hungry Soul: Eating and the Perfection of Our Nature*. Chicago: University of Chicago Press, 1999.

Kent, Bonnie. *Virtues of the Will: The Transformation of Ethics in the Late Thirteenth Century*. Washington, DC: The Catholic University of America Press, 1995.

MacIntyre, Alasdair. *After Virtue*. 2nd ed. Notre Dame: University of Notre Dame Press, 1984.

_____. *Dependent Rational Animals: Why Human Beings Need the Virtues*. Chicago: Open Court, 1999.

Maritian, Jacques. *Man and the State*. Chicago: University of Chicago Press, 1951.

_____. *Distinguish to Unite: or the Degrees of Knowledge*. New York: Charles Scribner's Sons, 1959.

McInerny, Ralph. *Aquinas on Human Action: A Theory of Practice*. Washington, DC: The Catholic University of America Press, 1992.

Moncher, Frank, and Craig Steven Titus (2009). "Foundations for a Psychotherapy of Virtue: An Integrated Catholic Perspective." *Journal of Psychology and Christianity* 28 (2009): 22–35.

Second Vatican Council. Pastoral Constitution on the Church in the Modern World: *Gaudium et spes* (1965).

Péguy, Charles. *The Portal of the Mystery of Hope*. Translated by David Louis Schindler, Jr. Grand Rapids: Eerdmans (1996).

Peterson, Christopher, and Martin E. P. Seligman, eds. *Character Strengths and Virtues: A Handbook and Classification*. London: Oxford University Press, 2005.

Pieper, Josef. *The Four Cardinal Virtues*. Translated by Daniel Coogan. Notre Dame: University of Notre Dame Press, 1966.

Pinckaers, Servais. *The Sources of Christian Ethics*. Washington, DC: The Catholic University of America Press, 1995.

Suggested Reading

_____. *The Pinckaers Reader: Renewing Thomistic Moral Theology*. Edited by J. Berkman and C.S. Titus. Washington, DC: The Catholic University of America Press, 2005.

_____. *The Pursuit of Happiness—God's Way: Living the Beatitudes*. Translated by M.T. Noble, O.P. New York: Society of St. Paul, 1998.

Scruton, Roger. *Sexual Desire: A Philosophical Investigation*. London: Phoenix Press, 1986.

Schmitz, Kenneth L. *The Texture of Being: Essays in First Philosophy*. Washington, DC: The Catholic University of America Press, 2007.

_____. *Person and Psyche*. Arlington, Virginia: The Institute for the Psychological Sciences Press, 2009.

Schockenhoff, Eberhard. *Bonum hominis. Die anthropologischen und theologischen Grundlagen der Tugendethik des Thomas von Aquin*. Mainz: Matthias-Grünwald Verlag, 1987.

Seligman, Martin, and Mihaly Csikszentmihalyi. "Positive Psychology: An Introduction." In *American Psychologist* 55 (2000).

Seligman, Martin. *Authentic Happiness*. Boston: Nicholas Brealey, 2004.

Sokolowski, Robert. *Moral Action: A Phenomenological Study*. Bloomington, Indiana: Indiana University Press, 1985.

Sweeney, Gladys, Craig S. Titus, and Bill Nordling. "Training Psychologists and Christian Anthropology." In *Edification: The Journal of the Society of Christian Psychology* 3 (2009): 51–56.

Taylor, Charles. *Sources of the Self*. Cambridge, Massachusetts: Harvard University Press, 1989.

Titus, Craig Steven. *Resilience and the Virtue of Fortitude: Aquinas in Dialogue with the Psychosocial Sciences.* Washington, DC: The Catholic University of America Press, 2006.

Vitz, Paul C. *Sigmund Freud's Christian Unconscious.* New York: Guilford Press, 1988.

_____. *Psychology as Religion: The Cult of Self-Worship.* Grand Rapids: Eerdmans, 1977.

_____. "Psychology in Recovery." In *First Things* (March 2005): 17–21.

Wittgenstein, Ludwig. *Philosophical Investigations.* New York, MacMillan, 1953.

Wojtyła, Karol. *Love and Responsibility.* San Francisco: Ignatius, 1981.

_____. *The Acting Person.* Translated by A. Potocki. Boston: D. Reidel, 1979.

Name Index

Adorno, Theodor, 248
Aeschylus, 140
Al-Farabi, Abu Nasr, 261
Aquinas, St. Thomas, 8n3, 11, 12, 19, 25–26, 32, 37–42,
    47–59, 63, 64, 66n54, 69–72, 76, 77, 85, 87, 89–93, 96,
    97, 100, 103, 105, 107, 110, 112n140, **118–137, 142–168,**
    171-199, 203–205, 207, 215, 217, 220, 222, 243, 248, 262,
    276, **281–291**
Aristotle, 57, 63n43, 65, 66n56, 77, 88, 91, 95, 98, 164, 183,
    187–192, 261, 276
Ashley, Benedict M., 10, 14, 281, 299, 305–306
Augustine, St., 85n92, 133n157, 158n180
Baumgarten, Alexander, 259
Beardsley, William, 297
Benedict XVI, Pope, 104, 145n166
Bentham, Jeremy, 182
Bernini, Gian Lorenzo, 251
Boethius, 260
Bonaventure, St., 175-177, 184, 186
Cather, Willa, 251
Cessario, Romanus, 5, 19n12, 32n18, 244–246, 299
Chesterton, G.K., 201–202, 214

Name Index

Marx, Karl, 252n247, 267
MacIntyre, Alasdair, 61–62, 82n88, 219n239
McInerny, Daniel, 26, 89n97, 200, 201, 283, 301
McInerny, Ralph, 38n25
Mill, John Stuart, 26, 182
Moses, 7
Mozart, Wolfgang Amadeus, 251
Paul, St., 103, 165
Pegis, Anton, 49
Péguy, Charles, 254
Percy, Walker, 222
Pieper, Josef, 242, 249, 251
Pinckaers, Servais, 91n101, 104, 157, 166, 176, 180n200
Pius XII, Pope, 5
Plato, 57, 63n43, 145, 211, 260
Pope, Alexander, 14
Ratzinger, Joseph Cardinal, 104. See also Benedict XVI
Sartre, Jean-Paul, 278
Scheler, Max, 259, **275**, 278–279
Schelling, Friedrich Wilhelm Joseph, 266, 271
Schiller, F.C.S., 266
Schleiermacher, Friedrich Daniel Ernst, 272–273
Schmitz, Kenneth, 15, 19, 56n37, 301
Scotus, John Duns, 175–178, 184, 186
Scruton, Roger, 11, 17, 247n270, 259, 301
Seligman, Martin E. P., 19n11, 31, 83n89, 161, 193,
    237n258, 293
Skinner, B. F., 289
Smith, Adam, 269
Strachey, James, 277
Sweeney, Gladys, 15, 19, 92n107, 142n162
Taylor, Charles, 221–222
Thompson, Christopher J., 23, 30, 31, 301

Subject Index

abortion, 229n248

agape, 145n166. *See also* charity; love

Aristotelian, 30, 49, 57, 84, 161, 262, 273

art(s), 14n10, 91, 97, 98, 228, 234, 239, 285

Augustinian, 49, 84, 229n248, 234n252, 275. *See also*
    Augustine, *Name Index*

authority, 75n78, 92, 252n274

autonomy, 164, 192, 267, 268, 270, 284

Baptism, 8. *See also* Baptism; sacrament

beatitude, 11, 42–45, 82n88, 112n139. *See also* happiness

Beatitudes. *See* Sermon on the Mount

beauty, 21, 114, 135, 145, 226, 229, 251, 252n274

Bible. *See* Scripture

Body: bodily goods, 146; body-soul unity, 12-13, 27, **49–59**,
    147, 154, 192, **260–264**; and emotion, 153, 176, 193,
    244; and mind, 281, 284, 287

capacities, 8, 12, 16, 59, **84-86**, **95–96**, 100-101, 150,
    237n258, 296

Cartesian, 146, 244, 263-264

Catechism of the Catholic Church (CCC), 13n8, 243n265

categorical imperative, 267–268

charity, 98n114, 106, 166, 296. *See also* agape; New Law

Subject Index

faith, **9–11**, 13, 98n114, 105–106, 272, 296. *See also* reason

Fathers of the Church, 260. *See also Index of Names*

fear, 26, 86, 88-90, 106, 110, 113, 144, 148–149, 151, 154–155, 165, 168–169, 176n195, 179n199, 181, 197–198, 205–209, 215–216, 253n274, 295

Fides et ratio, 13

finality, 95, 114. *See also* beatitude

forgiveness, 84n91, 94

fortitude, 26, 168. *See also* courage

Franciscan(s), 175

free choice, 25, **117–137**, 174–175

freedom, 25, 54n35, 76, 109, **117–137**, 168, 187, 225, 247, 253, 259, **262–268**, 270–271, 278–279, **282–287**, 290

friendship: natural friendship, 54, 77, 219; with God, 8–9, 42–43

gift(s), 9, 77, 91n101, 100n118, 109, 217, 241, 249–250

good: bodily, 143–145, 147, **150–156**, 163-64, 167, 173, 175, 184–189, **227**, 237; common, 75, 77–78, 90, 200, 214, 219–220, 227, **248–249**; difficult, 197, 208–210, 217–218; moral, 64, 68, **155**, 163, 171n192, 189, 219; natural, 241, 295; ultimate, 59, 45, 155–156, 192, 194. *See also* transcendentals

Gospel, 77. See also Beatitudes; Scripture

grace, 8, 75, 89n99, 97n114, 100, 105, 112n140, 137, 166, 296

habitus, 186–187, 190. *See also* virtues

happiness, 24–27, 30–32, 37, 42, 45. *See also* beatitude

holiness, 11, 156. *See also* Holy Spirit; sanctification

Holy Spirit, 91n101, 109

hope, virtue of, 20–21, 25, 85–86, 94, 98, 106, 129, 154, 181n203, 193, 197–198, 205, **207–210**, 222–223, 296

human nature, 7, 24, **48–49**, 60–61, 63n43, 65, 73, 75–76, 95, 114, 150, 152, 177, 193, 218n237, 227, 241, 245n267, **259–265**, 276, 282, 285. *See also* nature

Subject Index

moral obligation, 75n78, 179, 184

moral precepts. *See* precepts

moral virtue(s). *See* virtue(s), moral

moral theology, 104, 290

natural inclinations, **70–74**, 95, 99, 104, 106, 108, 178

natural law: and human nature, 60, 110, 214, 273; and the
    moral life, 62, **69–76**; and the New Law, 59, 78, 105;
    Thomistic approach, 62, 103, 220

nature: divine, 7; human. *See* human nature; rational, 44, 262;
    social, 73, 259, 278; and supernatural, 9, 11, 63, 65n53, 75–76

New Law (evangelical law, law of the Gospel), 75–77, 105.
    See also law

nominalism, 104

norms, 24, 61, 62, 83, 86. *See also* precepts

object, 25, 34–35. *See also* action

obligation, morality of, 75n78

Original Sin, 165

Our Father. See prayer

passion(s), **139–210**, 214–221, **242–251**, 268–269, 300

patience, 86, 216

peace, virtue/gift of, 276

perception, 87, 102, 120–121, **124–127**, 134, 151, 181,
    213, 280. *See also* sense

perfection, 8, 10, 42, 55, 66, 73, 77–78, **83–85**, 112n140,
    123, 129, **155–156**, 168, 185, 189, 191, 204, 243–244

person, human. *See* human person

persons, 8, 25, 27, 41, 65, 97, 99, 106, **133–136**, 141, 153,
    165, 192, **202–208**, 218, 227n247, 230, 234, 250, 254, 259,
    268–269, 275, **281–288**, 291

philosophy: basis for knowledge, 10, 36, 102; Christian, 15,
    17; integration with psychology, **20–23**, 138, 203, 211,
    225–228, 235–236, 249, 253; Kantian, 263–264, 266,
    268–270, 286–289

Subject Index

sin, 8, 42-43, 69n64, 87–88, 129n154, 165

social, 25, 48, 73, **80–88**, **101–114**, 196, 200–209, 218–221, 231–238, 248–252, **267–271**, 279–285

spirituality, 84

spontaneity, 101, 109, 278

Stoics, 156–257

substance, 49–50, 52n34, 56, 86, 260, 262, 264, 268

suffering, 86, 151, 152, 162, 165, 168, 171, 176n195, 201, 204, 216, 260, 278, 295

synderesis, 71, 103-104. *See also* conscience

technique, 102, 151–252, 170, 202, 236, 288, 294

temperance, 86, 88, 99–100, 168, 170, **188–191**, 226, 228, 231, 237, **240–245**, 248, 250, 253, 276, 283

theological virtue, 98n114, 106, 296

tradition: Aristotelian, 30; Catholic/Christian, 14–15, 17, 49, 138, 149, 226, 281; Kantian, **264**, 268–269, 275, 278; moral, 61–62, 68, 222, 231n249; philosophical, 22, 91, 279; Thomistic, 19, 30, **32–36**, 49, 69n66, 76; Western, 65

transcendental, 15, 21, 23–24, 27, 265

Trinity, 7

truth: about the human person, 13, 22, 34, 40–41, 44–45, 73, 87, 150, 169, 248; contemplation of, 11, 15, 34, 88, 90, 114, 211; and goodness, 21; longing/desire for, 54, **226–227**, 243; moral, 5, 66

utilitarianism, 26, 182–183

values, 28, 180n201, 238, 246, 260

vigilance, 113n142

virginity, 7. *See also* chastity

virtue(s): acquired, 96; cardinal, 66–67, 106, 242n263, 252n274, 276; infused, 85n92; intellectual, 97, 98, 167, 210; moral, 26, 67n57, 96, 98–99, 113, 130, 135–137, 161, **166–188**, 191, 193, 204, 210; theological, 98n114, 106, 296. *See also* habitus, infused moral virtue

Sophia Institute

Sophia Institute is a nonprofit institution that seeks to nurture the spiritual, moral, and cultural life of souls and to spread the Gospel of Christ in conformity with the authentic teachings of the Roman Catholic Church.

Sophia Institute Press fulfills this mission by offering translations, reprints, and new publications that afford readers a rich source of the enduring wisdom of mankind.

Sophia Institute also operates two popular online Catholic resources: CrisisMagazine.com and CatholicExchange.com.

Crisis Magazine provides insightful cultural analysis that arms readers with the arguments necessary for navigating the ideological and theological minefields of the day. *Catholic Exchange* provides world news from a Catholic perspective as well as daily devotionals and articles that will help you to grow in holiness and live a life consistent with the teachings of the Church.

In 2013, Sophia Institute launched Sophia Institute for Teachers to renew and rebuild Catholic culture through service to Catholic education. With the goal of nurturing the spiritual, moral, and cultural life of souls, and an abiding respect for the role and work of teachers, we strive to provide materials and programs that are at once enlightening to the mind and ennobling to the heart; faithful and complete, as well as useful and practical.

Sophia Institute gratefully recognizes the Solidarity Association for preserving and encouraging the growth of our apostolate over the course of many years. Without their generous and timely support, this book would not be in your hands.

www.SophiaInstitute.com
www.CatholicExchange.com
www.CrisisMagazine.com
www.SophiaInstituteforTeachers.org

Sophia Institute Press® is a registered trademark of Sophia Institute.
Sophia Institute is a tax-exempt institution as defined by the
Internal Revenue Code, Section 501(c)(3). Tax I.D. 22-2548708.